Individualized
Assessment and
Treatment for Autistic
and Developmentally
Disabled Children

Individualized Assessment and Treatment for Autistic and Developmentally Disabled Children

Volume II Teaching Strategies for Parents and Professionals

Eric Schopler, Ph.D.
Professor, Department of Psychiatry
Director, Division TEACCH
School of Medicine
The University of North Carolina at Chapel Hill
Chapel Hill, North Carolina

Robert Jay Reichler, M.D.
Professor and Head, Division of Child Psychiatry
School of Medicine
University of Washington
Director, Department of Behavioral Sciences
Children's Orthopedic Hospital and Medical Center
Seattle, Washington
and

Margaret Lansing, M.Ed.
Curriculum Coordinator, Division TEACCH
School of Medicine
The University of North Carolina at Chapel Hill
Chapel Hill, North Carolina

University Park Press
Baltimore

UNIVERSITY PARK PRESS
International Publishers in Science, Medicine, and Education
233 East Redwood Street
Baltimore, Maryland 21202

Copyright © 1980 by University Park Press

Typeset by University Park Press, Typesetting Division.
Manufactured in the United States of America by
The Maple Press Company.

Library of Congress Cataloging in Publication Data

Schopler, Eric.
   Individualized assessment and treatment for autistic
and developmentally disabled children.

   Vol. 2 by M. Lansing.
   Bibliography: p.
   Includes index.
   CONTENTS: v. 1. Psychoeducational profile.—
v. 2. Teaching strategies for parents and professionals.
   1. Developmentally disabled children. 2. Ability—
testing. 3. Educational tests and measurements.
4. Developmentally disabled children—Education.
I. Reichler, Robert J., 1937-   joint author.
II. Lansing, Margaret, joint author. III. Title.
[DNLM: 1. Autism, Early infantile. 2. Child
development deviations. 3. Psychological tests.
WM203.5 S373i]
HV3004.S36   362.7'8'3   78-13415
ISBN 0-8391-1521-0 (v. II)

Contents

Preface

The passage of United States Public Law 94-142 has mandated the right to education for all handicapped children, including an individualized educational program, developed with parental collaboration. With this law the attention of school systems throughout the United States has been drawn to children previously excluded, or educated according to the haphazard interests of individual school principals and teachers. At the same time new special education techniques and prescriptions for quickly meeting the needs of all handicapped children have multiplied by bewildering leaps and bounds. This volume is intended to present our efforts of the past two decades to bring a rational synthesis of these techniques to the treatment and education of handicapped children and their families.

It is not surprising that the most puzzling children with the most difficult behavior and the most uncertain educational outcomes have been the most neglected. These include autistic children and children with related disorders of development and communication. In the past schools have been encouraged to see these strangely behaving youngsters as belonging to the jurisdiction of mental health. If the mental health evaluation showed signs of brain damage or mental retardation, the child was then referred to a neurological or mental retardation service. Such services in turn often labeled the strange and difficult behavior the product of emotional disturbance, belonging to the area of mental health. Thus, too many of these children and their families were shunted from one service to another, in a cycle of increasing frustration.

In response to growing parental desperation we launched a 5-year research project aimed at ending this mindless and inhumane process. Supported in part by the Office of Education and the National Institute of Mental Health, our Child Research Project was initiated in 1966 at the Department of Psychiatry, School of Medicine, The University of North Carolina at Chapel Hill. In this project we demonstrated that parents of autistic and similar children could collaborate as co-therapists with professionals in order to devise an individualized program of special education and management, a program that could be incorporated into the child's special schooling when available. This project was dramatically effective and was extended by the North Carolina General Assembly to a statewide basis in 1972, thus making our program for the *T*reatment and *E*ducation of *A*utistic and *C*ommunication handicapped *CH*ildren (Division TEACCH) the first statewide service for these neglected children and their families. Since then, over 850 children and their families have been taught and helped in our program.

The material in this volume is based on the expertise of professionals representing many disciplines, including special education, behavioral psychology, language pathology, psychiatry, psychopharmacology, nutrition, and occupational therapy. It is not intended to replace the specialized knowledge developed in each of these disciplines.

Instead we intend to show how we have adapted such specialized knowledge for school and home use in a reasonably systematic way. The training and specialized interest of many experts has enabled them to develop scientific and detailed techniques. These come from a narrow focus, rarely possible or appropriate at home and school. However, many of these techniques have been invaluable to us for developing individualized teaching programs. Most of the teaching programs described in this volume follow a clear rationale, while others rely on trial-and-error experimentation. All of the techniques have helped some children. None of them worked for all.

The reader, parent or professional, interested in implementing the best special education and treatment for these children will find two major approaches reflected in reviewing the available literature. One is to find the best educational techniques for these children. In this direction you will find yourself following the path laid out by experimental science, paved by volumes of studies designed to demonstrate the cause of the children's disorder and the method used for reversing their disability. These studies have the effect of establishing techniques as scientifically verified, and often become more important than the children they are intended to help.

The second approach, on the other hand, starts with the handicapped child instead of the technique. Helpers come to recognize the individual differences among children and their home environments, and become aware of the many complex factors determining each child's learning skills and deficits, looking to the studies and experience of others that will best fit each individual child. The art of using that available knowledge to meet the needs of a particular child will be the most reliable guide for this second approach.

Our experience has informed us that it is most useful to give priority to the second approach. Special education as an art applied to individual children is a theme woven throughout this volume. However, by publishing our individualized assessment and educational programming procedures in order to make them available to many children, we are aiming for the thin line between the individual composition of educational programming and the empirical principles by which they will apply to others.

In line with this intent, no systematic review of the scientific literature is included in this volume. The reader interested in the most current review of the recent scientific literature may consult other sources, such as Rutter and Schopler (1978). Our references include only those most directly derived from our experience that shaped the content of this volume.

The first volume of this series presents our Psychoeducational Profile (PEP), the assessment instrument we devised for delineating individual learning profiles of children previously considered untestable by standard tests. In this second volume we delineate the principles, concepts, and procedures by which our assessment results are converted to an individualized educational program. After the Introduction, in Chapter 2 we review the information needed for developmental evaluation basic to any rational educational effort. In Chapters 3, 4, and 5 we review the formation of expectations, goals, and educational objectives needed for directing our educational program. In Chapter 6 we review the management of difficult behavior, which, if unattended, may negate the best educational program. In Chapter 7 we discuss specific strategies, techniques, and their rationale for achieving our goals and objectives; and in Chapter 8 we review some of the issues of implementing an individualized educational program at school and at home. Part II, Chapters 9-14, contains resource materials and suggestions useful for programming.

The content of each chapter in Part I is illustrated by the case material of one child, Tommy. It is followed by a form for readers to complete for practice application to a child they know and are concerned with. The sequence of chapters and summary forms does not necessarily conform to the sequence of information as it is acquired in real life. It is arranged for the sake of clarity, and in the expectation that it will stimulate understanding and planning in a most productive direction.

Eric Schopler
Robert J. Reichler
Margaret Lansing

Acknowledgments

This manual has evolved from three different drafts, with contributions from many TEACCH staff members and parents. Each of the contributions was made in the recognition that the development of new knowledge of the children's problems and how to teach them will require future revision. Some of our parents and staff have made extra efforts to make their successful teaching procedures available to other families. There are too many to name individually. We gratefully acknowledge each of their contributions.

Individual teaching programs for the first draft were compiled by Frank Robinson from the Western Center, the Piedmont Center, and the Eastern Center. Our Clinical Directors Bernard Harris, Lee Marcus, Jerry Sloan, and their staff made special contributions to the formulation of these programs.

Kenneth Daly reorganized this material in a second draft with additional contributions from our new Center Directors Hal Shigley, Jack Wall, and their staff. Our Director of Training, Greg Olley, read the manuscript and made several helpful suggestions. Developmental norms were laboriously compiled by Leslie Waters. Barbara Callahan and Evelyn Shaw cheerfully retyped the materials, and editorial assistance was provided by Martin Wilcox.

Special thanks are due to Michael Rutter of the Maudsley Hospital for his thoughtful reading of the manuscript and his helpful suggestions. Finally, the most constant questions and comments came from our parents and were generated from the crucible of the daily experience with their children.

Individualized
Assessment and
Treatment for Autistic
and Developmentally
Disabled Children

Part I.
Devising
Teaching Strategies

Chapter 1.
Introduction

Autistic children and those with related handicaps are now entitled to an education. This reasonable assertion represents a revolutionary approach to such children. In the recent past their options were few. Parents were considered the primary cause for their child's problems. If they were wealthy a few expensive residential schools were available for their child. If they were poor their child had access to large, impersonal, custodial institutions.

By contrast, today handicapped children are entitled to a public education. The curriculum should be individualized to fit the child's special educational needs. The children's parents are recognized as necessary partners in the planning of individualized curricula. Not only do parents usually have their child's best interest at heart, but they also maintain personal responsibility for a longer time period than anyone else. These new educational directions are mandated by Public Law 94-142. They constitute major political changes in special education.

However, if we were to design a service program for children with autism and related developmental disabilities from scratch, using as guidelines direct experience and research knowledge, we would arrive at a position identical to that advocated by PL 94-142. This is precisely what happened in our State Program for such children, developed during the past two decades in North Carolina. It is by no means a common occurrence for political and legislative decisions to coincide with clinical experience and research knowledge. Since we were privileged to participate in this fortunate convergence, we felt obliged to publish the results of our

This volume was developed by the Child Research Project of Division TEACCH, in part supported by grants from the Office of Education (OEG-0-8-070827-2633(032)) and the National Institutes of Mental Health (NIMH R01-MH15539).

experience: an account of how these educational aims can be achieved, the concepts from which they were derived, the ways and means of designing teaching programs tailored to the child's unique learning characteristics, and the particular environment in which the newly acquired skills will be applied. This is what this book is about.

BACKGROUND

The teaching strategies described in this volume originated during our work with autistic children during the early 1960s. At that time autism was considered a strange and obscure psychiatric disease, emotional illness, or early form of childhood schizophrenia. The children were thought to be suffering primarily from social withdrawal. Their lack of human relatedness, their poor communication skills, and other odd behavior were all considered to be their reaction against a hostile and stressful home environment. These children were usually considered untestable by standard psychological testing procedures. The diagnosis was made primarily at psychiatric centers and there was little agreement between one center and another. The home and the public schools were not considered the optimum place for teaching these children and helping them with their community adjustment. Placement in a residential school, away from the pathogenic influence of their parents, was usually considered the treatment of choice.

During the 1960s research evidence was developed, showing that the earlier understanding of autistic children was both incomplete and misleading. Autistic children's lack of developing appropriate relationships even during infancy was only one aspect of their basic problem. They also had difficulties with appropriate perception (Ornitz and Ritvo, 1968; Schopler, 1965, 1966), comprehension, and communication (Rutter, 1968, 1978a, b). Parallel to our increased understanding of the children's deficits came our better understanding of their parents. Research evidence showed that they did not suffer from more disordered thoughts and feelings than did parents of other handicapped children (Cantwell, Baker, and Rutter, 1978; Rimland, 1964; Schopler and Loftin, 1969a, b). On the contrary, they did not differ in any significant degree from other parents. They had the same range of hopes, frustrations, and struggles, with one major exception: they also had an extremely difficult child, one who did not respond in ways that their own past experience or their other children had led them to expect.

If these research data were valid, it should be possible to apply them in a different treatment approach to autistic and similar children and their parents. Instead of treating them with psychoanalytic therapy, used also with all kinds of other emotional disturbances, it should be possible to construct a psychoeducational treatment program in which parents functioned as co-therapists (Reichler and Schopler, 1976; Schopler and Reichler, 1971). This collaboration would be based on the frank acknowledgment that the specific underlying causes for any child's disorder are usually unknown, and probably rooted in multiple origins. The most knowledgeable and appropriate treatment would therefore come from a close collaboration between professionals and parents. The professional would bring to this partnership knowledge of the field and experience with many similar children. The parents, on the other hand, would contribute their special expertise on their own child and family situation, and also their motivation to raise their handicapped child without unnecessary family stress.

A research project to test this new kind of treatment relationship was launched in 1966, with the support of the Office of Education. Parents were taught special education approaches tailored to the needs of each child in their own family situation. They were also taught behavior management techniques to implement the curriculum and to help the child adapt to family routines.

The child's special learning needs were measured by our Psychoeducational Profile (PEP) (see Volume I). This diagnostic information was integrated with the priorities and interests of the child's parents. Each educational program was individualized in this fashion for each child and parents. The program was demonstrated by staff with the child, while parents observed the demonstration through a one-way observation screen. The program was written up for use by parents in daily sessions at home. As the child mastered new tasks, parents added new ones or discovered new teaching procedures, more effective than those prescribed previously. Parents would then demonstrate their use of the home teaching program while our staff observed them through the one-way observation window. In this manner a verbal and visual dialogue was carried on between staff, parents, and child, directed toward the optimum special education curriculum for each child and family.

This procedure was effective and useful. When the research grant expired in 1971, parents petitioned their legislators to make this program a permanent part of our state services. Senate Bill 383 was passed and subsequently five centers were mandated to continue this individualized work with families, along with 27 classrooms located in public schools, but under our program direction or consultation. Through parental involvement in both the centers and classrooms a relatively homogeneous learning environment could be developed for each child.

At the time of this publication more than 850 children and their families have been evaluated and taught in the TEACCH program, and more than 2,500 individualized teaching programs have been developed and implemented. The ways and means for constructing such teaching programs, described in this volume, are based on this past experience.

In order to understand our strategies of individualized teaching programs and how to develop them, it will be helpful to have a clearer idea of the children and the kinds of handicaps to which they are applied, the concepts they are based on, and the user for whom they are intended.

AUTISTIC AND DEVELOPMENTALLY DISABLED CHILDREN

There is now extensive literature on the nature and characteristics of autistic children, summarized most recently by Rutter (1978a, b). These children have intrigued and fascinated scientists, clinicians, and educators for over three decades. Leo Kanner (1943) was first to describe a series of children who drew his attention because of their most unusual characteristics. These included: 1) their lack of relating and responding to their parents from the very beginning of their lives; 2) not acquiring speech like normal children, often remaining mute or showing peculiarities of speech, impeding communication; 3) showing stereotyped behaviors at various levels of development, ranging from simple, repetitive body movements to more complex rituals of repeated behavior sequences; 4) showing problems in processing sensory information; and a host of other specific behavior problems.

Some fascinating case studies were reported. One preschool child was reported capable of accurately humming a Mozart aria, but incapable of meaningful speech; another showed unusual feats of memory without ability to use his recalled information. These remarkable case studies resulted in increasing research interest in the disorder; they also contributed to the increasing diagnostic confusion. It was the most unusual behavior that drew the most attention, precisely those behaviors that were expressed only by some autistic children but not others. There are, in fact, as many unusual behaviors reported as there are autistic children. Some flap their hands, others twirl objects or mouth objects. Some reverse pronouns, some are mute, others repeat television commercials endlessly, and some show different forms of language confusion. Hyperactivity may occur in some, whereas others are unresponsive even to painful stimuli. Autistic children may be deaf, blind, or suffer from neurological impairment, metabolic disorders, and a range of developmental disabilities. Because of this wide array of possible difficulties, many diagnostic labels have been assigned to these children historically. Over 20 such labels were reported by Laufer and Gair (1969), including childhood schizophrenia, symbiotic psychosis, borderline psychosis, and atypical children. There was little agreement among professionals on how these labels distinguish children. Some labels resulted mainly from theoretical considerations, whereas others emphasized only some characteristics and not others. Thus the limits of specific labeling for such children are now widely recognized.

Instead of using the diagnostic labels so popular in the past, the autistic features just described are now usually considered as occurring on a continuum of disabilities. Such children can also suffer from all degrees of brain damage and mental retardation. They may include epilepsy, some forms of cerebral palsy, language disabilities, metabolic disorders, and other severe disorders of childhood. The convergence of autism and other developmental disabilities has been acknowledged both politically and scientifically. The 1975 amendments (PL 94-103) to the 1970 Developmentally Disabled Services and Construction Act formally included autism with other developmental disabilities. In parallel direction the only scientific journal devoted to research on autism has changed its name from *Journal of Autism and Childhood Schizophrenia* to *Journal of Autism and Developmental Disorders* as of 1979. Our own experience included children who suffered from autism and the related spectrum of developmental disabilities. It is for children suffering from this broad spectrum of learning problems that the teaching strategies reviewed in this manual were developed.

In order to use the teaching strategies described in this volume, it is helpful to understand four underlying concepts: 1) the interaction model, 2) developmental perspective, 3) behavioral relativism, and 4) training hierarchies.

INTERACTION MODEL

For years clinicians and researchers have debated whether biological or environmental factors exert the determining influence in the development of children and their adaptational problems. More recently it has become increasingly evident that the search for a unidirectional cause of developmental problems, as suggested by the nature-nurture dichotomy, is an oversimplification. It offers limited help to research and frequent confusion for clinicians.

Important aspects of every child's development are directed by the interaction with his parents and teachers. With the normal child, parents usually gear their expectations to their child's age and developmental level. For example, a 6-month-old infant shows no interest in learning to ride a tricycle, and parents are not disappointed that he prefers plastic rings to tricycle wheels. Under normal conditions the parent-child interaction tends to be reciprocal. The parents tend to shape their child's behavior around parental expectations. The child, in turn, has an effect on the parents' behavior. The extent to which biological factors determine the normal child's effect on his parents depends largely on his age and developmental level.

More realistic planning can evolve from the recognition that development and problems in the process arise from a complex interaction of the child's biological and genetic makeup, with experiences shaped by parents, their socioeconomic situation, the cultural milieu, relatives, and teachers. The interaction concept enables us to look for the most important relationships in this interaction matrix, rather than confining us simply to an assumed cause.

Conceptually, the interaction model is more complex than the stimulus-response model of the behaviorists. It does not hold out the behaviorists' hope that, for each specific behavior problem, a scientifically established intervention can be found that when properly applied will produce the desired behavior. On the other hand, it has the advantage of admitting a wider range of factors when working out a particular problem. This may include a parent's acceptance of certain behaviors that do not interfere with the child's learning, rather than getting unrealistically sidetracked by searching for better techniques for modifying that behavior.

Accurate assessment of the child's developmental level is important for deciding through which side of the adult/child interaction to bring about improved adaptation. For example, if a 7-year-old child's language has developed no further than the level of an 18-month-old, his optimum adaptational level may be better realized when the adult accepts the language impairment and spends teaching efforts on nonverbal self-help skills. With limited learning-teaching time available, such priorities need to be set.

The interaction model is most useful for developing the teaching strategies presented in this volume. When a teaching program is focused on only one skill or behavior, as if it occurred in isolation, the best opportunities for fostering adaptation are often missed. Single behaviors and learning deficits can be identified more easily and dealt with uniformly. However, it is their interaction matrix that defines the individual child and his family. Particular needs and learning potentials can best be understood in this interaction context. The methods of developing teaching strategies presented here are directed toward observing, assessing, and finding the most appropriate interventions in the complex of interactions peculiar to a particular child in his own home and school environment.

The human infant is born with a biologically determined set of reflexes and responses. These appear in regular developmental sequences,
relatively unaffected by learned experience. Some of these reflexes, such
as the smile, are basic to social development. Even when their smiles are
still reflexive and not yet a social response during the first 6 weeks of life,
some infants smile a great deal while others smile less. Clearly, the infant's smile can influence and shape the mother's involvement. Frequent
smiles may reinforce the mother's sense of doing her job right, whereas
infrequent smiles may evoke unwarranted maternal feelings of self-
criticism. With an autistic infant who has impaired reflexes and social
responses, the mother is negatively conditioned for her mothering efforts. The interaction cycle is directed more by biological factors than it
is with the normal child. Even with the normal child, however, biological
factors direct interaction patterns more frequently at the early ages than
they do later on, when verbal communication and responses become
more complex.

THE DEVELOPMENTAL PERSPECTIVE

The developmental perspective serves as a reminder that children's adaptational skills and the manifestations of their handicaps are formed, at
least in part, by their age and developmental level. In practice, it means
looking at the handicapped child's level of development in different
areas of mental functions and formulating teaching responses appropriately. Some children may function uniformly in all areas at a lower developmental level than most children at their chronological age. Others may
have a handicap in only one area. Still others, like many autistic children,
may be operating at a number of different developmental levels, ranging
from slightly to extremely uneven.

This is not to say that the behavior of developmentally disabled children is like that of younger normal ones. On the contrary, the uneven
learning profiles characteristic of these children make them quite different from each other, and also from the experiences of most adults with
normal children. However, one sound and humane way to achieve the
special understanding needed by these children is to perceive their similarities and common needs with younger normal children. This comparison is a most useful component of understanding and teaching these
children. It also needs adjustment according to the idiosyncratic developmental patterns shown by each child. The identification of these peculiar
developmental patterns is demonstrated in the Psychoeducational Profile
(Volume I). The conversion of this understanding into individualized,
developmental curricula is covered in the following chapters.

BEHAVIORAL RELATIVISM

Teachers, therapists, and parents all would prefer to have the skills and social behaviors they teach their children carry over into other aspects of the child's life. The more a child can generalize learned skills, the more valuable and lasting are the teaching efforts. The desire for generalization, both of teaching techniques and learned skills, has led to many efforts to establish "scientific" techniques aimed at the establishment of general skills. Unfortunately, this kind of carryover does not always occur, particularly with developmentally disabled children.

The response repertoire of these children, because of their handicap, is less flexible and more context-determined than that of the normal child; but even normal children do not show their "best behavior" in every situation. Accordingly we have found it most useful for both children and adults to shape a child's behavior and skills relative to a particular context. A characteristic autistic behavior, like persistence in playing with jigsaw puzzles, may be adaptive during a free period at school and maladaptive during "show and tell" sessions. Other frequent autistic behavior, such as temper tantrums, may be maladaptive in most social situations. Nevertheless, the relationship between the behavior and the situation in which it occurs has to be considered in order to discover the most effective teaching strategy. In the example of the jigsaw puzzle play, two adaptive strategies might be: a) use puzzles during free period to help teach the child communication skills, and b) change the child's curriculum to postpone or eliminate "show and tell." Even the more persistent behaviors need relatively different solutions. Temper tantrums in the home may be resolved by timing out or isolation; tantrums in the supermarket may be resolved by making other plans for the child during shopping trips. This is not to say that we should not try to identify and develop generalizable skills in the child. However, we have found that this is most likely to happen when we are clear in defining adaptational problems for the child at home, at school, and in the community, and understanding the differences between the demands made on the child's learning in these different circumstances.

TRAINING HIERARCHIES

Priorities for setting particular curriculum tasks and behavior shaping procedures are individualized according to the child's learning profile, the requirements of his family's life-style, and the needs of his classroom. However, some general priorities need to be maintained, based on the risks posed to the child's survival and maintenance in his optimum and least restrictive environment.

First, one must give priority to problems that risk the child's life. These could include running onto a busy street, eating toxic substances, self-destructive behavior, and dangerously aggressive behavior against others. Improved adaptation in these situations can be produced by changing the child's behavioral response or by changing the conditions that create the risk to him. If, for example, risk to the child's life is created by his inability to cope with traffic hazards, his behavior may be changed by teaching him traffic signals, keeping him in the house when unattended, or fencing in the backyard. Choice of the most appropriate intervention should be guided by the developmental level appropriate to the child. At higher levels, symbols are the most efficient, when they can be used. Teaching the child spoken, written, and visual signals for traffic dangers is simpler, cheaper, and more appropriate than building backyard fences. On the other hand, in some circumstances, building a fence will be more appropriate than keeping him indoors or finding constant adult company for him outside the house. The problem needs first priority, but the method for resolving it is made on an individual basis for each child, family, and teacher.

Second in importance are risks to the child's living with his family. In our experience, direct threat to the child's life is less common than threat to his survival within his family. Difficult behavior problems tend to be the most serious threat to family adaptation. The range of such behaviors is wide, including temper tantrums, persistent sleeping difficulties, strange food preferences, messy eating habits, poor toileting habits, making persistent strange sounds, and excessive interference with siblings and their properties. Only the life-style the family is trying to build or maintain can define these survival problems. The handicapped child's survival in the family is best ensured if adaptations can be made with only minimum change for, and imposition on, the family, in addition to what is already required by his handicaps. Procedures for changing the child's behavior or the situation in which it occurs are discussed in Chapters 6 and 11. Some residential schools or institutions are a satisfactory alternative to keeping the most difficult children in their own homes, but these are few in number. Small group homes are being developed but are still too rare. The majority of children, especially in the preadolescent age range, are better off in their own homes than anywhere else.

Third in priority is the child's access to a special education program. Generally the child needs a minimum ability to get along with and tolerate other children, to use the toilet, and to show some responsiveness to the teacher. The child's chances for success and survival in a school program are enhanced when communication between school and home is open, and when efforts to socialize and teach the child in both places are integrated. All too often parent and teacher cannot agree on how to manage difficult behavior. The teacher is convinced that the child's most disruptive behaviors originate in the home, and the parents believe that the classroom is not providing adequate education. Teachers must recognize that some behaviors are acceptable at home but not in school, and parents must realize that classroom structure and peer group pressures may demand behavior controls not necessary at home. Parents and teacher should frankly discuss their respective standards for behavior, because a joint effort between home and school is most effective for teaching skills and social adaptation.

A fourth order of priority is the child's adaptation to the community outside the home and school. This involves going along on shopping trips and visits to friends, relatives, and doctors' offices. It also includes access to school experiences with normal children. Community adjustment is not necessarily less important than the other three areas cited above. In fact, it offers opportunities for increasing the child's level of independence. However, skills and social behaviors are required in this area that are not necessarily applicable in school and at home.

TEACHING GOALS AND EXPECTATIONS

Concerns over teaching priorities often arise at periods of management crises. With developmentally handicapped children these frequently result from poor fit between expectations for the child and the severity of his handicap. These crises usually come in the form of school expulsion, requests to medicate the disturbing child, increasing negativism, self-destructive behavior, and other forms of regression, and usually involve misunderstanding at various levels between the child, the teaching staff, and the family. Occasionally a child's disruptive behavior appears spontaneously, without any apparent reason. However, invariably the crisis also involves conflicting or inappropriate teaching aims set for the child by responsible adults. Learning expectations are either too low or too high. With autistic children parents sometimes have excessively low expectations. Sometimes they are discouraged with inappropriate diagnostic evaluations. Misguided professionals have advised them that their children are primarily emotionally disturbed because of parental attitudes and feelings. These professionals often studiously avoid giving specific management help. Instead parents are left with the impression that mysterious professional attitudes or theories will result in their child's improvement, while their own efforts will only continue to enhance the child's psychosis.

More common than under-expectation is the tendency to over-expect the capacities and abilities of these confusing children. This may be due in part to the many case studies in the literature reporting unusual abilities, such as extraordinary musical talents, mathematical and mechanical skills, or phenomenal memories. Such reports reinforce the suspicion that autistic children are potentially geniuses—if one could only remove the "autistic veil." Of course, there are handicapped children with unusual abilities, but they are more common in the literature than in real life. Even when such a child has an unusual skill, this does not necessarily result in satisfactory life adaptation.

Treatment aims for autistic and developmentally disabled children have much in common with those for retarded children, especially as the autistic symptoms diminish over time. Treatment aims will differ with every individual, but we cannot ignore information about levels of adaptation to be anticipated in adulthood by projecting the degree of retardation (Baroff, 1974). By dividing degree of retardation into mild, moderate, severe, and profound, we can describe the probable level of adaptation at 18 years or older as follows.

Mental retardation is defined by the combination of a low score on an IQ test, problems in adaptive behavior, and origin within the developmental period (Grossman, 1977). Degrees of retardation are defined psychometrically by the number of standard deviations below the population mean that an individual scores on an IQ test. Thus, the mildly retarded are those with scores between 2 and 3 standard deviations below the mean of 100 (52–67 on the Stanford-Binet, Cattell, or Bayley scales). The mental age and adaptive behavior of the mildly retarded are also proportionately low, although their individual abilities would vary greatly with age. For instance, the skills in independent functioning and communication of a mildly retarded 9-year-old would be similar to those of a severely retarded adult. Such individuals would be able to feed, dress, and maintain personal hygiene for themselves. They also would be expected to communicate in complex sentences and have some basic occupational skills (Grossman, 1977). This group accounts for over 6½ million people in the United States, or about 92% of all retarded persons (Haywood, 1979). Autistic children in this category tend to have the most variable skills. These include children with special peak skills, which sometimes can be developed into means for earning a livelihood. For example, several autistic children with musical peak skills have become piano tuners. However, because of the severity of their language impairment, few autistic children achieve this level of functioning. Most autistic children function at a moderate or severe level of retardation.

The moderately retarded score falls approximately between 36 and 51 on IQ tests. The adaptive behavior of moderately retarded adults may include self-feeding, bathing, and dressing, and communication in the form of simple conversations and limited reading. Occupational skills may be limited to routine chores (Grossman, 1977). These individuals are often placed in "trainable" classes in schools, and a minority of this group achieve independent living as adults.

Severe mental retardation is associated with IQ scores in the 20–35 range, and independent functioning would be expected only in limited areas, such as washing face and hands or running simple errands. Social and communication skills are greatly limited, and vocational activity requires careful supervision. The moderately and severely retarded comprise about 444,000 persons in the United States, or about 6% of the retarded persons (Haywood, 1979). In earlier years, the moderately and severely retarded were frequently placed in large residential institutions, but since 1969 that trend has been changing and community living arrangements are more common (President's Committee on Mental Retardation, 1977).

Those with IQ levels of 19 or below are considered profoundly retarded. Their numbers are relatively small—about 110,000 people in the United States, or 1.5% of the retarded (Haywood, 1979)—but their handicap is so pervasive that it makes them totally dependent in most areas of functioning.

The above categories are not absolute, but they do represent a developmental framework that should not be ignored. Children functioning in severely and profoundly retarded ranges need special education and training to attain the appropriate treatment goals for their group, just like the children with mild and moderate handicaps. However, their rate of learning will be slower, and they are more likely to have multiple handicaps and interfering behaviors that may limit their achievements.

The levels of mental retardation described herein offer a general perspective for long-range expectations. However, these should not be confused with short-term goals or teaching objectives (see Chapter 3). Variability among all developmentally handicapped children is sufficiently great that objectives and goals must be worked out on the basis of current assessment, rather than the more general long-term expectation. When parents can collaborate with professionals in defining realistically the short- and long-term aims of education for their child, the interaction among child, parent, and community can proceed without undue stress and without socially exacerbated management problems. In this way a humane life can be planned for the child while, at the same time, meeting the needs for both parents and community.

INDIVIDUALIZATION OF TEACHING

We have summarized guidelines for setting priorities in selecting teaching goals (elaborated upon in Chapter 3). We have also discussed long-term considerations of the developmental framework needed for shaping appropriate teaching structures. Although these long-term developmental projections are based on research data, they should not be regarded as absolute. It is possible for a child with an IQ of 40 to gain 10 or even 30 IQ points with good education. Such favorable development can best be produced when short-term teaching goals are set individually and modified according to his capacity to respond. This kind of dramatic improvement does not happen with most children. It can best be achieved when short-term individualized curricula are evolved within the appropriate developmental framework.

Many procedures for teaching autistic and developmentally handicapped children have been discovered and reported in the literature. In this country, where the schools are under increasing legislative pressure to educate all handicapped children, departments of public instruction have become desperate for systematic answers to the special learning and behavior problems of this population. Teachers and parents frustrated by their inability to use normally effective socialization procedures are eager for scientifically established techniques to remove the ambiguity from their daily encounters with these unusual children. However, in our experience, whenever any of the excellent special education procedures are used routinely for all the children in a special class and when these procedures are turned into techniques, they are likely to be counter-productive for some of the children and of only limited use to most.

The aim of this volume is to show how the limits of such techniques can be overcome by using the results of a developmental assessment of the child for formulating an individualized education program, tailored to his family and school. It may be helpful to compare this approach with some of the most popular special education techniques used with these children.

Operant conditioning remains one of the most widely used techniques. An extensive literature in scientific journals describes how positive reinforcement with various rewards increases certain desired behaviors while punishment reduces or suppresses undesirable behaviors. Formal evaluation of the child's developmental strengths and weaknesses is not part of this technique. Instead, it is replaced by counting or charting targeted behavior and applying the correct reinforcers. The technique rests on the assumption that, given enough time, any behavior can be changed if the correct reinforcement contingencies are applied. The oversimplified application of conditioning technology ignores some of the vital differences among children. When the behavior, shaped in this manner, does not appear in the house or at school, the failure to generalize is usually ascribed to parents or teachers. Concerns over the lack of generalization of the child's behavior have been published repeatedly (Lovaas et al., 1973). However, the problem may be more effectively defined as the overgeneralization of the conditioning technique. When behavior modification procedures are based on an understanding of the child's level of functioning in the context of a particular home and school, the frustration produced by lack of generalization into another setting can be reduced effectively.

Useful perceptual training procedures have been used and published by Dubnoff (1968) and Frostig and Horne (1964), among others. These have been effective for teaching children to reproduce controlled lines, figures, and letters, and other perceptual skills. However, when these procedures were turned into techniques for improving reading or writing comprehension, the results were disappointingly negative (Mann and Goodman, 1976). In our experience these techniques can be used effectively, for example, to improve certain clearly identified eye-hand coordination skills, but not to cure an underlying problem of perception or understanding.

Ayers (1973) has developed a variety of perceptual motor exercises organized along a normal sequence of maturational development of perceptual motor skills. These exercises are designed to overcome a deficit in sensory integration, assumed to be the child's underlying problem. However, many developmentally disabled children do not follow the developmental sequences outlined for the sensory integration technique. For example, we have seen children who can read slogans and spell words from memory but who cannot draw simple geometric shapes. Nevertheless, the specific exercises of this technique, using swinging inner tubes and obstacle course equipment, can be enjoyable and useful. They can improve gross motor skills and bodily coordination. However, the educational values to the individual child must be determined according to that child's profile of skills and deficits.

Considerable research and teaching interest have been generated in teaching strategies for communication skills. Some words and language functions can be developed effectively with operant conditioning procedures. However, these are not sufficiently effective for some children, such as autistic children functioning in the severely retarded range.

PARENTAL AND PROFESSIONAL INVOLVEMENT

This volume is intended for use by anyone involved in the teaching and socialization of developmentally disabled children, whether parent or professional. Anyone who is in a position to teach, manage, or socialize this kind of child for an extended time needs to learn about the child's behavior patterns in order to respond appropriately and offer direction toward improved adaptation for the child and his family.

Spontaneous teaching and management responses learned by most of us from our relatively normal interaction experiences are often misleading. The children's disabilities express themselves in unique learning deficits and adaptive modes. These require the special understanding of each child that can only be achieved from interacting with that child. For many this process involves challenge and excitement, satisfied by the discovery of how to improve interactions with a very difficult and different child. It also creates inevitable frustrations of repeated teaching efforts and a slow rate of change. We hope that our experience with many such children, summarized in this volume, will help to reduce these frustrations or false starts and enhance the rate of finding constructive teaching interactions. The discovery of how to use our experience will depend on your social role and the context in which you relate to the child.

Parents or substitute parents usually spend more time with these children than anyone else. They have primary responsibility for the children, but often lack the authority professionals acquire from special study and certification. Whether we like it or not, the parents' role demands more extensive teaching and management efforts over a longer period of time than are required from any professionals. For this reason most parents develop increasing understanding of their own child's handicap. They are less clear about what this means compared to the needs and treatment of similar children, nor are they able to use this wider experience for greater confidence and clearer direction in their own efforts. The principles and techniques discussed in this manual are intended to make our experience with many children accessible to parents and professionals struggling alone. With the establishment of PL 94-142 mandating education for all handicapped children, it should become increasingly unnecessary for parents to be alone in teaching and managing their child. With increasing help for these children in the schools and other agencies, this manual is intended to help parents play a more active and rational part in formulating an individualized educational plan with teachers and therapists. In our experience the most satisfactory progress results from active collaboration between parents and professionals; that is, when the professional has a good understanding of parental management and teaching problems, peculiar to the home and family living. Conversely, the child makes better progress when the parent understands the teacher's educational goals and the management needs of the classroom group structure. This can best be accomplished when tasks both at home and at school are geared to the variations in the child's mental functions and rates of learning as described and illustrated in this manual.

Therapists, including psychiatrists, psychologists, administrators, and others concerned with counseling and planning for these children and their families, are often less directly involved in the daily socialization efforts of parents and teachers. Nevertheless, they play a crucial role in directing efforts for improving the child's adaptation. This manual is intended to offer them a more detailed account of the relationship between individualized assessment, demonstrated with the Psychoeducational Profile of Volume I, and the application of this diagnostic information in forming the specific educational programs described in this volume.

There is no doubt that in our complex society many different roles and disciplines have evolved, all of which are involved in the teaching and management of autistic and developmentally disabled children. In addition to the professional roles cited previously, there are social workers, speech pathologists, occupational therapists, physical therapists, music therapists, play therapists, recreation therapists, dieticians, physicians, and others. Each of these specialties has a body of information and related procedures. Just which of these professional disciplines a child and his family will encounter often depends on accidents of location and information. The disadvantages of this professional diversity are several. Each professional tends to have a commitment to understand and treat the child in terms of his own special knowledge and experience. Because specialists have overlapping interests in the same child, confusion in planning treatment may result. Inevitably, decisions are too often made for reasons of professional territorial protection rather than the needs of the child and family. The positive side of the multidisciplines includes the availability of an array of interventions and services when no one special teaching technique has been established for all children. Future research and experiences will help to distinguish effective from ineffective procedures and will improve the prediction of effective procedures with particular children. In the meantime parents will continue to play an important part in defining and selecting optimum teaching strategies for their own child.

PL 94-142 acknowledges this state of the art. It also implies that there are rational processes for arriving at optimum individualized special education programs. It is the promotion of a rational approach among children, parents, and concerned professionals that this volume addresses.

Like cooking, teaching children can be a highly developed and sophisticated art form. Yet both activities are sufficiently important that roughly half of our adult population engages in these activities. While great cooks and teachers will continue to be rare, most of us can achieve a high level of competence. Many complex techniques and ingredients are available. The mastery of these improves with training and experience. Parents are called on to teach their offspring before and after they encounter teachers and other professionals. They use the information passed on to them by their parents and grandparents and modify this with their own experience and knowledge. The most important ingredient of all is love of teaching for its own sake and love for the child. Without love the best technical skills are often misapplied. With love the most esoteric teaching techniques can be learned and used for the individual child's optimum learning. Individualization is a widely recognized procedure preferable for most children. For the autistic and otherwise developmentally disabled children individualization is a necessity. Their peculiar learning patterns cannot be productively harnessed otherwise.

This manual does not include all relevant teaching techniques. To do so would require many volumes and an index the size of an unabridged dictionary. Instead we have included some specific examples for teaching in the areas we have found most useful in our statewide program in North Carolina for the past 10 years. These include individualized teaching programs based on careful evaluation of the child's learning and response patterns. These programs are formulated for developing skills in imitation needed for speech, perceptual functions, gross and fine motor skills, eye-hand integration, nonverbal comprehension, language skills, and behavior management needed for teaching. However, the main purpose of this volume is to convey the most effective approach we have evolved over the years, that is, strategies for selecting and developing the right educational program for a particular child.

Parental Involvement

The strategies and techniques discussed are intended to make sense for both parents and professionals. Parents will not usually test and evaluate their own children with formal testing. They do need to understand their child's reaction to learning tasks at different levels of development or difficulty. The child's learning is greatly facilitated when parents understand and take part in forming specific teaching goals. When parents and teachers work out joint teaching goals, it becomes easier for parents to detect the difference between a child's unwillingness to work on a task and a deficit that makes the task especially hard for the child. Most important, this manual is intended to help parents understand the principles of individualized special education and to participate in the following activities:

1. To help teachers and school systems comply with PL 94-142 (Turnbull, Strickland, and Brantley, 1978) and to hold them accountable for working out an individualized educational program for their child
2. To collaborate with teachers and other professionals in understanding or identifying the child's peculiar learning strengths and handicaps
3. To enable parents to furnish information to professionals that will help in planning and making appropriate educational goals
4. To help the child's learning by working on a home teaching activity or otherwise carrying through on the individualized education program

Professional Involvement

This manual is also intended for teachers, school psychologists, speech therapists, and other professionals working with the child. Often their specialized training and techniques give them insufficient opportunity to adapt their expertise to all aspects of the child's life in the community, at school, and at home. The rational and flexible approach to the formulating of appropriate goals, the use of developmental evaluation with the Psychoeducational Profile, and the procedures for collaborating with parents in carrying out a unified teaching effort could contribute to more effective application of special professional knowledge and techniques. It should lead to the following activities:

1. To engage parents in their efforts to comply with PL 94-142 and to enlist parental cooperation and support in carrying over professional efforts into the home
2. To help parents understand the child's special learning problems observed in class or clinical setting and to help translate effective interventions for use in the home
3. To help parents in finding and collaborating in the achievement of both specific teaching objectives for a semester or less and the broader long-range goals for a year or more
4. To draw from the extensive literature of special education and treatment techniques those procedures that best fit the child's special needs and learning readiness

In summary, this manual is for parents and professionals whose love of teaching is combined with their commitment to the education of the autistic or developmentally disabled child. With these two qualities the strategies described next should enable them to find better ways to understand the child's puzzling and difficult behavior, and to find the needle of appropriate education in the growing haystack of special techniques.

CASE ILLUSTRATION

The principles and information covered in subsequent chapters are illustrated with clinical information obtained from one child, Tommy D., summarized at the end of each chapter. His diagnostic assessment information is summarized at the end of Chapter 2, the selection of his teaching goals in Chapter 3, his specific teaching objectives in Chapters 4 and 5, behavior management procedures in Chapter 6, and his IEP in Chapter 8. Tommy is included in this volume for two reasons. First, his summaries are an applied example of the information covered in each chapter. Second, they are also meant to provide a format for you to complete a parallel case review of a child known to you. A blank form, like the one used for Tommy, is provided for this purpose at the end of subsequent chapters.

In order to introduce Tommy Dodd to the reader, a brief summary of his referral to our program is presented.

Case of Tommy Dodd

Name: Tommy Dodd

Referral: Mrs. W., a school psychologist, referred Tommy for evaluation. She was concerned whether he could be placed in a local kindergarten. His parents had brought him to the kindergarten for a preliminary visit, and the teacher felt that he was not ready to start school. She was concerned because Tommy would not look at her nor answer her questions. Instead he made odd screeching sounds and stared at the fingers of his right hand. He did not go to the bathroom, soiling himself instead. He did not interact with any of the other children, but lined up books after repeatedly flipping their pages.

Family Background: His father, Mr. R. D., is 28 years old. He completed high school and works as a mechanic in a local mill. He is on the day shift and earns about $10,000 annually. His mother, Mrs. S. D., is 25 years old. She completed 2 years of high school and works as a threader in the mill on the 3 to 11 pm shift, at an annual salary of $5,500. They have one other child, John, 3 years old. He is described as normal, but is frequently fussy with Tommy. They often fight with each other.

Mrs. D.'s mother has been living with the family, taking care of the children while parents are working. Parents have been quite concerned about Tommy's lack of speech and slow development. However, the maternal grandmother told them not to worry because her own brother was also a slow talker. She believes that Tommy is quite bright but prefers to be alone. He will be all right and talk when he is ready.

Developmental Background: Pregnancy and Tommy's birth were normal according to parents. They had no concerns about him until he was 2½ years old, the time John was born. He showed no interest in the new baby. He began to be irritable and cried frequently. He played more and more by himself, lining up sticks, and rolling cars. Sometimes he seemed to be deaf and did not respond to interruptions of his play. Other times he was restless and continuously moving. Before John's birth he was heard to say a few words, "car," "coke," "Tommy." Now he only makes sounds as he moves about.

Parents' Concerns: Parents became concerned about a year ago when he was 4 years old. His behavior seemed to become more difficult. As his brother began talking, parents noticed that he was able to do things that Tommy was not yet doing. John, then 1½ years old, had begun to say words, liked to play with his father, and showed enjoyment of affection. When John tried to approach Tommy he screeched, sometimes had a tantrum, and began biting his own hand.

Current Behavior: Parents reported that he is usually happy when eating or left alone to play as he likes. He enjoys taking a bath, watching the water run out, stacking blocks, and lining up sticks. He likes to be outdoors, but has to be watched. Often he will not stop when called. He urinates into toilet when reminded, but still has bowel movements in trousers, usually going to his room for this. He has used the toilet when mother was there to help him.

Parental Expectations: Parents stated that Tommy is not as well advanced as his brother, except in physical activity. They suspect he is below the normal development of most 3-year-olds in mental and social behavior. They believe he will need a special class, and expect him to learn fast once he starts to talk and pay attention. They are eager to help him but don't know how.

Chapter 2.
Assessment and
Evaluation

OVERVIEW

In a time when there is an overabundance of tests, scales, and question-naires evaluating and reducing to numbers our performance in almost every sphere of life, from work to sex, evaluation has come under attack in many quarters. It is therefore necessary and appropriate in a chapter on assessment to explain the need for evaluation and explicitly how it is to be used with these children. It is almost mundane to state that, before an optimal plan of action can be taken, some appropriate assessment of the situation is necessary. In the simplest condition it may mean checking the flow of traffic before crossing the street. In more complex situations, such as building a house, flying a plane, or investing money, it means taking into account many different factors through the best techniques, preferably objective and measurable, that are available. This is essen-tially the process we attempt to teach children, normal and developmen-tally handicapped alike: stop and observe carefully; integrate the infor-mation available; check if further information is required; develop a list of actions; set priorities for action; select action and implement; and re-assess the situation (results). This chapter identifies the areas to be eval-uated and techniques for evaluation necessary for the development of an individualized educational program. In the following chapters we show how these observations are translated into goals and objectives, and fi-nally into a specific program.

Frequent resistance to evaluation evolves from confusion between functional assessment and diagnostic labeling based on theoretical or nosological concepts. Such labels are then often assumed to suggest a specific treatment, but this is rarely the case without an individualized functional assessment (Reichler and Schopler, 1976). Diagnostic labels can either be names or numbers. Although they do have research and occasional social and political value, as applied to developmental disabilities they are at best rough boundaries identifying a group of children, and at worst impediments to appropriate programming.

In this chapter we are talking about a holistic and functional assessment. In order to develop a good individualized education program we need to take a careful look at the whole life of the handicapped child and his family, their assets and liabilities. These observations will enable us to identify what aspects of the child's *present* level of functioning and behaving we might reasonably expect to change, what aspects his parents want to change, and what resources the child, his parents, and community have to contribute toward making these changes. This process follows the principles of interaction and development described in Chapter 1. We decide what to observe and how to sift our observations from four points of view: what is known about normal and variant patterns of development; our experience with autistic and similar children; how this child's development uniquely and specifically differs; and what his parents want and can do. The processes involved in answering the question of "Where are we now?" may be arranged in three areas: 1) developmental evaluation, 2) observation of behavior patterns, and 3) talking with parents.

DEVELOPMENTAL EVALUATION

Tests

The diagnostic evaluation includes standardized intelligence and developmental tests, such as the Bayley Scales of Infant Development, Merrill-Palmer, Peabody Picture Vocabulary Test (PPVT), Wechsler Preschool and Primary Scale of Intelligence (WIPPSI), Wechsler Intelligence Scale for Children—Revised (WISC-R), and Leiter International Performance Scale. Although these tests by themselves do not provide sufficiently detailed information for specific training, they do indicate the *developmental range* within which the child is functioning. They also suggest areas of deficit. Care must be taken in choosing tests that are appropriate to the child's level of function and that are not significantly limited by a major deficit. For instance, with a nonverbal child, a test requiring significant language understanding or ability would essentially measure the child's language handicap but would be insensitive to his other strengths and deficits. We frequently find it useful to administer more than one test to overcome the limitations of any single instrument. Similarly, the Vineland Social Maturity Scale provides information on the child's strengths and weaknesses in areas of self-help and social skills.

Additional information is gained if the age of attainment of skills is noted on the Vineland instead of using the standard pass-fail notation. This provides information on significant periods of delay and on the rate of development: Has there been continuously slow development? Was there a major delay with subsequent development? Is development proceeding at a slow, regular, or accelerated rate? Even in unusual instances where it is not possible to administer a standardized test completely, *structured* estimates of function can often serve well. We have found that estimates of developmental level of specific functions, indicated as age equivalents, can be highly accurate, whether provided by parents or professionals (Schopler and Reichler, 1972).

Testability Many children are readily labeled "untestable" when initial efforts at testing have failed. This means that, when asked to perform a specific act, they have refused, cried, screamed, or "tuned out" the adult. The inference is quickly made that they are too scared, angry, rebellious, stubborn, or "withdrawn" to perform. This judgment is usually unfair and presumptuous. Directions, especially verbal ones, are often too difficult or complicated for the child to comprehend, and the tester must explain the request in simpler or nonverbal ways. Alternatively, the task may be well beyond the routine ability of the child. When the child can understand the adult's request and when he has the skills needed for success, the response is quite different. For example, the tester might place several blocks and a box on the table and say, "Put the blocks in the box." If the child does not understand the language, he will be confused and may stack the blocks, hold them, mouth or throw them, simply not respond, or even leave the table. The tester then makes the task easier by pointing to a block and the box, saying, "Put." The tester may put a few blocks in himself, or move the child's hand through the motion required. The tester will praise and reward the child. Significant error in evaluation of children occurs when the tester assumes the resistant child *could* perform the tests "if he wanted to" rather than that the resistance occurs when the task is either too difficult or confusing for the child. This error commonly occurs for two reasons. First, the examiner believes that a child is either uncooperative or unable to do a task. In real life children tend to be uncooperative precisely in the area of their deficits. Second, the examiner assumes that the child should perform at the same developmental level evenly across all functions and skills.

Functional Developmental Testing Clinical and parental experience with autistic, psychotic, and other developmentally disabled children repeatedly confirms the finding that development in these children is uneven. Thus, within the same child, various functions operate on different developmental levels, and the evaluator is unable to predict performance in every skill area. Therefore, the most relevant teaching techniques can often be best approximated from the appropriate methods for a particular developmental level for a particular skill. For example, if a 5-year-old child has the motor coordination of a normal 5-year-old but has the language comprehension of a 2-year-old, this child can be taught to ride a tricycle by using simple speech appropriate to his language level. While developmentally disabled children do not necessarily resemble normal, younger children, their problems can be understood in terms of similarities with and common needs of chronologically younger children. For example, a psychotic 8-year-old who obtains an age equivalent score of 2 years in the language area of a diagnostic test neither functions like nor resembles a normal 2-year-old. What his score does mean, however, is that the normal 2-year-old's verbal skills can offer a starting place for planning appropriate responses to the child's special educational needs.

The principal instrument used to make this assessment is the Psychoeducational Profile (PEP) (Schopler and Reichler, 1979). The PEP is an inventory of behaviors and skills designed to identify uneven and idiosyncratic learning patterns. It is most appropriately used with children *functioning* at preschool-age level within the chronological age range of 1 to 12 years. The PEP determines the child's developmental function in seven areas, defined in Chapter 3: 1) Imitation, 2) Perception, 3) Fine Motor, 4) Gross Motor, 5) Eye-Hand Integration, 6) Cognitive Performance, and 7) Cognitive Verbal.

At times you may have to make rough approximations of the child's developmental levels in these function areas before testing with the PEP, for example, in order to complete the practice assessment form at the end of this chapter. For this purpose informal observations of a child can be compared with the scales for normal development provided in Appendix A. This information can be used for making a rough and preliminary estimate of a child's learning profile.

There is also a Pathology Scale to identify degrees of behavioral pathology in affect; relating, cooperating, and human interest; play and interest in materials; sensory modes; and language. One can supplement this with the Psychosis Rating Scale (Reichler and Schopler, 1971). As noted in Chapter 1, we have designed this individualized education programming manual for use with the PEP. Although programs can be developed using other methods of evaluation, we have found that these seven areas encompass important developmental functions for treatment of handicapped children.

The PEP consists of a set of toys and play activities presented to a child by an examiner who also observes, evaluates, and records the child's responses. At the end of the test the child's scores are distributed among the seven function scales, yielding a profile depicting relative strengths and weaknesses in different areas of development and behavioral pathology.

Successful teaching is based on using the child's relatively strong skills to foster growth in his handicapped functions. Therefore, it is essential to know exactly what he can and cannot do in all areas mentioned. For example, a child with strong visual skills who readily learns to recognize words might use this skill to help increase his understanding of spoken language. This could be achieved by placing large printed labels on most common objects in the home or classroom, and requiring his reading of labels, such as "milk," before he can obtain the desired object.

Whether the child is put into a test situation or observed in his routine environment at home or school, it is crucial to identify in each area the skills he can perform easily and those he cannot. Between these two points (easy tasks and impossible tasks) lies the area critical to learning. Whereas most tests evaluate a child on only two levels, passing and failing, the PEP provides a third and unique level known as "emerging." An emerging response can be defined as a response that shows that a child has *some* knowledge of what is required for the task but does not have the *full* understanding or skill necessary to complete the task successfully. To express this concept in another way, when a child demonstrates that he has some sense of what a task is about or if he can partially complete it but does so in a peculiar way, his response is scored as "emerging." The educational program is focused on these "emerging" abilities. This makes it possible for the child to experience success while directing his efforts toward the acquisition of new skills.

The PEP has some significant advantages over other methods of evaluation. The items are developmentally arrayed, and were selected from a range of teaching activities that have been empirically established as suitable for the target population. In addition, the items in the PEP do not have to be presented in any set order, providing flexibility in administration, which allows the examiner to respond to the child's interest and responses. Language requirements are minimal both in directions for tasks and for responses. Furthermore, the scoring system takes into account responses, often idiosyncratic, that ordinarily are disregarded on other standardized tests. These responses can be used to develop individualized programs. Last, the PEP allows the opportunity to try to teach the child the task in order to identify his readiness and ability to learn a new skill.

LANGUAGE DEVELOPMENT IN AUTISTIC CHILDREN

Although this manual has been written so that our approach to home programming and teaching can be generally applied to different types of handicapped children, we have been working primarily with autistic and communication-handicapped children. Since language is a primary deficit for these children, training in this area is commonly a major teaching focus.

As in all areas of teaching, the basis for an individualized language program is the accurate assessment of what the child currently can understand and express, and the knowledge of what next steps are within his range of emerging ability. Language is a highly complicated process involving a wide range of behaviors or skills difficult for the autistic child: listening, observing others, waiting, initiating, remembering, integrating sights, sounds, and touch. While these behaviors are important to language development, they also apply to other teaching objectives as well. In this section we discuss the language deviations of autistic and similar children and some special language assessment techniques.

Patterns of Language Deviations

Most language problems involve developmental delay, peculiarity of expression, or a combination of these. The most extreme form of delay appears in the child who never developed speech as a toddler, and whose noises seemed random, without clear communicative intent. There are also some children who appeared to listen and understand some language, and who communicated their wants with a few words, such as "mama," "go car," "bye-bye." However, between 2 and 3 years of age these words disappeared or were replaced by jargon. There are other children who gradually acquired new words, phrases, and even sentences that never approximated normal language use. However, only rarely do these children use language simply like a younger child. They often show other peculiarities of speech, such as echoing words or television commercials. They may reverse pronouns or use words and phrases in the wrong place.

Flexibility   Many of our children appear to learn their language in a rote, inflexible manner. A word tends to retain the precise original meaning with which it was learned. For example, the word *chair* may mean only the bright green chair a child sat in when the word was first taught. These children do not generalize language from one situation to another. They cannot use words in new combinations but stick with a phrase learned by rote. For example, "Want milk" is repeated even when the offered food is juice, cola, or cookie.

Communicative Intent   Autistic children show little interest in communicating with others. This characteristic is one component of the frequently described deficit in human relatedness. Even when they have the vocabulary to express their needs, they often do so only when pressured by the adult. This lack of interest or initiative discriminates them from other children with delayed language skills.

Gestural Communication   Autistic children fail to develop a gestural system to compensate for their lack of speech. They often have to be taught to point or use other hand signals for communication. Communicative facial expressions are also slow to develop. In contrast to the deaf child's vivid smiles, frowns, and grimaces, these children show a blank facial expression.

Abstract Concepts   Words that represent abstract concepts, such as time, color, size, and feelings, are difficult for autistic children to understand. Questions (who, what, where, when, why) are confusing. Even when they have the vocabulary to answer a question, they cannot choose the correct one (for example, "Who is throwing a ball?" Answer: "Ball.").

Auditory Memory   Short-term memory is often very good, and autistic children can parrot back long phrases they do not understand. However, they often have great difficulty retrieving from their long-term memory even short phrases they do understand. They may be able to produce certain linguistic structures (sentences) in random situations but be unable to produce them on demand, even when they are motivated to do so. This presents a confusing picture to the adult who knows the child can produce a phrase from memory, but wonders why he does not do so when he needs it.

Visual Memory   Since visual memory is often exceptionally strong, some children are able to read and even spell words that are not understood in spoken language. Their comprehension of the written word is rarely ahead of their verbal receptive language, however.

Speech   Many children remain nonverbal. Those children who do learn to form phrases and sentences continue to have limited vocabulary and to lack variety in syntactic forms (grammar). Babbling, jargon, and echolalia continue long past the appropriate developmental stage. The use of both immediate and delayed echolalia, phrases that are often far above the child's meaningful speech, may make expressive language appear misleadingly high. Voice quality may be monotone, sing-song, or copied from an adult in the child's environment. Articulation of autistic children is often more accurate than that of non-autistic children at a similar level of language development. With some children, articulation may be clear in their echoed speech and defective in their spontaneous speech.

Special Assessment Techniques   For the reader who is not using the Psychoeducational Profile (PEP), some general principles for assessment of language may be helpful. The basic rule is: never make assumptions about how much language a developmentally handicapped child understands until you test it out in a variety of situations. The level of receptive understanding ability must be known before expressive demands are placed on the child. Since autistic children often have good memories for routines and can follow gestural, situational, and other nonverbal cues, they can carry out a verbal direction without actually understanding the meaning of the words. Such directions as "Shut the door," "Turn on the light," and "Put on your coat" can be followed, giving the impression that they understand the language. However, if the examiner gives the same direction when the action is not anticipated and without gestures, the child is often unable to understand. (For example, ask the child to "Shut the door" in the middle of a play period without looking toward the door.) If such a direction is understood, the examiner then has to determine if the child gains meaning from just one word or from the whole phrase. The examiner would then vary the direction ("Touch the door," "Put on your hat," "Give me your coat"). A series of such directions would be given using names for objects, furniture, and prepositions ("Put the shoe under the table"), verbs, and two-step directions. For higher level children, pictures are useful for testing out receptive vocabulary of less familiar objects and actions ("Touch 'man pushing the wagon'"). It is important to start at a very simple level in order to teach the child the procedure and gain his cooperation. Difficulty is gradually increased until the child appears confused and makes mistakes. Once the general level of receptive understanding is determined, the tester then looks at the child's expressive abilities.

Since echolalia and short-term memory skills often give a misleading impression of expressive language ability, it is important to test out the child's expressive abilities in two other ways. Placing the child in a comfortable structured routine (lotto game, for example), the examiner asks the child to name pictures to be placed on the board or objects to be put in a box. The examiner gives frequent help at first, preventing frustration or fear of failure from stressing the child. Gradually the examiner delays giving help in order to judge the child's expressive ability in varying situations of comfort/stress. Second, the examiner writes down any spontaneous language heard during the testing session. The vocabulary and sentence structures used in spontaneous communication give important information on which to base a language program. It is helpful to note the intent of these spontaneous utterances. Are they communicative to the tester? Are they a form of "talking to oneself"? Are they echoed phrases unrelated to the events of the session?

OBSERVING BEHAVIOR

The goals of a successful program should extend beyond the narrow target of specific skill acquisition. Although it is useful to develop "eye contact" on command, or to initiate a motor movement like clapping, teaching can develop a much broader range of essential behaviors. For example, a child needs to learn to look for objects, such as his toys. He must become aware of his body and observe his hands and feet when dressing. He must learn to imitate his parents in order to participate in even simple tasks around the house.

Developmentally handicapped children often do not automatically generalize newly learned skills beyond the immediate context in which the skills were learned. Thus a child may only perform the new skill in the situation in which he originally learned it, or only with objects originally used or very closely associated with it. There is risk of the child developing a narrow repertoire of isolated, relatively useless skills. In part this is overcome by coordination of training programs in the clinic, school, and home, and by varying the materials (discussed in Chapter 8). The acquisition of broader integrating skills can facilitate appropriate generalization. Thus, the assessment of these areas of the child's functioning is important in the planning of the individualized education program.

Information concerning these areas of behavior comes from several sources. They include reports from parents, teachers, and others actively involved with the child, and from direct observation. The child's behavior is observed throughout the testing as well as during nonstructured periods. We watch the child in the waiting room with his parents for 10 minutes or so before testing, and for at least one 5-minute period midway through the test. During this "testing break" the child is told to "go play" while the tester marks the score sheet. This withdrawal of demands and adult impingement and structure gives the child time to relax. His behavior at these times provides information about his ability to organize himself, his preferences in play, and his need for social interaction. Throughout both nonstructured and structured periods we note the child's main interests and preoccupations, his activity level and length of attention to any specific activity, his ability to organize and control his impulses, and his preferences in the use of his senses (vision, hearing, touch, smell, and taste) and modes of behavior (motor movements). Some of these are scored directly on the Pathology Scale of the PEP.

These behaviors and functions are usefully organized in the categories of learning skills, organizational skills, and social skills. In addition, negative or pathological behaviors that may interfere with success are noted separately.

Learning Skills

The examiner must assess the child's ability to organize visual attention (look at materials, scan a range of materials, ignore irrelevant details, observe the adult's face and hands); his ability to imitate (copy motor movements, language or auditory stimuli, and the use of materials); his degree of curiosity and ability to use initiation and exploration in play; and his ability to use trial-and-error techniques and to self-correct his errors.

The teacher must be aware of the child's strong and weak areas in learning skills in order to utilize his assets and supplement or strengthen weak areas. The program will have specific learning skills as one goal and the structure of teaching can facilitate improvement in this area (e.g., exercises to develop scanning—looking over several items in order to select the most appropriate choice).

Organizational Skills

In order to assess organizational skills the examiner must observe the child's memory for routines (When test routines are repeated, does he anticipate or initiate the next step?); awareness of causal relationships (Does he relate consequence with his or tester's actions, and does he use this understanding to control the situation on repetition?); ability to recognize the organization or sequence within a specific task (Does he see where to begin, how long to continue, and where to stop?); and ability to use materials appropriately (Does he use objects as functional wholes or use only a part of an object or use it "inappropriately"?).

These organizational skills depend on the ability to recall past experiences and to recognize and recall the sequence or order of occurrence. The teacher must know about the child's abilities in this type of thinking. He cannot expect the child with no memory for sequential order to carry out tasks independently. Yet the teacher should expect and train independent work habits in the child who is able to recall such a sequence of events. This skill is not an all-or-none phenomenon but may be achieved at various degrees of difficulty, and the program expectations must be geared to the appropriate level of skill.

Social Skills

The examiner should note the following: the child's awareness of the adult's presence and response (Does he alter any behavior following the adult's actions, affect, or communication?); the child's recognition of his role in the interaction (Does he recall the adult's past reactions and show his awareness of causality by changing his behavior in the future?); the child's response to social praise (Does he notice and enjoy the adult's verbal praise, e.g., "Good work," "That's nice"? Does he smile or seem to enjoy being touched? Does he understand that a reward—food or toy—is a form of praise?); the child's dependence on the adult (Does he ask for help, accept help when given, and accept the adult's control and limitations on his behavior?).

All teaching, regardless of the goal of the lesson, is dependent on the child's motivation to attend and to perform. The teacher may need to motivate the child by increasing his "enjoyment." The teacher must know what rewards (food, a pat, hug, smile, verbal praise?) will be "understood" and how often they are required.

Negative Behaviors

The examiner notes behaviors that may interfere with learning, social acceptance, or that may place the child in danger. As stated in the introductory chapter, we give priority to behaviors that create risks to the child's life, to the child's living within his family, or to access to education. Stereotypic, manneristic, or other "peculiar" behavior (hand flapping, rocking, walking on toes, posturing, grimacing, wriggling) is noted, but such behaviors are not usually the primary target of the educational program. Many such behaviors can, if necessary, be altered through careful and consistent modification procedures. However, we focus on these "problem" behaviors only to the extent that they significantly interfere with the development of new skills and new pro-social behaviors, or if they are critical to survival of the child in his home or classroom. More commonly there is a spontaneous decline in the "bizarre" behaviors as the child develops understanding and competence in other areas. (A child does not flap his hands when they are usefully occupied in arranging or using materials.)

We expect these observations to provide guidance in answering the following questions: What does this child find most interesting? What gives him pleasure, enjoyment, or satisfaction? How does he learn something new? What is his optimal rate of learning? Under what conditions does he give his best attention and energy? What is the optimal length of attention? Under various conceptual frameworks these concerns would be identified as learning style, attention, conditionability, cognitive ability. These problems and their management are described in greater detail in Chapters 6 and 7.

TALKING WITH PARENTS

Parents are not only a major source of essential information concerning the development and behavior of their children. Their role as active agents in their child's development is critical to the success of helping their handicapped child. We must be particularly concerned to learn what interests and priorities they have for their child's development and what behavioral problems are most bothersome to them.

While the goals for the child are determined by his current level of ability, the program must also take into account the family's life-style and its immediate priorities. Initial success for parents, as for teachers, clinicians, and the child himself, contributes significantly to motivation to maintain the long-term effort required.

The home program component of the individualized educational program is precisely what the name states—activities to be done at home. As such, home programs have to be formulated for the particular home in which the teaching will take place and for the people doing the teaching. In order to accomplish this we need to keep in mind the parents' work schedules (Are both working? What shifts?), occupations, income level, education (although one should abandon simplistic stereotypes), communication styles, thinking abilities, and preferred activities (athletic, intellectual, artistic, practical). We also need to consider the number, sex, and ages of the siblings in the house (Is there a young child requiring much attention?), their personalities, and coping styles. It is important to know the size and physical layout of the child's home (Does he have his own room? Are there dangerous objects in the house? Is there an area for teaching free from distracting sights and sounds? Is there a safe outdoor play area? Does the neighborhood contain appropriate playmates? Are there dangerous dogs or traffic?). Community resources also need to be identified (Are responsible babysitters, day care, schools, relatives available?). When the program is developed for use in settings other than home, such as school, these questions are still important. In most instances, parents should and will be essential partners in programs centered at school or other institutions. In such situations, it is critical for success that programs at home and school be coordinated. Long-term success will still depend on taking parental priorities into account. Even for programs conducted exclusively in institutional settings, questions concerning the child's school, institutional, and living environments remain essential (see Chapter 3).

CONCLUSION

The initial assessment consists of three parallel steps in gathering information: testing the child's level of abilities, observing the child's behavior, and finding out about family and parental needs, priorities, and general life-style. Professionals will find a home visit a helpful method for increasing their understanding of the child in his home. Parents who create an individualized home teaching program without help from others will still want to take time to assess all aspects of their own child: his skills, his behavior, and the expectations and style of their family. Chapter 3 contains further elaboration of these elements of assessment as the selection of goals for teaching is discussed.

Figure 1 is an example of an assessment summary based on the information presented in this chapter. It is similar to the PEP form in Volume I. The format for the summary is the same as in the blank form (Figure 2) provided for your use with diagnostic data from a child you are familiar with. This will enable you to review your understanding of our assessment discussion. At the same time we hope that this exercise will clarify your diagnostic understanding of your particular child. You may have to get some additional information on your child to complete the form. You may also be able to make some educated guesses. As long as you replace your estimate with more direct diagnostic information as you collect it, such estimates can be quite helpful. Even the most thorough diagnostic evaluation is only based on the best information available. Hence it too is subject to revision with the development of new data.

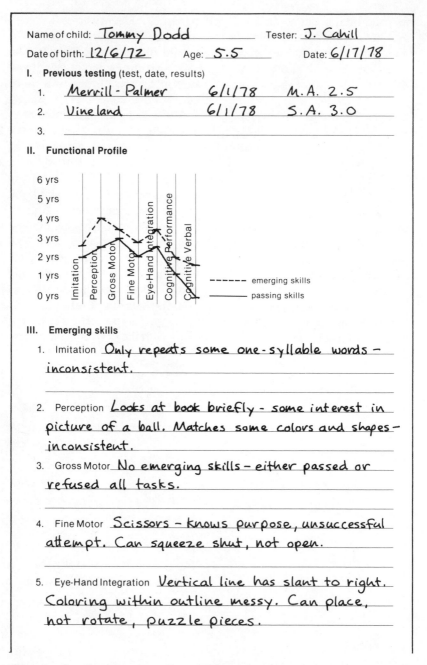

Name of child: **Tommy Dodd**   Tester: **J. Cahill**

Date of birth: **12/6/72**   Age: **5.5**   Date: **6/17/78**

I. Previous testing (test, date, results)

1. **Merrill - Palmer**   **6/1/78**   **M.A. 2.5**
2. **Vineland**   **6/1/78**   **S.A. 3.0**
3. _____

II. Functional Profile

6 yrs
5 yrs
4 yrs
3 yrs
2 yrs
1 yrs
0 yrs

Imitation · Perception · Gross Motor · Fine Motor · Eye-Hand Integration · Cognitive Performance · Cognitive Verbal

------ emerging skills
——— passing skills

III. Emerging skills

1. Imitation **Only repeats some one-syllable words — inconsistent.**

2. Perception **Looks at book briefly - some interest in picture of a ball. Matches some colors and shapes — inconsistent.**

3. Gross Motor **No emerging skills - either passed or refused all tasks.**

4. Fine Motor **Scissors - knows purpose, unsuccessful attempt. Can squeeze shut, not open.**

5. Eye-Hand Integration **Vertical line has slant to right. Coloring within outline messy. Can place, not rotate, puzzle pieces.**

Figure 1. Completed Assessment Form for Tommy.

6. Cognitive Performance <u>Hands 2 of 5 objects named.</u>
<u>Responds to "come" "give" gestures only.</u>
<u>Matching inconsistent.</u>

7. Cognitive Verbal <u>Vocalizes when playing - variation</u>
<u>in pitch, mostly vowel sounds, however. Echos</u>
<u>his name: "To--eee." Echos single words on demand.</u>

IV. **Behavioral Description**

1. Communication <u>Gestures wants by reaching or</u>
<u>moving adult's hand.</u>

2. Social interaction <u>Fleeting eye contact. Laughs</u>
<u>when tickled or swung. No initiation of</u>
<u>contact.</u>

3. Attention, use of sensory modalities <u>Hyperactive -</u>
<u>attention ½ - 1 min. Visually distracted.</u>
<u>Ignores sounds when playing.</u>

4. Interests, preferences <u>Lines up objects. Dislikes</u>
<u>change or interruptions. Repetitive play.</u>
<u>Likes all foods.</u>

5. Bizarre mannerisms <u>Stares at hands and fingers.</u>
<u>Bites hand when stressed. Some rocking.</u>

6. Response to structure <u>Cooperative when he understands</u>
<u>task. Learns from demonstration and physical prompts.</u>
<u>Some understanding of task-reward sequence.</u>

V. **Family Description** (name, age, occupation)

1. Father <u>Robert J. 28 yrs. Mechanic (8-5 shift)</u>
2. Mother <u>Susan D. 25 yrs. Millworker (3-11 shift)</u>
3. Siblings <u>John   3 yrs. at home - normal</u>

4. Others in home   Grandmother (mat.) Mrs. Downy –
at home

5. Classroom, teacher   to be decided

VI. **Parent Concerns** (problems, expectations, current management)

1.   Toilet training. Urine daytime OK 50%,
Bowel accidents frequent. Requires constant
supervision – scolding unsuccessfull. Does not
undress to sit on toilet.

2.   Dressing. Some skill with shirt, requires
prompts and help with pants. Parents want
independent dressing (except shoes).

3.   Behavior. Opens refrigerator, can't wait for
anything, tantrums, fights with brother.
Spanking and scolding ineffective. Isolation
not tried.

4.   Ignores others – no language. Parents
want more response and speech, don't know
how much he understands – they usually
yell at him.

Name of child: _____   Tester: _____

Date of birth: _____   Age: _____   Date: _____

I.   **Previous testing** (test, date, results)

1. _____

2. _____

3. _____

II.   **Functional Profile**

6 yrs

5 yrs

4 yrs

3 yrs

2 yrs

1 yrs

0 yrs

Imitation | Perception | Gross Motor | Fine Motor | Eye-Hand Integration | Cognitive Performance | Cognitive Verbal

III.   **Emerging skills**

1.   Imitation _____
_____
_____

2.   Perception _____
_____
_____

3.   Gross Motor_____
_____
_____

4.   Fine Motor _____
_____
_____

5.   Eye-Hand Integration _____
_____
_____

Figure 2.   Blank Assessment Form.

6. Cognitive Performance _____
   _____
   _____

7. Cognitive Verbal_____
   _____
   _____

IV. Behavioral Description

1. Communication _____
   _____
   _____

2. Social interaction _____
   _____
   _____

3. Attention, use of sensory modalities _____
   _____
   _____

4. Interests, preferences _____
   _____
   _____

5. Bizarre mannerisms _____
   _____
   _____

6. Response to structure _____
   _____
   _____

V. Family Description (name, age, occupation)

1. Father _____
2. Mother _____
3. Siblings_____
   _____
   _____

   4.   Others in home _____

_____

   5.   Classroom, teacher _____

VI. **Parent Concerns** (problems, expectations, current management)

   1.   _____

_____

_____

_____

   2.   _____

_____

_____

_____

   3.   _____

_____

_____

_____

   4.   _____

_____

_____

_____

Chapter 3.
Expectations, Goals,
and Objectives

In Chapter 2 we discussed the systematic evaluation of the child by assessment of the present level of functioning and behavior in specific skill areas. A holistic approach was emphasized, taking into account not only the child's interest and abilities, but the parents' needs, goals, abilities, and the availability of resources. During the *initial* assessment we collected information about what the child can do, what he is ready to learn (emerging skills), and what his parents would like him to learn. In this chapter we focus on the process of identifying and selecting both long-range and short-range goals for the individualized educational (and treatment) program from this assessment.

Setting an appropriate direction is an especially important aspect of special educational planning, because parent and teacher expectations, goals, and objectives for a particular child tend to affect all aspects of the curriculum or set the tone for teaching interactions. It can range all the way from the attitude that any teaching program is fine as long as the children don't misbehave, to the expectation that all children can be mainstreamed if only the right techniques are used. Clearly, a different curriculum would evolve from each of these aims. From our experience we have learned that neither of these expectation extremes serves to maximize individual adaptation for our children. In order to achieve this basic purpose of our efforts, even the most tentative goals need to be based on the most rational understanding possible of the child and his family.

Expectations, goals, and objectives all involve some kind of prediction of the results we anticipate from our teaching efforts. We know that it is difficult to make such predictions specifically and with any certainty. It is extremely difficult to predict what we ourselves or the child we are teaching will be doing 10 years from now. There are too many as yet un-known determining factors for us to make many specific estimates. On the other hand, we can expect to predict a great many details for tomor-row and the rest of the week. For these reasons we have found it useful and important to distinguish three kinds of rational goals: 1) long-range expectations, 2) intermediary goals for 3 months to a year, and 3) imme-diate teaching objectives (discussed in Chapters 4 and 5). We have found that, when these three levels of planning are contradictory, the result is often increased strange and psychotic behavior in children and demorali-zation, frustration, and even mental illness in teacher-parents. On the other hand, when these three levels of planning are reasonably coordi-nated with each other, the basis for appropriate special education, even for the most difficult child, can be established.

LONG-TERM EXPECTATIONS

Long-term expectations most often reflect parents' hopes and expecta-tions for their child and professionals' understanding of the prognosis for various handicaps. However, such expectations are likely to be gen-eral and fewer in number than the more immediate goals. Clearly, the more the parents know about their child, and the more the professional knows about children like the particular one, the more reasonable their long-range expectations are likely to be. Thus, a moderately retarded child will not be expected to attend college. Schopler and Reichler's (1972) investigation of parents' understanding of their own children's de-velopment showed that they were usually quite accurate. They could pre-dict their child's current abilities and developmental levels accurately when compared with subsequent test results. However, their predictions of future achievement were often highly discrepant from their current as-sessment. Their long-range expectations seemed to be affected by their hopes and desires for major therapeutic and educational effects, not lim-ited by their child's current disability.

This was especially true of the parents of the younger child. As the child grows older, the future increasingly becomes the present, and pre-diction and expectation more closely approximate current reality. Pro-fessionals have similar difficulties, but are highly diverse. Many primary care clinicians reflect high future expectations similar to those of the par-ents. Teachers also often project high future expectations for their charges. In part, this reflects their need for optimism in order to main-tain their own demanding efforts with the child. Unrealistically high ex-pectations have also been supported by earlier writers and theorists who believed most of these children to be unusually bright. They felt the child's "true high potential" would be released once the "psychiatric" barriers were overcome.

Other professionals, and at times parents, forecast unreasonably poor prognoses, often leading to hopelessness and minimal efforts for the child. We now have considerably improved data to provide more realistic long-term expectations for children as a group, but caution is still warranted. We know, for instance, that lower overall function, as reflected in IQ or developmental assessment scores of less than 50, generally predicts more limited outcome. Also, when speech continues to be absent for many years, prognosis is more guarded. However, predictability from IQ and developmental data becomes less reliable when the child is functioning above the IQ level of 50. There are often individuals who show sudden and unexpected rapid development despite initially low levels of performance, and children who make significant progress even with severely delayed speech.

We generally find that emphasis on long-term expectations can be detrimental to effective programming for children. Because of the complexity and difficulties in future predictions discussed above, such emphasis more often than not leads to inappropriate immediate expectations of the child. Despite their awareness of the child's current limitations, those with highly optimistic expectations frequently place unrealistically high demands on the child and expect progress to occur more quickly than is possible. This usually leads to a continued sense of failure for child, parent, and teacher, and increasing "resistance" by the child.

Over the long run, this distorts the situation so that the child is perceived as "refusing" rather than "unable" to perform, and the parent's or teacher's frustration turns into anger. The teaching task changes from a helping one to a battle of "wills." On the other hand, unreasonably poor expectations lead to decreased effort and inadequate demands on the child. He is not challenged at his optimum learning level, and progress does not occur. At times expectations fluctuate between over-optimism and pessimistic hopelessness, responding to immediate successes and failures.

For these reasons we find it most useful to defer issues of long-term expectations and outcome to those times when such planning is required. Optimal effort occurs more often when regular success is experienced. When the focus is on shorter term goals and immediate specific objectives geared to the child's emerging abilities, immediate success is more likely to be experienced, programs develop gradually and systematically, effort is more stable and sustained, and hope remains positive.

TEACHING GOALS

Unlike long-term expectations, short-term goals refer to progress expected to occur over a span of 3 months to 1 year. A greater number of such goals can be formulated than for longer time periods, and they can also be more specific. However, usually goals have to be broken down into more immediate teaching objectives to be realized. Short-term goals also refer to the time period for the Individualized Education Program (IEP) prescribed by PL 94-142. There are two kinds of goals: those that pertain to curriculum content and those that involve the management of difficult or strange behavior. Since our children frequently express odd behavior during teaching sessions, the two goals tend to overlap. However, it is useful to consider them separately.

Curriculum Goals

Whether we are formulating a teaching program for the home or the classroom, we need to know the child's current skills and deficits, his parents' needs and concerns, and reasonably achievable goals. We start with the assessment question "Where is the child now?" in order to answer the next question for goal selection, "Where do we want to go with him?" The reader who has little teaching or child-rearing experience may find it difficult to select goals from the information gathered at the initial assessment. In Chapters 4 and 5 we discuss in some detail the specific objectives and tasks by which to reach our goals. The focus on these short-term objectives also facilitates the regular reevaluation of our goals. This allows us to readjust our plans to changes or lack of changes in the child, his parents, their home situation, the school, or other supplementary programs.

Such changes in short-term goals do not jeopardize continued hope and effort. We have seen unpredictable spurts in learning; for example, a child jumps or combines steps we had expected to follow one after the other in orderly sequence. We have also seen a lack of expected change, where child and parent-teacher seem "stuck in a groove." Such situations arising in the course of home teaching (or school teaching) necessitate flexible adjustments. It is detrimental to both parent and child to spend time on activities that are either so simple that they are boring or so difficult that they are highly frustrating. The selection of goals is a statement of intended purpose, not a fixed requirement. They can and should be changed whenever they are clearly no longer appropriate. However, the formation of goals provides an operating framework or guideline for selecting specific objectives for preparing a specific teaching program.

Behavioral Goals

Management of the child's behavior becomes a primary teaching goal for two distinct reasons. Frequently a major concern of parents or teachers that brings them to seek help is one or more difficult behaviors the child presents at home or at school. A second reason for focusing on behavior is when it seriously interferes with the process of the teaching program.

Developmentally disordered children often have a variety of behaviors that concern parents and others responsible for their care. These range from behaviors that are simply peculiar or annoying to those that disrupt the lives of those around them and endanger the life of the child or others. It is important to carefully identify individual behavior problems and distinguish the nature of the problem that they present. The problem will not be solved if we try to work at some diffuse, global level; rather we have to single out particular behaviors and work on them one at a time. Not only does such a focus make the problems more tractable, but solving a single behavior problem tends to have effects beyond the target area—not only for the child, but also for the parent-teacher, who gains confidence with every success in managing the child's behavior. The training hierarchies presented in the first chapter determine priority.

Not all possible target behaviors, initially identified, require immediate attention. As indicated in Chapter 1, alternative solutions are sometimes preferable to direct behavioral interventions. For instance, it might be better to latch the door for a child who wanders off than to intervene behaviorally before certain commands like "stop" and "no" are understood. Likewise, until a child understands and responds to these commands it may be easier to provide a fence or supervision for his safety in the yard. Houses and classrooms can be made relatively "child proof" from a safety standpoint, much as one would for a mobile 2- or 3-year-old child.

In order to teach a child, he must be able to sit for some specified period of time or, for some activities, at least stay in the proximity of the parent-teacher. Sitting, orienting, and attending behaviors inevitably become an issue in teaching. Similarly, some compliance to requests is essential for teaching to progress. Often these behaviors are initially best dealt with in the circumscribed context of the teaching situation, and, as some progress is achieved, they can be generalized to other situations. The need for success for both child and parent-teacher should always be kept in mind. For a child who is constantly on the move, sitting still for even a few minutes may be a major accomplishment. Excessive expectation far beyond the child's initial ability will lead to failure and frustration. As with teaching in other areas, only one or a few behaviors should be worked on at a time. If too many problems are targeted at once, parent and child are continuously engaged in a conflict, with resulting frustration and failure and little opportunity to experience success and pleasure in their interactions.

Those common behaviors that are peculiar and annoying, such as hand posturing, spinning and flipping objects, and self-stimulation, should generally *not* be made specific targets for behavior management unless they directly interfere with teaching. We have observed that such behaviors tend to diminish as the child becomes oriented to the teaching task, and, even further, as new skills are learned. For such behaviors, then, the teaching structure itself may serve as a control and not require additional management efforts. These behaviors become easier to handle when the child has more skills. Attention to every peculiar behavior too early will divert effort from more important goals and increase the probability of frustration, conflict, and failure. As the child gains in other skills, these behaviors become less important to him and more tolerable to the parent who achieves success in other areas.

Even for behaviors that are dangerous to the child or to those working with him, it is preferable first to attempt to control them through the use of appropriate teaching structure and educational goals before deciding to use aversive and painful procedures. However, when the behaviors involve high risks, as with repeated aggression in older children, throwing objects, and fire setting, they need to be targeted for change independent of other teaching goals. When behavior management becomes a specific goal of the program, certain principles must be applied similar to those underlying the educational goals. They should be based on observable problems formulated in specific behavioral terms. The goal should have the potential for being implemented with consistency and within the child's ability to respond appropriately.

CONSIDERATIONS IN GOAL SELECTION

At this point a relatively large number of possible goals may be identified. A smaller number of manageable goals must be culled from this list. Final goals for the program should be decided with the following considerations: 1) realistic for the child, 2) classroom relevance, 3) parents' priorities and needs, and 4) probability of successful results.

Realistic

Many skills and behaviors are more readily accomplished when certain prerequisites have been met. For example, before a child can be expected to respond consistently to a verbal command, some ability to understand the language used is necessary. The behavioral expectations must take into account the child's developmental level much as would be necessary for a normal child. This applies both to the nature of the behavior as well as to the level of achievement expected. While a child functioning at a 2-year-old level might be expected to sit relatively still, one would not expect him to do so for 15 or 20 minutes under most circumstances. Similarly, a child who has just begun to sit still during the teaching period may not immediately be able to do so in other situations, especially strange or more complex and stimulating situations as in church or when his extended family is visiting the home.

Observed emerging abilities form the basis for selecting realistic goals. Many concrete clues can be obtained from emerging scores on the PEP. Newly developing self-help skills can be reported by parents. For example, "Child tried to pull off his shoes and socks when he arrived home from school. . . . Child pushed his chair and tried to climb to reach the peanut butter. . . . He poured juice into a glass. . . . She got mother's pocketbook when it was time to go out. . . . He tried to use a rake after watching his father work in the yard." These recent changes indicate the child's readiness for further progress in the same skill area. We then need to ask ourselves: What will offer additional practice for a partially learned skill? How can a learned skill be used for teaching a new one?

Classroom Relevance

A number of goals are likely to improve the child's adjustment at school and also at home. Others are especially important for improved school adjustment. These are likely to involve getting along and working with other children and being able to use classroom routines. Does the child need practice in sitting in a chair, walking with the group, holding another child's hand, attending to the teacher's directions, communicating his needs? Does he need help with stopping and coming on command, controlling his impulses, taking turns? Does he have the necessary skills for marking with a crayon, for carrying a tray in the cafeteria, using the toilet, getting dressed, following through on work routines? We need to consider whether a particular goal can be worked into a group activity.

Family Priorities

Just as there are certain goal priorities that apply especially to the classroom, others have special significance at home. We would ask: What are the parents' immediate priorities for improving the child's safety and home adjustment? Do they want improvement in sitting at the table for meals, staying out of a sister's room, accepting affection from relatives, dressing himself for school, decreasing tantrums? Do they have strong feelings about controlling impulses and funny behaviors in public places, playing with siblings, demanding less attention? Do they need help with keeping him out of the street, out of neighbors' houses, out of Daddy's study?

In order to define the most immediate family goals, it is helpful to consider special interests of parents and other family members. What do they enjoy doing that could be useful for involving and teaching the child? Mother may enjoy playing records, dancing with her children, baking, or gardening. Father may enjoy carpentry, drawing, playing the guitar, sports, or table games. Often the extended family or siblings can be involved in play and teaching activities with the handicapped child.

Probability of Success

The parent-teacher shares with the child the need to experience success and to develop a self-concept of competence. It is therefore helpful to begin the home or school teaching with a *few* activities that are *easy* for the child to learn so that both parent-teacher and child can experience success together. Occasionally a parent will give top priority to a behavior or skill that is beyond the child's developmental level. Although it is important to accept this priority as a longer range goal, the professional must translate it into preliminary activities that the child is ready to learn, thus enabling the teaching experience to be one of success. During the subsequent course of home teaching, care should be taken to point out success, especially when things seem to be going slowly. For both school and home teaching the likelihood for success can often be increased by using the child's interests and skills, even if they are sometimes unusually repetitious. If he is especially interested in objects that turn, wiggle, or move, these may be used for further learning. If he likes to arrange blocks in a line, this can be used for teaching other organizational skills. The observant and inventive parent-teacher can find ways of using the child's special interest in food, telephone books, maps, puzzles, toys that come apart, favorite TV shows, or jewelry to make the teaching goals more interesting and their achievement more likely.

GOAL SEQUENCE AND INTERACTION

It is possible to begin teaching any skill at the child's emerging level of function, but the most effective and efficient teaching program will be achieved if attention is paid to prerequisite skills. By prerequisite skills we mean the recognition that most tasks are more easily learned if the child has already mastered some of the skills required for the task. The assessment of function areas already assures that an easier necessary skill in that function will be accomplished before a more difficult task is attempted in the same function area. For instance, difficult fine motor tasks, such as tracing a complex figure, will not be attempted before more basic fine motor skills, such as holding a crayon and making simple strokes, have been attained.

In addition to sequencing factors, it is also important to recognize that goals for different mental functions are interdependent and overlap with each other. Staying with the same example, for instance, the child not only requires basic fine motor skills, but also must have some basic eye-hand coordination before he is ready to learn to trace complex figures. This is in keeping with development in normal children as well as the handicapped, and follows from the developmental basis of our approach. Development, even in normal children, is not a smooth, continuous process in every skill and function area. Rather, one or more skill areas develops to a certain level and then ceases further progress, while there is a rapid development in others. When some skill areas reach an appropriate level of development there is often a sudden spurt of progress in skills that had been temporarily arrested. Frequently, new areas of skill rapidly begin to emerge as a result of the interaction of two or more functional areas. Certain skills may be relatively basic to a wide range of later learning and need to be emphasized in early goals. The skills are discussed in relative developmental order.

Imitation

The imitation learning modality is basic to acquiring language and new words. It has the advantage of being conducted either verbally or nonverbally. It involves cooperation and can facilitate all future learning. Imitation also provides early opportunity for the child and parent to experience *pleasure* in interaction and fosters motivation for accomplishment (competence motivation). Imitation skills also increase the sensitivity to careful observation. They may require some perceptual and motor skills. However, imitation tasks can usually be programmed at very early levels of development.

Gross Motor

All responses require some motor ability and this is often the area most intact in autistic and developmentally disabled children. Gross motor activities also serve to increase alertness in withdrawn and hypoactive children and dissipate excess energy in hyperactive children. They are also used in both interactional and self-occupying activities. They help focus the child's attention in a structured, self-controlled manner. In these ways, they will facilitate development in a wide range of areas and be useful in future efforts, such as self-help skills.

Perceptual

Perceptual skills are essential to the learning process since they are the major means by which we communicate intent to the child and are critical for the child to "know" his environment. Perceptual skills are necessary for fine motor development and perceptual-motor integration because they provide feedback for the child to check his performance. Ultimately, perceptual skills are essential for differentiating functional use of objects and are critical to cognitive development, allowing planning and organization of the environment. Increased perceptual ability at every level serves to decrease fearfulness and increase flexibility, making all teaching easier.

Fine Motor

Fine motor skills are used in many areas as learning advances. They enhance perceptual development and imitation ability. Fine motor skills are necessary for the development of self-help skills, writing, and most vocational skills. They are critical when sign language is used in a simultaneous communication program. Fine motor skills also increase the potential for the experience of pleasure, encourage the development of self-occupying play activities, and significantly increase the potential behavioral repertoire of the child.

Eye-Hand Integration

Eye-hand integration represents the interaction and integration of skills in perceptual and motor functions. The development of eye-hand integration facilitates further development in all preceding areas, allowing more fine tuning of performance. The child's ability for execution of ideas and impact on his environment is considerably enhanced. Communication and interaction with others are stimulated and the opportunity to experience pleasure is increased. Eye-hand coordination is essential for significant cognitive development.

Nonverbal Cognitive

Nonverbal cognitive skills include matching, categorizing, and sequencing. While some cognitive organization occurs early, real development in this area reflects the integration of functional areas previously identified. Cognitive nonverbal skills facilitate increased understanding of the environment and the development of planning and cause-and-effect relationships. Cognitive skills reflect the child's increasing ability to organize his environment to form symbols and construct mental models of his world. Social relationships and communication are enhanced. As a result, the world becomes more predictable, fearfulness is decreased, and flexibility is increased. All learning is facilitated and generalization is promoted.

Verbal Cognitive

Language represents the major interaction of all prior skills, as well as the integrating skill for all other functions. It includes both receptive and expressive abilities. Verbal ability not only facilitates all interactions with the environment and other people, but it is also a major organizer for internal mental processes. Language allows for increasingly subtle and sophisticated differentiations, including the identification of emotional states. This encourages the expression of needs, desires, and feelings in a modulated manner, and tends to have a temporizing effort on all behavior. Language is so essential that it is dealt with here in greater detail.

Previously discussed guidelines for goal selection also apply to language: 1) they must be realistic for the child, 2) they must be relevant to the classroom vocabulary and sentences, 3) they must be understandable and relevant to the parents' speech, and 4) they must have optimum likelihood for success. Because language is so important and efficient for human adaptation, parent-teachers tend to place great emphasis on teaching it. However, language goals must differ according to the child's language development and readiness. This may be clarified by separately discussing lower and higher level language abilities.

The low verbal level child may be mute except for sounds and squeals, even though his chronological age is well above 2 years. Sometimes parent-teachers will use most of their teaching time to condition the child to say a new word. Even though they eventually succeed with that word, the child may not necessarily use it appropriately. This does not represent optimum educational programming. If a child is profoundly retarded, he is not likely to achieve functional language (see Chapter 1). He will, however, need self-help and social survival skills, which can be neglected by focusing on inappropriate language goals. Instead, goals should aim at preverbal skills. The achievement of these will also be useful for other areas, without ruling out some gradual language acquisition.

Realistic skills prerequisite to language include imitating sounds or even body movements. The ability to sit, to wait, and to follow simple directions with gestures is part of a realistic start. The child may learn the meaning of pointing, nodding, shaking head, and other meaningful signs. Beginning facial and mouth exploration, sound exploration, verbal imitation, and beginning understanding of simple words all contribute toward language goals achievable through simultaneous use of sign and spoken language. Some prerequisite skills are needed for goals in this area. The child must show evidence of visual memory, such as looking at a picture of an object and getting that object from across the room. He should have some kinesthetic recall, such as being able to repeat a movement like hand clapping. Motivation is also an important consideration, and goals should include things the child likes and wants. However, the child can also be taught by manipulating his hands through meaningful motions or "signs."

Preverbal goals in the classroom are more readily achieved when the other children also use certain signs, and when these refer to objects and activities that are part of the classroom routine. Preverbal and signing skills can then be realized more readily through peer and classroom activity. Generalization between school and home is desirable for any language goal. Beginning signs should be usable both at home and at school. The sign for "drink," for example, is more general than one for "milk," and can thus be used whenever the child is thirsty.

Parents may need assurance from the professional that signing and preverbal skills are not a substitute for talking, but an aid to developing communication and speech. At this early level of development, it is especially important to coordinate home and school teaching efforts. For example, if signs are used, these can best be achieved if parents also use them at home. Thus goals should be set that lead to actions considered desirable both at home and at school.

The success of both preverbal and signing skills is most likely to occur when the goals relate to activities for which the child has shown a preference or special motivation, as, for example, words or signs for favorite toys, activities, and foods the child really wants.

The parent-teacher has somewhat more flexibility in establishing higher level language goals than those for the lower levels. The child already uses language ranging from short phrases to long sentences, both expressively and receptively. He may have a good vocabulary, including nouns, verbs, prepositions, pronouns, and auxiliary words. Such a child asks and understands meaningful questions ("what," "where," and "who" coming first, "how," "when," and "why" being more difficult). He understands one- and two-step directions, and knows some words for abstract concepts (color, size, shape, amount). Even though a child with emerging language may also use some more advanced phrases in the form of echolalia, jargon, or "TV talk," goals for the language program will focus on meaningful communication that is of immediate importance to the child and his social situation. For example, it may be important to develop a few labels for emotions (happy, sad) to help him explain his behaviors, or some social responses ("Please," "Thank you," "What is your name?" or "How are you?") to promote social interactions. Appropriate goals for training such a child are to fill in any gaps in the list of language skills; to expand the range and variety of sentence structures; to develop descriptive language so that the child can talk about events that occur in his life; to be able to answer yes/no questions; to focus the child on the present and his concrete surroundings in order to eliminate his inappropriate language ("TV talk," jargon, and echolalia); to develop sequencing skills (the ability to tell a story with a beginning, middle, and end); to develop the ability to give out practical information (address, phone number, mommy's name, name of school, teacher); and to develop social conversational abilities.

SPECIFIC OBJECTIVES

In this chapter we have discussed how we develop an appropriate direction to our teaching efforts in three time frames. Long-range expectations extend beyond 1 year. They are few in number and general in nature. They affect the parent-teacher's hopes, expectations, and emotional set, which needs to be positive and optimistic without being clearly unrealistic. Goals encompass our teaching aims for 3 months to a year. They must consider the child's uneven levels of development in various areas of function, the school and home context in which the skills are to be developed, and the preferences that are likely to optimize success. Although goals are generally more specific than long-range expectations, they are still not as precise as the actual objectives of the teaching activity by which we expect the child to achieve the goals set.

These specific teaching objectives determine the daily curriculum. They constitute any one of several steps that must be accomplished in order for the child to achieve a stated goal. Objectives are formulated at the step(s) where the child is experiencing some difficulty, but where he is also showing some emerging skill for achieving the step(s).

An example from the area of self-help skills illustrates the process of selecting specific objectives. Suppose that bowel training is selected as an appropriate goal. This means that the child has shown some bodily awareness of the need to evacuate. He must now be able to remove his clothing, place himself on the toilet or potty chair, remain seated and maintain balance sufficiently to be physically relaxed, do his job, and so on. We have observed him go toward the bathroom when he feels the need. He has not removed his pants without his mother's help, but he is able to balance himself in a sitting position for a reasonable period. The immediate objective of the toileting goal would be to remove his pants. If he has trouble in accomplishing this step it could be further reduced to the following objectives:

1. To place thumbs inside waistband of pants
2. To push thumbs downward
3. To bend body and push pants below knees
4. To push down and step out of pants

Regardless of the child's developmental level or the goals selected for him, successful teaching depends on carefully observing the child's emerging skills, careful analysis of the steps required for achieving this goal, and using this information for stating clearly the specific objectives to the lesson plans. In Chapters 4 and 5 we discuss some of the details for developing specific objectives. Additional illustrations are presented in Chapter 12.

RATIONALE FOR SELECTION OF GOALS FOR TOMMY

Our goals for Tommy were selected on the basis of the three criteria described in this chapter: 1) relevant to his home and school environment, 2) in line with his parents' concerns and priorities, and 3) realistic and possible within the range of his emerging abilities.

The initial assessment told us what general level of skill to consider possible. We saw that Tommy was generally developing slowly, at about half the normal rate. We would not expect him to make a year's progress in 1 year. By looking through the scales of normal development (see Appendix A) we found various skills at his emerging level, and these gave us a clearer idea of what we might realistically expect Tommy to learn.

Considering relevance, we saw Tommy just about to enter school. At home he needed to deal with changes in routines and a younger brother's interruptions. The goals were aimed at improving skills and behaviors that could help him adjust to his immediate environment and could build preacademic skills necessary for future progress.

The parents' priorities were then considered with goals set for the teaching program that would facilitate improved self-help and social skills, ones they most wanted next.

In the goal selection form in Figure 3, the rationale for each set of goals is specified as it applies to Tommy. You can then apply these principles to selecting goals for your own child on the blank form (Figure 4).

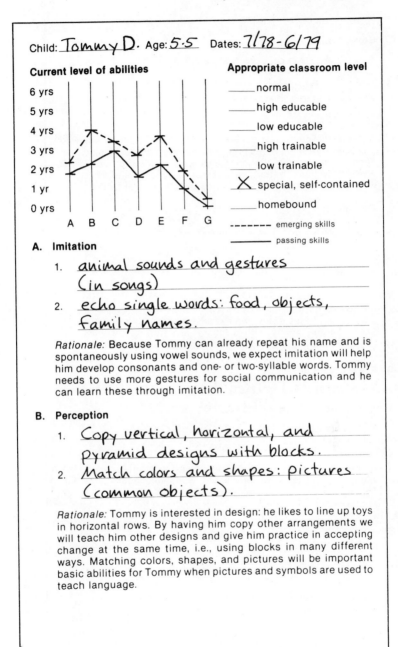

Child: _Tommy D._ Age: _5·5_ Dates: _7/78 - 6/79_

Current level of abilities

6 yrs
5 yrs
4 yrs
3 yrs
2 yrs
1 yr
0 yrs

A B C D E F G

Appropriate classroom level

_____ normal

_____ high educable

_____ low educable

_____ high trainable

_____ low trainable

__X__ special, self-contained

_____ homebound

------- emerging skills

———— passing skills

A. Imitation

1. _animal sounds and gestures (in songs)_
2. _echo single words: food, objects, family names._

Rationale: Because Tommy can already repeat his name and is spontaneously using vowel sounds, we expect imitation will help him develop consonants and one- or two-syllable words. Tommy needs to use more gestures for social communication and he can learn these through imitation.

B. Perception

1. _Copy vertical, horizontal, and pyramid designs with blocks._
2. _Match colors and shapes: pictures (common objects)._

Rationale: Tommy is interested in design: he likes to line up toys in horizontal rows. By having him copy other arrangements we will teach him other designs and give him practice in accepting change at the same time, i.e., using blocks in many different ways. Matching colors, shapes, and pictures will be important basic abilities for Tommy when pictures and symbols are used to teach language.

Figure 3.   Goal Selection Form for Tommy.

C. Gross Motor

1. Ride tricycle (independently)

2. Balance one foot, squat, touch toes

Rationale: Tommy is hyperactive and will need controlled physical movement in his program. Riding a tricycle was chosen because it will help him join in games with his brother. Goal 2 contains actions that are necessary to taking off and pulling on his pants, an important skill for independent toilet training.

D. Fine Motor

1. Work large buttons and zippers

2. Cut on line with scissors

Rationale: Buttons and zippers are important to dressing and toileting and they are within his emerging ability level. He also has emerging ability with scissors, and cutting on lines will enable Tommy to participate in classroom table activities.

E. Eye-Hand Integration

1. Color within outline, copy vertical and horizontal lines

2. Thread large beads, work inset puzzles (no help)

Rationale: All skills are within his emerging level. Goal 1 trains skills used in copying letters and numbers. Goal 2 teaches Tommy to manage materials that will be used to teach concepts at a later time.

F. Cognitive Performance

1. Match and sort by size, color, and shape

2. Sort objects, same name (shoes, cups, etc.)

3. Point to, give to, adult: objects, body parts, family members.

4. Follow verb commands: sit, come, give, stop, wait, go get.

Rationale: Goal 1 requires attention, organization, and trial-and-error work skills; all important for Tommy. Goals 2, 3, and 4 pertain to increasing his understanding of a basic vocabulary. Since Tommy is weakest in language and this is the top priority for both home and school, all aspects of his program will focus on teaching a basic receptive vocabulary (words he can understand).

G. Cognitive Verbal

1. Respond to questions: "What this?" "What want?" — verbal response

Rationale: Although Tommy can repeat a word, he has not yet used one to express his own thoughts or needs. Single-word approximations that communicate important meaning will therefore be the focus of expressive language tasks.

H. Self-Help

1. Put on / take off: pants and shirt (unaided)

2. Complete urine training. Bowel training with prompts.

3. On command: put away toys, carry cup / plate to sink.

Rationale: Dressing skills are essential for independent toileting, a priority for home and school. Goal 3 was chosen because these tasks would give Tommy practice in listening to directions, moving slowly with organization and purpose, and accepting routines and arrangements of others. At the same time these "helping" routines would make him appreciated at home and at school.

I. Social

1. Take turns (in structured games)

2. "Look" at adults when told.
   Carry objects to others.
3. Gesture for help and initiate
   tickle, hug, physical play.

Rationale: When Tommy can learn to "take turns" (goal 1) in a structured game, this skill can then be used to help increase play skills with his brother. Goal 2 teaches behaviors that increase social interactions and facilitate communication. Goal 3 was chosen because Tommy clearly likes a tickle but cannot ask for anything. He needs to initiate requests for what he likes. When a child will look at, give to, and laugh when playing with another person, he will naturally receive more attention from others: parents, teachers, and children. This, in turn, stimulates his desire to communicate.

J. Behavioral

1. Sit for 5 min. (for meals and
   tasks)
2. "Wait" for 1 min. without tantrum

3. Decrease length and frequency
   of tantrum behaviors

Rationale: Although Tommy cannot sit as yet for 2 minutes, it is important to increase this, and it can be done gradually with daily lessons, which are gradually lengthened. The ability to "wait" is a necessary skill for playing with others, managing school routines, and going into public places. Goal 3 is a top priority for family survival, and also for school.

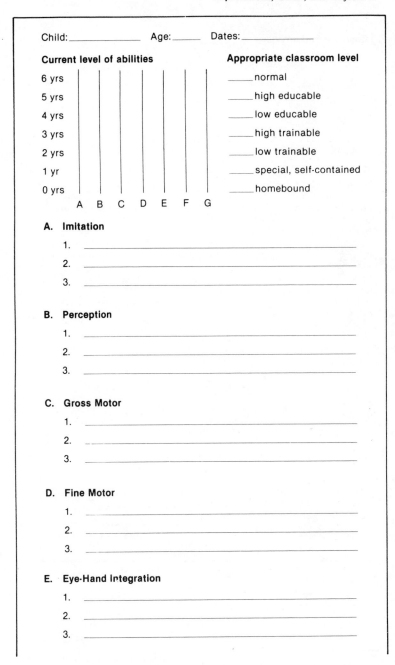

Child:_____   Age:_____   Dates:_____

Current level of abilities   **Appropriate classroom level**

6 yrs   _____ normal

5 yrs   _____ high educable

4 yrs   _____ low educable

3 yrs   _____ high trainable

2 yrs   _____ low trainable

1 yr   _____ special, self-contained

0 yrs   _____ homebound

        A   B   C   D   E   F   G

A. Imitation

        1. _____

        2. _____

        3. _____

B. Perception

        1. _____

        2. _____

        3. _____

C. Gross Motor

        1. _____

        2. _____

        3. _____

D. Fine Motor

        1. _____

        2. _____

        3. _____

E. Eye-Hand Integration

        1. _____

        2. _____

        3. _____

Figure 4.   Blank Goal Selection Form.

F. Cognitive Performance

    1. _____

    2. _____

    3. _____

G. Cognitive Verbal

    1. _____

    2. _____

    3. _____

H. Self-Help

    1. _____

    2. _____

    3. _____

I. Social

    1. _____

    2. _____

    3. _____

J. Behavioral

    1. _____

    2. _____

    3. _____

Chapter 4.
Lower Level
Teaching Objectives

At this point you are familiar with the process of assessing the child's developmental level and learning problems in several areas of mental functioning (Chapter 2). We discussed ways of identifying appropriate teaching goals in Chapter 3. In this and the next chapter we focus on how to translate goals into specific teaching objectives for immediate use with the child. We discuss the selection of specific objectives under each of the seven function areas represented in the Psychoeducational Profile. This scheme is used primarily to help organize large numbers of teaching possibilities. The categories will obviously overlap with each other, and are not the only possibilities for grouping.

This chapter includes objectives in the areas of imitation, perception, and motor activities. These involve skills that usually develop during preschool years in normal children. These lower level skills will reflect less in their curriculum during the elementary school years than will higher level skill training in areas of eye-hand coordination, cognitive performance, and language, including both receptive and expressive abilities. Autistic and developmentally disabled children may have difficulties in all of these areas. However, for the sake of clarity, we cover the four lower level skill areas in this chapter and the three higher level ones in Chapter 5.

From our assessment we have some clear ideas of what a particular child can and cannot already do. We also know some of the tasks he is struggling with, not yet successfully but with clearly emerging skills. It is from the goals for these emerging skills that we will want to select our specific objectives. This is a most important step for selecting the individualized curriculum, and we have found it useful to bear in mind several considerations.

First, it is helpful to gain some idea of the reason for the child's specific learning problem. This does not mean knowing or attempting to diagnose the cause of the child's developmental disability. Even if it were possible to do so, and it usually is not, such diagnostic formulation does not necessarily have any direct bearing on teaching objectives. If a child has difficulty with bowel training, he may suffer from brain damage, genetic aberration, autism, or mental retardation, and the problem of formulating appropriate teaching objectives remains the same.

On the other hand, an analysis of the task and the child's response to the task will offer the best clues for understanding the child's specific learning problems. Following the bowel training illustration, a task analysis will show steps like: 1) recognizing the need to go, 2) going to the right place, 3) pulling down pants, 4) sitting on toilet, 5) using paper to wipe, and 6) getting dressed. Other steps could be added to the list depending on how detailed the analysis needs to be. If the child's response to the bowel training problem shows that he has trouble with step 3, pulling down pants, a further task analysis is needed of this particular task. This might include the following steps: 1) place thumbs of both hands inside waistband of pants, 2) push downward with both hands, 3) bend body to push pants below knees, 4) push down to floor and step out. If the child's response to pulling down pants shows that he has trouble bending his body (step 3), the teaching objective will be different for this goal than if he has trouble inserting his thumbs inside the waistband. In either case, good observations of the child will usually show a usable cause of a particular learning problem, which can be corrected by selecting an appropriate teaching objective. This cause will usually have no direct bearing on the cause of his disorder. In fact, over-concern with theories of learning problems can often lead to unnecessary and unproductive teaching exercises.

Sometimes it is not possible to infer a reason or even a hypothesis for why a child has difficulties with a particular task or objective. In this case, trial-and-error experimentation with different objectives can still lead to a successful teaching interaction. The parent-teacher need not be afraid to try out ideas for variation in objectives. The child will not be harmed by such experimentation as long as his responses are observed and the parent-teacher changes strategies when they are clearly not productive. This kind of experimentation is essential to the continuous evaluation necessary to finding the best and most productive teaching strategies.

In the following examples, several different objectives are given for achieving teaching goals in the areas of Imitation, Perception, Fine Motor, and Gross Motor.

IMITATION

The achievement of goals in the area of imitation requires a number of basic skills. The child must look at or listen to another person; he must understand the concept of matching; he must be able to organize his movements to make them match what he has observed. Difficulty with any one of these basic skills will prevent successful imitation. Although all teaching activities in this manual develop some of these basic skills (observation, matching, and organization), here we discuss objectives that specifically pertain to several major goals in imitation: copying the use of a material, copying a physical movement, and copying a sound. When a child gets no pleasure from the copying process itself, the adult has to teach it with "external reinforcers." This usually requires setting up a repetitive game and rewarding him with edible treats or praise.

Some children learn to imitate physical movements more easily than to imitate sounds. For others the opposite may be true. It is important to keep in mind that one learned response does *not* meet the goals of imitation. It is often easy for the child to learn a specific action, such as clapping hands, or a specific sound, such as "bye," without understanding the imitative element. Effective imitation requires that the child can *change* from one action/sound to a different one according to what he observes the adult doing. First he is taught two or three actions or sounds. Then he is asked to copy alternating or varying actions/sounds. When this is successful the adult can assume that the child has the necessary understanding for this imitation goal.

The following teaching activities illustrate some typical objectives used to develop imitation goals. The reader will see that the specific objective of each activity represents one step toward reaching the goal stated for the child.

GOAL 1:   TO DEVELOP IMITATIVE USE OF MATERIALS

Objective A: To turn, push, pull knobs; copying adult's movements.
Materials: "Busy box" (infant activity board with knobs used in a variety of ways)
Procedure: Sit next to the child. Ask him to "look" as you move one knob; then say "Do it" and help him; praise and reward. When he can repeat this one action after you, teach a second action. When he can use at least three knobs in different ways, alternate them in random order, telling the child with word or gesture to copy you.
Objective B: To use one object in two different ways, copying adult.
Materials: Car, clay, spoon, and pan

Procedure: Place one object/toy on the table. Do one action with it, then ask the child to copy you. Now take the toy and do a different action with it, asking the child to copy this new action. For example:

Toy car—push back and forth/pick up and bang down.

Clay—roll into coil/flatten into pancake.

Spoon and pan—stir or tap edge of pan.

Objective C: To arrange a set of materials in three different ways.

Materials: Building blocks (four to six for each person)

Procedure: Teach the child three different arrangements: 1) a tower, 2) a train, 3) a square block. When he can copy all three, begin to alternate arrangements so that he copies whatever one you have just made.

Considerations in Selecting Objectives. In all these examples the child is asked to choose between two or three possibilities: a certain object, a certain action, or a certain arrangement. We do not want him to simply memorize what to do, we want him to watch and copy what he has just observed. Individual children will find some imitation tasks more difficult than others. For example, a child who dislikes changing routines or who has a strong attachment to certain objects will find it difficult to give up his own preferences in order to imitate the adult. If he is strongly driven to always stack blocks he might find it easier to imitate the arrangement of some other materials, such as pegs or coins. If a child dislikes touching sticky surfaces he would not be asked to imitate the use of clay. Teachers and parents must be sensitive to the reasons why some activities do not work easily for a specific child. They must be ready to make changes to accommodate the child's particular needs and limitations.

GOAL 2: TO IMITATE PHYSICAL MOVEMENTS

Objective A: To clap hands, slap knees, touch feet, and stamp feet, copying the adult's movements.

Materials: None

Procedure: Sit facing the child. Ask him to "look" as you do one movement. Help him to copy you. Reward and praise him. Continue until he can easily copy one movement. Then teach a second movement in the same way. When he has learned three different movements, begin to alternate, praising him for copying the one he sees you do.

Objective B: To touch face parts: nose, mouth, ears, hair; copying the adult's movements.

Materials: None

Procedure: These movements are taught separately, in the same way as the preceding activity. Then they are presented in random order and the child must "look" and then copy.

Objective C: To make various strokes with chalk, down, across, dots.

Materials: Chalk and chalkboard

Procedure: Stand next to the child. Place his hand on top of yours as you make a mark, stating the direction, "Down." Then hand him the chalk and ask him to do the same. Repeat one movement until he has learned it and can copy you without physical assistance. Then teach the second movement. When he has learned three, begin to alternate them.

Considerations in Selecting Objectives. When we ask a child to imitate physical movements, we must consider his gross motor skills and coordination, his awareness of different body parts, and his ability to visually observe movements in others. The rationale for selecting objectives and procedures A, B, and C follows.

Objective A teaches physical movements that the child can observe himself making. He therefore has visible confirmation that he has matched the adult's movements. These movements can all be done while seated. They are appropriate for children who do not have a good understanding of their body parts and who have difficulty controlling their balance and their attention when standing up.

Objective B asks the child to make movements he cannot observe himself making. He must learn through touch that he has matched the adult's actions. It may be necessary to help a child with this step by working side by side in front of a mirror.

Objective C teaches a child to make movement that results in a visible mark. The emphasis is placed on the direction of the movements. This may be difficult for children who do not track the direction of moving objects easily. In the procedure we ask the child to feel the movement of the adult's hand at first, thus giving him additional information through his kinesthetic senses.

GOAL 3: TO IMITATE SOUNDS

Objective A: To imitate sound approximations of "wheee," "boom," "down."

Materials: None

Procedure: Repeatedly play a physical game the child enjoys and use one sound at a predictable point in the action. When the child learns to expect this sound, delay the next physical action slightly as you indicate by touching the child's lips that you want him to also make the sound. For example, bounce the child on your knee four times, then say "wheee" as you swing him backward down and up again. When learned, begin to delay the swing until he makes some sound. A variation of this could be done with "ring around the rosey" emphasizing the word "down" as you fall to the floor.

Objective B: To imitate "zii-ip," "zoo-om," and "oh-oh" during a crayon task.

Materials: Crayons and paper

Procedure: Sit with child and take turns making marks on the paper. Make a special sound with each particular mark and exaggerate the dramatic inflection of the sound. Do so with obvious enjoyment. When you hand the child the marker for "his turn," hold it a moment, preventing movement, as you indicate he is to make the same sound.

Objective C: To imitate the animal sounds "moo," "bow-wow," "meow."

Materials: Toy animals (cow, dog, cat)

Procedure: Move the toy cow along the table toward the child, repeating the "moo" sound. Hand him the cow and indicate it is his turn. Encourage him to make the sound by moving his lips open and repeating sound yourself. When this is learned, proceed to the next animal.

Objective D: To imitate sounds without physical movements, "ma-ma," "ba-ba," "coo-kie."

Materials: Box of rewards (food he likes or small toys)

Procedure: Sit opposite child with the rewards in your lap. Say "look" and point to your mouth as you make a sound, "ma-ma." Then point to the child's mouth and reward him as soon as he makes the sound in imitation. At the beginning, reward the child for any sound he makes. Gradually begin to expect more accuracy.

Considerations in Selecting Objectives. The goal of increasing sound imitation is vital to the development of speech. The four sample objectives we have just described illustrate some different ways to work on this important step. The choice of which to start with will depend on several factors: how much vocalizing and babbling the child is already doing, whether he is aware of producing sounds and uses them to gain attention, whether he enjoys physical movement or music, whether he understands the sequence of task-reward. For example, Procedure A is chosen for a child who enjoys being bounced and swung and can remember the sequence of this game. He learns that a specific sound is part of the routine and he is therefore motivated to make this sound in order to continue the game he enjoys. For those children who vocalize only when they are in a state of urgency, the excitement of physical play encourages sound production. Children who enjoy music often make their first sounds as part of a song or musical game.

Procedure B is appropriate for a child who does not enjoy physical contact and is not interested in music. This child enjoys making designs and is primarily interested in visual stimuli. He is encouraged to produce sounds because they are part of making the design he likes to see.

Procedure C is chosen for a child who likes animals and has some skill with pretend play. This child is more aware of the sounds made by animals, cars, and machines than the sounds made by humans. The sounds that a child listens to are appropriate ones to ask him to imitate.

Procedure D is chosen for a child who has begun to vocalize and show some interest in experimenting with sound production. We are now asking him to concentrate on more and more exact articulation, on more variety as we introduce two-syllable babbling sounds. Each sound is rewarded so that he understands that we want him to copy our sounds.

PERCEPTION

Many developmentally disabled children suffer from disordered use of perceptual abilities, and the goals for teaching are directed toward improving this use. While all teaching activities utilize sensory modalities, there are some specific techniques that have been helpful in providing special training in perceptual skills that are not functioning effectively—skills that the child is able to use physically but is not using functionally. The following objectives pertain not to physical disability of the eyes and ears but to problems of attention and organization of those stimuli that he can perceive. We will be discussing objectives to meet the goals of tactile, auditory, and visual perception. Difficulties children have around perceptions involving smell and taste can often be dealt with as behavioral problems; for example, excessive tasting of salt, refusing new foods, not distinguishing edibles from non-edibles.

Tactile Perceptions

GOAL 1:   TO INCREASE ACCEPTANCE OF TACTILE STIMULI
  Objective A: To touch and explore two new textures.
  Materials: Play-do, furry puppet
  Procedure: Gradually introduce the child to making contact with:
  1.   Play-do: - push a stick into a clay "cookie."
              - push a ball of play-do onto a spoon.
              - poke a fingertip onto the surface, pressing in a nut.

                    - pick up the "cookie" with his fingers.

                    - roll, squeeze, and pinch play-do.

2.   Puppet: - watch adult stroke puppet.

                    - place hand over adult's while stroking.

                    - touch fingers to fur while stroking.

                    - stroke puppet independent of adult.

(*Note:* Quite frequently a child will overcome an initial fear by repeated experience; on the fourth day he may be quite pleased with an activity he disliked the first three times.)

Objective B: To accept new tactile stimuli on many body parts—neck, back, legs, arms, hands, and cheeks.

Materials: Lotion, powder, brushes, sponges, feather

Procedure: Start with the material that the child finds most enjoyable. Use it on his foot or leg, gradually increasing the pressure. Teach him to use it on himself. Once this is accepted, begin to touch him on other parts, gradually approaching the neck and face. Once he is familiar with the routine, allow him to choose the material he likes best and show you where to touch him.

Objective C: To discriminate among different stimuli.

Materials: Hairbrush, feather, soft sponge (two of each)

Procedure: Place the three objects (one of each) on the table and ask the child to feel them. Describe them if the child understands language. Now take one of the duplicate set and rub it on his body where he cannot see (a leg under the table, a hand behind his back). Ask him to tell you (by gesture or word) which one he feels.

Considerations in Selecting Objectives. The choice of objective will depend on the child's current response to tactile stimuli. Some children are fearful of or actively dislike touching certain textures (play-do, paste, chalk, fur). These children are highly sensitive to textures of clothing and may refuse to wear certain clothes because of a slight scratchy quality. They may dislike having their hand held, sitting on a lap, being washed, or having their head touched. They may be excessively ticklish and appear to reject all affectionate contacts. They defend themselves against tactile stimuli. Objectives for these children focus on developing their acceptance of tactile stimuli. Activity A is chosen for a child who fears letting his hand touch these surfaces (clay and fur). Activity B is appropriate for a child who may be willing to handle different materials but who dislikes having other parts of his body touched. By presenting the new stimuli very gradually and through repeated structured games, fear is reduced. Once relaxed, the child can organize his attention to the actual perception of the tactile stimuli.

In contrast to the overly sensitive child, Objective C is chosen for the child who shows no interest in or awareness of tactile sensations. He may not notice or feel pain or changes in temperature. He is unaware of his clothing and does not notice being wet or soiled. Physical contact goes unnoticed until it becomes unusually strong. In this activity he is given a matching task, one that is dependent on the perception of tactile stimuli. He learns to identify these sensations, either by pointing out the object being used or by verbally describing the sensation.

Visual Perceptions

GOAL 1:   TO SCAN AN AREA TO LOCATE A GIVEN OBJECT

Objective A: To scan the table to locate a correct puzzle piece.

Materials: Four-piece inset puzzle

Procedure: Place a simple puzzle on a cleared table, putting each piece at a different location around the table. Point to each piece in turn, directing the child to put *that* piece in. Once he understands that he is to place the pieces as you direct, then name each one, e.g., "put banana," or point to the hole that needs filling. Now the child will have to scan the area to find the correct piece.

Objective B: To scan the room to locate a given object.

Materials: Apple, ball, shoe, cup

Procedure: Place the objects around the room so that they are clearly visible to the child. Then sit next to him and ask him to "get apple." (If he has no receptive language, hold another apple up, showing him what to get.) The child now has to look at a distance, find what he wants, and move across the space without becoming distracted.

GOAL 2:   TO INCREASE VISUAL TRACKING

Objective C: To observe a moving object.

Materials: Bubbles, ball, balloon, flashlight.

Procedure: Ask child to "look" at each object, and then take action.

Bubbles—Blow them into the air; child pops them with his fingers.

Ball—Sit on floor facing the child. Roll the ball to him, asking him to "catch" it. Gradually roll it slightly to the right or left side so he must reach over to catch it.

Balloon—Pat it into the air and teach child to pat it up again.

Flashlight—Seat child in one place, hand him the flashlight, ask him to make the light "hit" the place you name, i.e., a picture on the wall, a toy across the room, a person.

GOAL 3:   TO MAKE SHIFTS IN VISUAL ATTENTION

Objective D: To look from one object to another, around the room.

Materials: Five objects the child knows by name, e.g., shoe, cup, apple

Procedure: Place these objects around the room. Ask him to "point to" the object as you name it, then quickly name the next object so that he continues visual scanning to keep up with your pace.

GOAL 4:   TO MAINTAIN VISUAL ORGANIZATION

Objective E: To find one object in a cluttered background.

Materials: Kitchen or desk drawer filled with common objects

Procedure: Ask the child to "find" a certain tool or object from the drawer: "Find spoon...baster...eggbeater" or "Find pencil...paper clip...rubber band." If the child does not know the object by name, hold up a similar one and say, "Find this."

Objective F: To find all similar objects in group.

Materials: Box filled with buttons, bobby pins, beads, etc.

Procedure: Show the child one button and put it in a bowl. Now ask the child to get out *all* the buttons and put them into the bowl.

Objective G: To point to one detail of a "busy" picture.

Materials: Pictures of activity, people doing things, many details

Procedure: Ask him to "look at the picture" and then to point to one item, e.g., the boy, the bird, the man raking, etc.

Considerations in Selecting Objectives. A number of visual perception difficulties are addressed in the preceding example objectives. Some children are highly stimulated by visual stimuli but their attention is scattered. This type of child is constantly scanning his environment, but he does not maintain his gaze on one thing for more than a few moments. He is quickly distracted by the slightest movement, a bright color, a shiny surface. He gives only fleeting glances to people or materials, yet he may be extremely quick to observe a tiny crumb or a piece of candy on the floor. He may be distracted from his work by a speck on the table. His scanning and tracking abilities are well developed but he has little control over his attention.

Other children are unusually slow to shift their visual attention. They attend to only one stimulus for long periods, e.g., a wiggling stick, a spinning record, a string being flipped. They gaze intently at the edge of a table, a Venetian blind, running water, and occasionally people's faces. One child may have difficulty looking around the room for an object he wants, or may be unable to follow the movement of a ball. The objectives chosen give practice in the visual perceptual skill that is weak, and are at a level where the child can obtain success.

Objectives A and B train visual scanning at different levels of difficulty. A child first learns to find objects nearby before he can scan the distance effectively. Objective C presents four ways to practice tracking a moving object. The choice of material here depends on what visual stimuli the child finds most interesting and what action he most enjoys doing: popping, pushing, or patting. Objective D is planned for a child who is slow to shift his gaze, one who tends to stare at objects for overly long periods. Objectives E, F, and G train the child to discriminate one particular stimulus from many in front of him. They are presented in order of difficulty but additional considerations must be given to the choice of stimuli used in these activities: The child will have more success with objects that he knows by name, with objects that are obviously discrepant (bright colors, different shapes), and with objects that interest him (food, toys).

Auditory Perceptions

GOAL 1.   TO LOCATE THE SOURCE OR AGENT OF A SOUND

Objective A: To associate three animal sounds with a correct animal.
Materials: Toy cow, dog, and cat
Procedure: Place one animal (cow) on the table. Make the sound "moo-oo," then teach the child to pick up the cow. When this is learned, teach him to do the same with the other two animals. You are teaching him to listen to the sound you make, then pick up that animal.

Objective B: To discriminate between three sound makers.
Materials: Rattle, bell, whistle (two of each)
Procedure: Present one instrument at a time, encouraging the child to first listen to the sound, then make it himself. Next present two instruments, teaching him to use only the one he has heard you use. Finally, place all instruments out of sight. Use one of them, telling him to "listen"; then have him choose the instrument he just heard.

Objective C: To identify the source of a common sound and touch the correct picture.
Materials: Pictures of a telephone, TV, and vacuum cleaner
Procedure: Place the three pictures taped to a wall. As soon as one of these sounds occurs, cup your ear and say, "Listen. What do you hear?" Ask the child to touch the correct picture or name the source.

GOAL 2:   TO RECOGNIZE THE IMPLICATION OF A SOUND IN TERMS OF WHAT HAPPENS NEXT

Objective D: To respond to three sounds with an appropriate action.
Materials: Bell, buzzer (on oven), whistle, glass
Procedure: Teach the child that one particular sound is always heard before a familiar routine occurs by consistently making that sound.

For example, ring a bell before meals, blow a whistle before going out in the car, bang on a toothbrush holder before starting a bath. When the child begins to associate these sounds to a specific routine that follows, then begin to remove them from the child's sight as a signal that he is to come.

Objective E: To carry out an action following an alerting sound.
Materials: None
Procedure: Train the child to carry out some simple actions following an alerting sound associated with these actions. Once he has learned the routines, delay him by gesturing, but expect him to begin the action again when he hears and attends to the alerting sound.

a.   Knock on the door—child opens it.
b.   Ring a bell—child sets the table.
c.   Start the vacuum—child gets dust cloth.
d.   Start the washing machine—child gets clothes.

Considerations in Selecting Objectives. Some autistic and developmentally disordered children seem to be hypersensitive to auditory stimuli. They are distracted and sometimes disturbed by them. They can only work in a quiet environment because they notice the slightest sound (footsteps in the hallway, a cellophane wrapper being opened in another room, etc.). Yet even with their acute hearing they do not always attend to loud noises nearby, such as verbal commands or the telephone. Their attention is highly selective and it is particularly difficult for them to notice sounds when they are engrossed in a visually interesting play activity. Their ability to attend seems to improve when they understand and are interested in the sounds that occur.

We have divided the previous objectives into two general groups. The first group was chosen to increase the child's understanding of a variety of sounds, e.g., those made by the human voice, those made by sound makers, and those made by common household equipment. The second group of objectives was chosen to increase the child's interest in sounds by associating them with an activity he enjoys. Objective D teaches the child that a certain auditory stimulus (bell) is a signal that something is about to happen. Objective E carries this understanding of sequential events one step further, and teaches the child that the sound (bell) is a signal for him to start doing something, part of a familiar routine he enjoys.

GROSS MOTOR

Goals for gross motor development commonly are part of every child's teaching program. Although gross motor skills of autistic and developmentally disordered children are often relatively well developed, their energy, strength, and agility may be far more advanced than their judgment or understanding of verbal and social restraints. This increases problems with managing their behavior. However, a number of these children do have specific problems with gross motor skills. In addition, they all enjoy moving around, and gross motor activities provide an excellent way of teaching verbal and nonverbal cognitive development. Physical movement is essential to the development of the child's awareness of his body and of its relation to his environment. Many school systems and communities can provide special resource programs directed by physical therapists and recreational therapists, but parents and teachers also need to include gross motor activities in their program plans. The following objectives pertain to problems we have frequently observed in our clinical work: 1) lack of energy and muscle strength, 2) poor control of balance, 3) clumsiness when maneuvering around obstacles, and 4) poor control of speed and strength, often placing the child in danger.

GOAL 1:   TO INCREASE ENERGY AND MUSCLE STRENGTH

Objective A: To increase running and kicking skills.

Materials: A large ball

Procedure: First demonstrate by kicking the ball yourself. Take the child's hand and pull him along, running to get the ball. Help him kick it, and run together to catch it. Reward the child after each time you reach the ball; repeat.

Objective B: To bend down and reach up, lifting objects.

Materials: Bags of groceries

Procedure: Include the child in the daily routine of taking groceries out of a bag and placing them on a counter. Place the bag on the floor so that he must bend down. Ask him to put some items on a shelf high enough so he must reach up above his shoulders. Gradually increase the weight of the items you give him.

Objective C: To fall down and get up rapidly.

Materials: None

Procedure: Play "ring around the rosey," taking the child's hands and circling as you sing. Fall down together as you sing "we all fall down," then get up quickly and start again.

Objective D: To run and stoop repeatedly.

Materials: Large bowl filled with five potatoes.

Procedure: Teach the child, by demonstrating, to run to the bowl, stoop down to pick up a potato, and run back and put it on the table. Repeat until all potatoes are moved. This game can be done simultaneously with the adult or with other children.

Objective E: To strengthen stomach, back, and leg muscles.
Materials: None
Procedure: Ask the child to join you in daily calisthenics, imitating you with occasional prompts. Suggested actions are sit-ups, touching toes, knee bends, jumping, running in place.

Considerations in Selecting Objectives. Two main factors must be assessed when selecting objectives to achieve Goal 1. First, we need to know how the child uses his body, which muscles are well developed and which are not, and what actions the child needs to perform in order to be successful in home or classroom activities. Second, we must consider the child's interests so that we can provide motivation or enjoyment of the activities. Hypoactive, "lazy" children get little pleasure from exercise; therefore the gross motor activities must have some point or interest apart from physical movement.

Coordination and muscle strength improve with daily practice. The sample objectives were reached because the activities were individualized to each child's interests in the following ways: Objective A was used with a child who particularly liked to watch and handle this large ball; Objective B was for a child who liked food, who enjoyed lining up cans in rows; Objective C was used with a child who loved music; Objective D worked well for a child who liked repetitive routines, whose play consisted of dumping and filling objects into containers; Objective E was for a child who understood imitation, who was already trying to copy some actions he saw his father doing.

GOAL 2:   TO IMPROVE BALANCE AND COORDINATION

Objective A: To walk forward on balance beam.
Materials: $2'' \times 4''$ board, $5'$ long
Procedure: First demonstrate the action, ask another child to do it, then help the child to walk on the beam. It will be important to analyze the task, giving help at the point of difficulty, and then withdrawing help gradually as his skill increases. An analysis of steps in this task might include standing on the board, placing one foot in front of the other, shifting balance to the forward foot, taking two steps independent of help, and walking the entire board. An analysis of the amount of help might include holding both hands, holding one hand, supporting a stick that the child grasps, or simply walking beside the child with no contact.

Objective B: To balance on one foot.
Materials: Blocks of wood or solid boxes.
Procedure: Lay the blocks on the floor in a "pathway." Ask the child to step over each block as he comes to it. If necessary, reward him at

the end of the pathway. When this is successful, place the blocks farther apart, and ask the child to step up onto each block with one foot and down to the floor with the next foot. Increase the difficulty by placing the blocks so that the child uses first his right and then his left foot to step *up*. Further difficulty is presented when blocks of different heights are used.

Objective C: To counterbalance, adjusting to different angles.

Materials: Swing made from a tire, canvas strap, hammock

Procedure: Place the child in the swing, feet touching the ground. Provide only slight movement until the child gets used to the sensation and begins to move his body in an effort to counterbalance against the swinging motion. Gradually increase the motion and encourage him to use his feet to push backward, then release to swing forward. (*Note:* The same exercise can be provided without a swing by holding the child and tilting him over to one side, then to the other, tilting him forward, then backward, and swinging him around.)

Objective D: To turn upside-down and back without fear.

Materials: None

Procedure: Demonstrate each step of a somersault, then help the child position his body for this, and help move him through it. Care is given to presenting this task one step at a time, giving the child time to get used to each position before pushing him to the next step. For example: 1) kneel with forehead on floor, 2) kneel with top of head on floor, 3) head down with hips up and legs straightened, 4) elevate legs above head, 5) bend neck as legs go over head.

(*Note:* For variation, try the "wheelbarrow" game. This involves picking up the child's feet and pushing forward gently as he walks on his hands.)

Considerations in Selecting Objectives. The choice of objectives for Goal 2 requires an analysis of all the skills the task requires of the child, an analysis of the type of physical help that will be most productive in encouraging him to increase his own physical skill, and a respect for the child's fear or hesitation. Many physically active and strong children show marked clumsiness, fall down easily, or avoid heights or using moving toys, such as wagons or tricycles. Some show marked fear when held up, swung around, or tipped sideways. *We* know there is no danger, but they are unconvinced. Such fear is overcome through frequent experiences with procedures that are exactly at the step the child can manage with help, and therefore accept without fear. Once the task becomes familiar and the child becomes confident, then the adult's help is gradually reduced. Examples of this process of analyzing both the steps of a task and the type of help given are contained in the above objectives. Usually a new step is not taught until the child has mastered the preceding step without needing the adult's help. For example, a child would not be asked to step up onto a block until he had learned to step over a low block without holding the adult's hand.

GOAL 3:   TO INCREASE ABILITY TO MOVE AROUND OBSTACLES

Objective A: To go between two obstacles without touching.

Materials: Household furniture

Procedure: Place the furniture so that the child can go between pieces with 1 foot of clearance. Lay a red string on the floor to mark the pathway. Demonstrate walking down the pathway, making exaggerated movements that illustrate "avoiding" touching the furniture. Ask child to walk without touching, and correct him if he does touch. You may need to control his speed or give physical prompts at first. Once the task is understood, then gradually reduce the space between the obstacles.

Objective B: To watch and place feet on designated spots.

Materials: Colored shapes or "footprints" placed on floor

Procedure: Place the footprints in a pathway. Demonstrate how to walk, placing each foot on one footprint. Help the child to copy you. At first, space the footprints to match the child's natural gait. Once the task is understood, vary this spacing so that he must look, and consciously adjust his gait to fit the visual directions.

Objective C: To carry out a sequence of directional movements.

Materials: None

Procedure: Ask the child to "sit" and watch you as you carry out a sequence or "course." For example, walk between the sofa and table, go around the chair, and lie down on the rug. Now ask the child to "do the same." This activity should include some actions that will be challenging and some that will be fun. The child will now have to look not only where he is going, but also keep track of what to do next. This helps to increase his awareness and organization of movements in relation to his immediate surroundings.

Considerations in Selecting Objectives. These objectives all require the child to pay close visual attention to his surroundings. They also exercise his control, balance, and speed of movement to match the demands of these surrounding limits. Many children with good energy and strength who seem well-coordinated and enjoy physical activity still show poor judgment in moving through their surroundings. Such children do not predict how near or far they are from furniture or how fast or slow they are moving. They may run into things, stumble over a rug, or knock objects or people down unintentionally because they are not attending or judging their size and speed in relation to these obstacles. The appropriate objective is chosen in order to train skill and judgment in specific situations in which the child has been observed to be lacking these skills.

FINE MOTOR

Fine motor skills in this chapter refer to the child's use of his hands—his fingers, his wrist, and the coordination of both hands together. Fine oral motor skills are included under language. Most activities require gross motor and eye-hand integration skills as well and are, therefore, overlapping. Autistic and developmentally disabled children commonly have poorly developed fine motor skills. While they may enjoy watching their hands and fingers move, they often are not skilled in handling, moving, and arranging materials. Developing fine motor skills becomes an important focus of teaching. Children learn about the properties of materials, size, shape, texture, and weight through playing with objects. They are handicapped in learning when they cannot manipulate materials like a normal child. In addition to their difficulties with fine motor tasks, these children often lack the curiosity and persistence that lead to normal exploration of new materials. They ignore appropriate toys and may play for long periods with very simply grasped objects like sticks or coat hangers. Therefore they do not practice new skills like a normal child and are unable to improve their abilities without structured help from others.

In order to choose helpful teaching goals and objectives, the adult must observe how the child handles objects and where he has both difficulties and emerging skills. We have grouped the more common problems under the general goals that follow. The objectives chosen to reach each goal are listed generally in order of difficulty. They are also selected with consideration for a particular child's skill and the new skills that are likely to be an appropriate next step to learn. The numerous objectives presented are not a complete list, but rather illustrations of the process of analyzing the many steps contained in each goal.

GOAL 1:   TO INCREASE GRASPING AND PINCHING SKILLS
   Objective A: To pick up and release various sizes of objects.
   Materials: Shoe, paper napkin, blocks of different sizes
   Procedure: Ask the child to pick up the shoe and hand it to you, pick up the napkin and put it in the trash can, pick up the blocks and put them in a box.
   Objective B: To pick up and release different weights.
   Materials: Grocery items, such as cans, boxes, packages, and books

Procedure: Ask the child to pick up grocery items out of a bag and hand them to you. Ask him to take different books off the shelf and put them back on the shelf.

Objective C: To pick up small objects using a pincer grasp.
Materials: Peanuts, dried beans, cereal bits, buttons, bobby pins
Procedure: Ask the child to transfer the objects from a plate to a bowl, or from a box to a jar.

Objective D: To pinch (squeeze) with strength enough to open.
Materials: Clothespins
Procedure: Demonstrate how to open clothespin and put it on a box edge. Then place your hand over the child's as you help him to squeeze. Gradually use less pressure as he begins to use his own muscles.

Objective E: To carry large objects a distance.
Materials: Any large object you need to have carried
Procedure: Ask the child to carry your pocketbook from the car to the house, a bag or box from the house to the car, father's newspaper across the room.

Objective F: To keep objects level as he carries them.
Materials: Plate, tray, glass, bowl, pitcher
Procedure: Ask the child to carry to the table a plate of cookies, a bowl of cereal, a glass or pitcher of liquid, a tray with a plate or a glass on it.

Objective G: To maintain grasp while pressing downward.
Materials: Blunt table knife, large spoon, spatula
Procedure: Ask the child to hold a blunt knife and press down to separate a coil of dough into bits (for cookies). Ask him to hold a large spoon to stir a pudding. Ask him to hold a spatula to press down on dough bits to flatten them.

Objective H: To squeeze shut and open scissors.
Materials: Blunt-ended scissors, child size
Procedure: Demonstrate the squeezing motion by placing your hand over the child's to help him feel the movement. Teach the opening motion by placing your middle finger between the scissors grip to pry them open without letting go of the scissors. Make a fringe on a piece of paper so the child sees the results of his movements.

Considerations in Selecting Objectives. The preceding objectives each address one aspect of the general goals of grasping, pinching, maintaining the hold, and releasing. They were chosen with the following problems in mind: 1) The child who dislikes holding objects and prefers to keep his hands free. He may kick off his shoes but dislike using his hands to take off his clothing. 2) The child who is constantly holding an object in each hand and dislikes letting go, or cannot release it appropriately. 3) The child who eats with his fingers but is not willing to hold a spoon. 4) The child who can grasp easily but who is not able to maintain his grasp long enough to carry anything a small distance. 5) The child who lacks the muscular strength necessary to carry out common self-care procedures, such as brushing teeth, pulling up clothing, fastening belt.

GOAL 2:   TO MAINTAIN GRASP AND RELEASE EXACTLY TO PLACE OBJECT ON A TARGET
 Objective A: To place objects over a hole and release.
  Materials: Coffee can with plastic lid, with hole cut in lid to fit blocks or beads
  Procedure: Ask the child to pick up each block or bead and place it over the hole, then release it so it drops through.
 Objective B: To stack large and medium size objects.
  Materials: Shoe boxes, cereal boxes, cans, blocks
  Procedure: Ask the child to stack these objects. He will need to carefully "center" them to balance since they are of different sizes.
 Objective C: To place objects upright into a hole.
  Materials: Small soda bottles and six-pack box, pegs and pegboard
  Procedure: Ask child to lift up and place down bottles into the container. The same skill is used in the pegboard activity.
 Objective D: To place a flat object directly over a matching one.
  Materials: Lotto board, pictures to go on board
  Procedure: Place the board on the table and show the child where to put each picture. The emphasis is on the motor skill needed to make an exact placement "over" the match.

Considerations in Selecting Objectives. These objectives were chosen for the child who can grasp objects tightly but who has difficulty releasing his grasp at exactly the right time to make objects fit together. Children with this difficulty will make a "stab" motion while fitting pegs in a board, or will "bang" down the blocks when building a tower, thus knocking it over. They lack coordination between the arm movement, the visual information, and the release-of-grasp movement.

GOAL 3:   TO ROTATE WRIST WHILE GRASPING
 Objective A: To unscrew the lid of a jar.
  Materials: Baby food jars, or ones that open with one turn of lid

Procedure: Present child with the jar and show him the movement needed to take off the lid. Place your hand over his to help him feel the rotation of wrist movement. Place an edible in the jar so he will be motivated to do this for himself.

Objective B: To screw and unscrew nuts and bolts.

Materials: Plastic nuts and bolts

Procedure: First hold the bolt while the child works the nut. Guide his hand to help him maintain pincer grasp as he turns. Gradually give less help, then have him hold both nut and bolt.

Objective C: To turn knobs to open doors.

Materials: Any doors you want the child to be able to open

Procedure: Demonstrate by placing your hand over his, gradually giving less help. For larger knobs the child may need to use both hands.

Objective D: To rotate puzzle pieces to make them fit.

Materials: Inset puzzles with large pieces, form boards

Procedure: When the child places the piece in such a way that he needs to rotate it to make it fit, say the word "turn" and use a gesture that you have already used in unscrewing tasks.

Objective E: To make continuous rotations to unscrew.

Materials: Jars requiring several turns to open

Procedure: This task requires the child to rotate, release, and rotate again. At first the child may forget to release and so will screw the lid on again. Provide coaching by touch or word to remind him to release his grasp after each rotation.

Considerations in Selecting Objectives. The ability to grasp and rotate the wrist is necessary to the development of scribbling and writing, as well as to many assembly tasks. The parent-teacher must consider the level of the child's judgment when selecting an objective. If we teach a child to open a door or open a jar, he will do it whenever he wants. It is important to train wrist rotations using a material you can trust the child to use independently. Therefore, for a child who is apt to run away or swallow inedibles, one would work with puzzles or plastic nuts and bolts.

GOAL 4:   TO COORDINATE THE USE OF TWO HANDS

Objective A: To thread one object into another.

Materials: Large beads and string, Tinker Toys

Procedure: Teach the child to hold one bead steady while he moves the other hand (holding thread or stick) toward the target.

Objective B: To tear paper strips.

Materials: Newspaper or paper bags

Procedure: Demonstrate the tearing process. Then place your hands over the child's to teach him the movement necessary. He must start with both hands together, and move them in opposite directions simultaneously.

Objective C: To hold and position paper while cutting.

Materials: Scissors, paper

Procedure: For the child who can manipulate scissors, the next step is to hold the paper firmly and rotate it appropriately as the cutting line demands.

Objective D: To use one hand continuously in stacking.

Materials: Blocks, pegs, puzzles

Procedure: To prevent the child from using both hands for stacking blocks or fitting pegs or puzzle pieces, the adult holds the less dominant hand flat on the table. This technique is used for any activity in which the child tends to use alternating hands, although one hand is more dominant; for example, eating with a spoon, using crayons.

Considerations in Selecting Objectives. All of these objectives are helpful to the child who has not developed a clear hand dominance. This child may use either hand or may use both hands at the same time in different actions and be unable to organize them appropriately. He may, for example, grab a puzzle piece with each hand and try to put both pieces into holes at the same time, being unable to watch what either hand is doing. He may move a spoon to his mouth with one hand while the other one is picking up food. He may draw alternately with each hand, or be unable to hold the paper steady with one hand as the other uses the crayon.

Although teaching objectives in the areas of higher level goals are presented in the next chapter, these areas overlap and are often taught concurrently. The objectives for Tommy's lower level functions follow (Figure 5), and those for his higher level functions are presented at the end of Chapter 5.

Child: Tommy D. _____   Date: 9/10/78 _____

GOAL 1:   IMITATION OF ANIMAL SOUNDS/GESTURES IN SONGS
Objective: Move cow/kitty to make appropriate sounds.
Materials: Toy cow and toy kitten
Procedure: Move cow and make "moo" sound. T. does same. Prompt him to look at your mouth position, and touch his cheeks to prompt imitation. When learned, put to music: "This is the way the cow sounds ... mooo ... mooo." (T. joins in.) Repeat for kitty, "meow."

GOAL 2:   IMITATE SINGLE WORDS
Objective: To repeat "juice, nut, bread, grape."
Materials: Juice in glass, apple bits, raisins
Procedure: Put food on table out of reach. Ask "What?" and help T. point to food he wants. Pick it up, say the name "juice," and prompt him to repeat by touching his lips; give food as soon as he makes same sound. At first accept approximation.

GOAL 3:   TO PERCEIVE DIFFERENCES IN BLOCK ARRANGEMENTS
Objective: To make vertical/horizontal lines with blocks.
Materials: Ten blocks of same color
Procedure: Arrange five blocks, vertically or horizontally, as T. watches. Give T. five more, and help him arrange them in the same pattern. When understood, ask him to copy the pattern without seeing the demonstration.

GOAL 4:   GROSS MOTOR SKILLS—RIDING A TRICYCLE
Objective: To place feet on pedals and push.
Materials: Tricycle, large rubber bands
Procedure: T. sits on tricycle. Put one foot on pedal and place rubber band to hold it there. Hold leg as you push trike so T. feels the pushing motion. Repeat with other foot. Decrease help until he pushes himself, then remove rubber bands.

GOAL 5:   TO IMPROVE BALANCE NEEDED FOR PUTTING ON PANTS
Objective: Balance on one foot for 2 or 3 seconds.
Materials: Three wooden blocks (2" high), three shoe boxes (4-5" high, pants)
Procedure: Place blocks on floor and have T. step up and over each block. Hold his hand to help balance. Decrease help by holding his elbow, then just touch his elbow. Repeat same with shoe boxes. Finally, have T. lift his foot up and into pants without holding on to you. Repeat with other foot.

Figure 5.   Objectives Form for Tommy.

GOAL 6:   FINE MOTOR SKILLS TO WORK ZIPPER AND BUTTONS
Objective: To pull down zipper
Materials: Pants and coat
Procedure: Place T.'s finger and thumb on zipper and help him pinch tightly and then pull downward. Gradually decrease help until he pinches while pulling without help. Repeat with other zippers, including those on other adult's or children's coats.

GOAL 7:   FINE MOTOR SKILLS USING SCISSORS
Objective: To shut and open scissors independently.
Materials: Scissors and paper
Procedure: Place scissors in T.'s hand. Help him open by prying them with your fingers, saying "open" as you do this. T. can shut them himself, but as he does, say "shut." Decrease help as he begins to use his own muscles to open the scissors. Now let him use them on the paper, cutting a fringe in several single cuts.

Child: _____   Date: _____

GOAL 1: _____

Objective: _____

Materials: _____

Procedure: _____

_____

_____

_____

GOAL 2: _____

Objective: _____

Materials: _____

Procedure: _____

_____

_____

_____

GOAL 3: _____

Objective: _____

Materials: _____

Procedure: _____

_____

_____

_____

GOAL 4: _____

Objective: _____

Materials: _____

Procedure: _____

_____

_____

_____

Figure 6. Blank Objectives Form.

GOAL 5: _____

Objective: _____

Materials: _____

Procedure: _____

_____

_____

_____

GOAL 6: _____

Objective: _____

Materials: _____

Procedure: _____

_____

_____

_____

GOAL 7: _____

Objective: _____

Materials: _____

Procedure: _____

_____

_____

_____

GOAL 8: _____

Objective: _____

Materials: _____

Procedure: _____

_____

_____

_____

Chapter 5.
Higher Level
Teaching Objectives

EYE-HAND INTEGRATION

Eye-hand integration begins to develop during the first month of life, when the child first reaches out to grasp an object he has seen. This integration between his muscles and his visual perceptions continues to develop as more and more complex activities are attempted. We have frequently referred to the child's need to "watch what he is doing" during the discussion of gross and fine motor objectives. In this section we discuss some difficulties the child may have with eye-hand integration as he attempts higher level tasks, especially writing.

Many autistic and developmentally disordered children who show emerging skill in these pre-writing tasks do not make continuous progress. We are surprised by how difficult the next small step seems to be for him. At this point, the parent-teacher must carefully analyze the task and the child's response in order to pinpoint the problem that the task is presenting. Objectives are then chosen that will focus on this particular problem area, either by providing additional exercises or by teaching the child ways to use his stronger skills to supplement his disability. To illustrate this process, we discuss two of the more common problems: 1) the inability to make a line go in the intended direction, and 2) the inability to copy a design by assembling materials.

GOAL 1: TO CONTROL THE DIRECTION OF LINES

  Objective A: To connect two dots with a line (left to right).

    Materials: Paper, felt pen or crayon

    Procedure: Make four sets of dots, 2 inches apart (see Figure 7). Color left-hand dot green (place to start) and right-hand dot red (place to

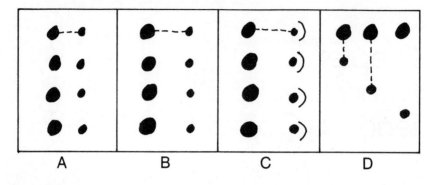

A   B   C   D

Figure 7.   A, Four sets of dots, 2 inches apart. Left-hand dots are green ("start") and right-hand dots are red ("stop"). B, Space between dots is gradually widened. C, If child continually overshoots target, insert "boundary" (ridge of tape). D, Repeat procedure for vertical lines.

stop). Demonstrate and then guide the child's hand to go "over" and "stop" on the dot. Once he can make his line without help, the space between dots is gradually widened. The same procedure is used for vertical lines, using the phrase "down and stop."

Variations: If the child starts in the wrong direction or heads for the wrong target dot, have him touch both the "start" and "stop" dots with his finger before he uses the crayon. If he cannot stop accurately but continues to overshoot the target, make a small ridge of Plasticine or tape just beyond the stop mark, so he can *feel* the boundary limit.

Objective B: Use vertical and horizontal lines to make a picture.

Materials: Worksheets (see Figure 8), felt pen or crayon

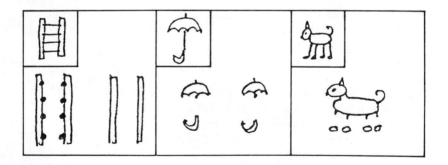

Figure 8.   Completed models are in upper left-hand corner of each frame. Ask child to complete the pictures, making them the same as the models.

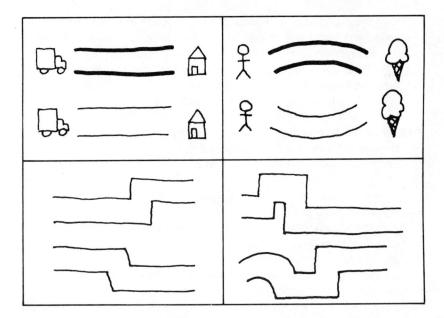

Figure 9.   Mazes. Ask child to go between the lines from left to right. For children who find this difficult, make a ridge of glue on boundary lines (see top row of mazes) to make a "wall." Gradually increase difficulty of maze.

Procedure: Show the child the completed model and name the picture. Ask him to "finish" the pictures, or "make them the same." Help at first by making small dots to show him where to go. Withdraw this help when you see he understands the task and the picture.

Variations: Whenever possible use simple drawings of objects the child sees frequently, e.g., rungs on a chair, doorways, windows, the legs on a dog.

Objective C: To direct a line between boundary lines and complete a "maze."

Materials: Worksheets (see Figure 9), crayon or pencil

Procedure: Ask the child to "follow the road" or "go between the lines" from left to right. Guide his hand at first, and gradually decrease the amount of help until he can proceed independently. (*Note:* the four mazes in Figure 9 represent rapid jumps in degree of difficulty. Intermediary steps commonly would be used, making the increased difficulty more gradual.)

Variations: For children who do not understand the concept of "between the lines" and cannot visualize the maze lines as a "road," it is helpful to make a ridge of white glue on the boundary lines. When this hardens it provides a physical "wall" that reminds the child of the boundary. Repetition is helpful, and this is accomplished by asking the child to repeat the maze, using each of the eight colors of crayons. This technique also helps the teacher observe improvements with each repetition. Motivation is increased by adding pictures that make the maze represent a meaningful journey, such as a trip to school or a walk to get ice cream.

Objective D: To make several lines to complete a picture.

Materials: Worksheets (see Figure 8 for sample), crayon or pencil

Procedure: Ask the child to look at the model picture, name it, and, when language permits, name the various details (eyes, mouth; wheels, window; handle, brush). Help him find what is missing on the worksheet, and tell him to "make it the same."

These tasks are more interesting when the pictures represent toys or objects the child uses in his daily life (favorite stuffed animal, a coat hanger, toothbrush).

(*Note:* No artistic talent is necessary to make these worksheets. Simple shapes without detail are preferable.)

Variations: As the child's skill improves, more and more lines are left out for him to complete. Some children begin simple drawing of a complete schema by this gradual process.

Objective E: To direct a line through sand, mud, or clay.

Materials: Pie plate of wet sand or play-do (see Figure 10), stick

Procedure: Place two marks on the rim of the pie plate. Demonstrate how to draw the stick through the sand from one rim to the other. Assist the child in tracing over your line. Erase and ask him to do the same without help.

Variations: Rotate the pie plate so that he is making vertical, horizontal, or diagonal lines. More marks can be added to the rim so that he now makes both horizontal and vertical lines to form a "cross." Outdoor play provides an excellent opportunity to vary this exercise, using long sticks to make lines in the dirt, sand, or mud.

Objective F: To make lines according to verbal directions.

Materials: Chalkboard or easel, chalk or brush

Procedure: Have the child stand next to you at the chalkboard or easel. Hold the chalk, place his hand over yours, and get ready to make a line down. Say the word "down" as you make the movement (and line) downward. Now give him the chalk, hold his hand, and repeat the word "down," asking him to say it also. Repeat this word and directional line until he is able to make the line downward without any physical prompts. New directions are taught in the same manner: over, around, up.

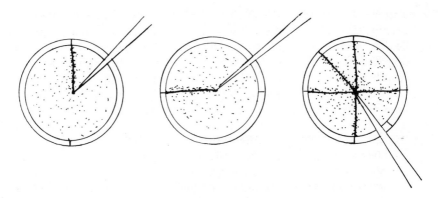

Figure 10.   Fill pie plates with wet sand and place two marks on rim. Draw a stick through sand from one rim to other. Rotate pie plate to make vertical, horizontal, or diagonal lines.

Variations: Once this is taught in a vertical plane, the same directional words are used as the paper is moved to a horizontal plane (e.g., placed on a table).

Considerations in Selecting Objectives. Although you may not know why a child has difficulty controlling the direction of his line, you can try out these various exercises and observe which seem to make the task easier for him. Objective A (dot to dot) shows the child very clearly where to start and where to stop; his only task is to make one short, straight line. When a child is first asked to make a specific directional line, and if he cannot learn this through imitation or free drawing, it is helpful to make the first lesson extremely easy, and very gradually increase the distance between the two dots or pictures. In Objective B, the child is still given cues to the direction of line, but now he can see that his line is an important part of a meaningful picture. Objective C (mazes) is particularly helpful for children who make swift marks that either miss the target or go beyond the final point. Mazes require him to make a continuous effort to control his line as he is asked to make curves, right angle turns, and diagonals. Objective D (adding details to pictures) asks the child to make more complete designs (circles, squares, curves) without providing him with dots. He must now decide for himself what kind of line is needed, and then produce it. Objective E (drawing in sand) requires the child to use more pressure to make a line, since the sand or clay provides resistance. This helps in two ways: it puts a brake on the child's movement, giving him time to watch his hand as it moves, and increases use of his muscles, providing more information through the sensations of movement—information that may be easier to recall than what he can get from his visual memory. Objective F (verbal directions) is also helpful for children who cannot recall a visual image of what a design should look like. They may be able to recognize the letter T and name it, but may still not remember how to form it, given a blank sheet of paper. These children can often remember directional words, however, and can tell you how to make it: "down, across." By teaching them the words to describe the directional lines, we give them a way of supplementing their weak visual memory.

GOAL 2: TO COPY A DESIGN USING MATERIALS

Objective A: To arrange clay coils to match sample.

Materials: Play-do or Plasticine

Procedure: Have the child roll out short coils of clay. Ask him to arrange two coils the same way you do, doing this one step at a time. When this is easy, ask him to make a design that you show him, but one he has not seen you make. Start with the simplest, working gradually to more complex patterns that require four or five coils to make. **Variations:** This can be done also with pipe cleaners or short popsicle sticks (see Figure 11A).

Objective B: To arrange blocks to copy a design.

Materials: One-inch cubes, all the same color, and paper squares

Procedure: Place a paper square in front of child and one in front of you. Take three blocks, line them up vertically, and ask the child to do the same on his paper. Gradually change the designs to include more blocks and more variations (see Figure 11B). This task can be used to teach the child to notice the complete shape of letters.

Objective C: To assemble paper shapes to make a picture.

Materials: Colored paper cut into shapes (circles, squares, triangles, rectangles)

Procedure: Assemble a design, shape by shape, asking the child to copy you step by step. When this is done, take the design apart and prepare to paste it onto plain paper. Watch to see if the child can remember the design. If not, help him step by step as you both paste and place the pieces. When this is understood, give the child a completed design to copy; he should be able to paste his own pieces with only minimal help. (See Figure 11C.)

Considerations in Selecting Objectives. In Objective A solid materials like clay or sticks are used to represent lines that do not require the child to control directional movement. They do require him to observe the relative position of lines in a design and to make decisions about his arrangements. It is helpful to children who need practice in making designs, but whose poor motor control prevents further progress in this area. For Objective B we ask the child to assemble small square blocks to form a

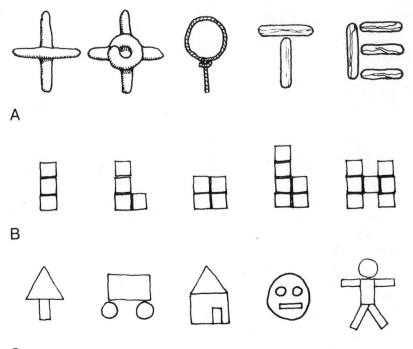

Figure 11.   A, Designs made with clay, pipe cleaners, and popsicle sticks. B, Block designs. C, Pictures made from paper shapes.

solid design. This is helpful to children who do not realize that a line represents the boundary to a solid shape. Once they have made solid shapes they are better able to understand the representative nature of line drawings. For Objective C, the assembling of paper shapes requires the child to organize the relative position of several familiar shapes, which together form a meaningful whole. This is helpful to the child who is ready to proceed with his recognition of pictures and symbols, but whose poor writing skill prevents further progress. A child who cannot form a letter T with crayon or pencil may be able to assemble paper strips to make a T, or even assemble cut-out letters correctly to spell his name.

There are many published materials available that contain excellent worksheets and activity suggestions for pre-writing skills. Appendix B contains a list of those that have been useful most frequently in our clinics and classrooms. The need to individualize to the child's ability and special interests often means drawing original pictures and designs. They will be more meaningful to him when they represent familiar objects or situations.

COGNITIVE PERFORMANCE

In this section we are concerned with higher levels of thinking. These involve the organization and remembering of perceptions and the comparison of incoming sensory information with memory for the purpose of anticipating and carrying out appropriate actions. This is a very complex process made up of many different skills. We confine our discussion to categories of skill training we have found especially useful. They include: 1) recognition of similarities and differences, 2) sequential order of events in time and also in space, 3) recognition that objects have several qualities or attributes, and 4) ability to select appropriate attributes by matching and sorting.

Normal children develop such skills without special effort from daily routines and play experiences. They notice and remember that spoons, forks, and knives are kept in one drawer and conclude that this is because they are all used for setting the table. They remember that one event follows another in a predictable order and can understand and therefore accept the rules of sequence, "First. . ., then. . ." Developmentally disabled children, on the other hand, often have difficulty in getting the underlying rule from these same experiences. They may be able to arrange their own belongings or their own sequence of actions by rote, in a rigid order, but they do not notice this same organization in the belongings or actions of others. They may be able to put all the spoons, forks, and knives in a certain drawer once taught to do this, but be unable to put a new spoon in the same drawer. They can only perform those actions that have been directly taught and memorized.

Some of our children have excellent rote memories, and this peak skill enables them to memorize where things are kept or what will happen next. They give the impression of more reasoning and intelligence than are actually the case. The parent-teacher is sometimes surprised or even angered when the child does not apply a rule to a new situation. The child's lack of generalization is often attributed to lack of cooperation, when in fact he has only learned the procedure by rote, without understanding the reason. Such misunderstanding usually leads to increased negativism. In order to avoid this, we suggest ways to check on the child's understanding of underlying concepts and his ability to use them in new situations in the following discussion of objectives.

GOAL 1:   TO RECOGNIZE SIMILARITIES AND DIFFERENCES
Objective A: To select objects of the same shape.
Materials: Solid pieces (squares, circles), five of each shape, all the same color

Procedure: Place two containers on the table. Place a square shape in one and a circle shape in the other. Hand the child one shape at a time, showing him how to place it in the correct container. If he places it incorrectly, hand it back to him and ask him to try again. Continue in this way until all the shapes are placed correctly.

Variations: Ask the child to sort groups of objects that are similar in two ways: 1) same shape, same function: spoons, cups, combs, shoes; and 2) same shape, same color: red beads, blue blocks.

Objective B: To associate (pair up) objects by use.

Materials: Shoe and sock; toothpaste and toothbrush; soap and washcloth

Procedure: Put all objects in a box. Pick out one (shoe) and put it on the table. Ask the child "What goes with the shoe? What do we need?" and then ask him to get it. Pantomime putting on shoes to help him understand what you mean. Do the same with the other objects.

Objective C: To match objects of the same color.

Materials: Colored blocks, colored beads or pegs

Procedure: Put two containers on the table. Place a red block in one and a blue block in the second. Hand the red and blue blocks to the child, one at a time, showing him how to place them according to their color. Use the same procedure with the beads and pegs. Present the child with all three materials (three red blocks, beads, pegs, and three blue blocks, beads, pegs) and ask him to place all the materials into two containers on the basis of color. Now he must ignore the shape difference and attend to the color.

Objective D: To match objects of similar color.

Materials: A variety of toys or small objects that are one solid color (not striped), primary colors only (red, yellow, blue)

Procedure: Ask the child to sort into containers the various objects according to their matching color. They will all be of different shapes, sizes, and functions, but will be of the same or similar color.

Considerations in Selecting Objectives. The objectives have been listed roughly in order of difficulty, based on the experience with our children. They understand similarities of shape and match pairs of objects that are used for the same purpose, providing they have used these objects themselves. Objective A teaches the child about similarity of shape and Objective B teaches about similarity of function. Objective C teaches the child to observe similarity of color, starting first with objects that are exactly the same except for their color. Once the child has been successful in recognizing color differences, we then ask him to attend to *only* this attribute, ignoring the shape of the objects. In Objective D we ask the child to place a block, bead, and peg all in the same container because they are all red. If this is a difficult step for a child, make sure he understands the concept of color matching (Objective C) before moving to Objective D.

Occasionally we see children for whom color is a very strong stimulus, and they find it easier to match on the basis of color similarity than on the basis of shape similarity. Individual differences will become obvious as you watch the child work.

GOAL 2: TO RECOGNIZE AND REPRODUCE A SEQUENCE OF OBJECTS

Objective A: To stack blocks in the same sequence as the model.

Materials: Four different shapes of blocks; squares, rectangles, cylinders (two sets of each)

Procedure: Give one set of four blocks to the child and keep one for yourself. Begin to stack, asking the child to stack his blocks in the same order. Begin to work one step at a time, but gradually expect him to see your completed tower and reproduce it without help.

Variations: The same task can be done arranging the objects in a horizontal line. Always move from left to right. The sequences can be based on attributes of shape, color, or size, depending on what concepts the child has learned.

GOAL 3: TO UNDERSTAND THE SEQUENCE OF EVENTS

Objective B: To carry out actions in the sequence stated.

Materials: Pictures of objects or actions (coat, coat hanger, and chair; faucet on, soap, faucet off)

Procedure: Tell the child what he is to do, laying down each picture from left to right as you give the directions: "First get coat [lay down coat picture], then get the hanger [lay down hanger picture], and last sit down [lay down chair picture]."

Variations: Pictures in sequence can be used to teach a child any sequence of self-help skills that he needs help with, such as washing his hands and turning off the water, or using the toilet and then flushing it.

Objective C: To arrange pictures in a sequence that shows how they usually occur.

Materials: Pictures of events (bare feet, socks on feet, shoes on feet)

Procedure: Ask the child to look at all the pictures, then to find the one that happens first, second, and last. Place them in order from left to right. With verbal children, this arrangement is then described as a story: "The boy is barefoot. Now he puts on his socks. Now he has his shoes on."

Considerations in Selecting Objectives. Objective A requires the recognition of a visual order—from top to bottom or from left to right. Objective B presents a temporal order—first, then, and last. Here the child is given the sequence and asked to carry it out. In Objective C the child must use his memory of past experiences and arrange past events in a sequential order. Our children vary in their ability to understand the order of these two types of sequences; some find visual sequencing the easiest, whereas others find temporal sequencing the easiest. In addition, the ability to remember sequential order develops at widely different ages with these children. You can gain clues to your child's readiness to comprehend sequential arrangements by observing his daily behavior. Emerging skills are apparent when you see the child begin to arrange his own toys in an intentional order or when he develops his own routines. However, even though he is able to sequentially order his own actions, he will need help in remembering the sequence of routines the adult directs. This child may have to be told what to do next even for very familiar daily routines, such as "Go to the bathroom...take off your clothes...get in the tub...take the soap..."

Children can often increase their ability to remember temporal sequences by having visual cues provided. When they understand that pictures in a row represent a sequence of actions or events, then picture charts can be used to remind them of what to do next. The objectives illustrate ways to develop this understanding of picture sequences.

GOAL 4:   TO RECOGNIZE THE MOST RELEVANT ATTRIBUTE AND TO SHIFT WHEN APPROPRIATE

   Objective A: To sort same material by color or shape.
   Materials: Pegs and blocks, two red, two blue, two yellow
   Procedure: Place three containers on the table and tell the child to put the objects into them according to color. Then take the same objects and ask him to sort them into two containers, this time according to shape.
   Objective B: To select objects on the basis of two attributes.
   Materials: Colored shapes
   Procedure: Tell the child to "listen," then to give you a "blue triangle," "red square," etc. If he attends to only one attribute, repeat the direction giving special emphasis to the part he ignored, i.e., "RED square" or "blue TRIANGLE."
   Variations: This exercise is used with each new concept as it is taught; for example, big spoon, new shoes, big red circle.

GOAL 5:   TO IGNORE IRRELEVANT STIMULI

   Objective A: To leave unsorted objects that do not match.

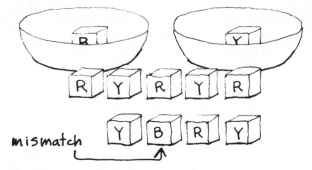

Figure 12.   Ask child to match blocks. R, red blocks; Y, yellow blocks. The blue block (B) is the mismatch.

Materials: Two bowls, five red and five yellow blocks, one blue block
Procedure: Place the two bowls on the table, and place one red block and one yellow block in each bowl. Hand the child all the other blocks and tell him to "put them where they go." Watch what he does with the blue block. If he leaves it alone then you know he really understands the reason or rule underlying the sorting task. If he places it in one of the bowls regardless of mismatch, you need to show him why there is no match, and give him a place to put this odd block (see Figure 12).
Objective B: To decide which attribute is most relevant.
Materials: Beads, blocks, pegs, and shapes in various sizes and colors
Procedure: Give the child several objects in a box and two empty containers for him to sort them into. Select your objects so that there is only one way in which they can be divided into two groups—for example, various sizes and shapes of objects that are either red or blue, or blocks and beads of various colors and sizes.

Considerations in Selecting Objectives. As we have mentioned, the autistic child is often able to master a number of tasks by memorizing the procedure. The parent-teacher cannot assume he has mastered the concept until observing him successfully reasoning out a new task that he has not been taught previously. Goals 4 and 5 suggest tasks that require the child to use the concepts he has learned in new situations or in new ways. It may be quite difficult for a child to sort a group of objects by shape, for example, if he has been taught to sort them by color previously. This child then needs practice in observing the two or three attributes of each object and reasoning out for himself which one is important to the task he is given. He must also be able to decide for himself that an object may have no similarity to the group, and be confident enough of his judgment to discard this mismatch.

ADVANCED CONCEPTS

As the child progresses in his understanding of similarities and differences, in his ability to associate objects by function or organize them in sequences, he can be given more abstract attributes to learn. Receptive language skills play an increasingly important role, and are discussed next. Other more advanced concepts would include age, amount, gender, affect (happy/sad), time (day/night), seasons, temperature, speed.

Language

Deficits in communication are among the most serious handicaps of autistic and developmentally disordered children. Therefore the improvement of communication skills becomes a major focus of most teaching programs. The choice of goals, based on the assessment of both the child's receptive language (understanding of what is said to him) and his expressive language (what he says to others) has been discussed in Chapter 3. In this section we describe some language activities in order to illustrate the selection of teaching objectives. Additional language objectives and activities are presented in Chapter 12, pp. 210–218.

First we discuss teaching objectives for the lower level child who is nonverbal or just beginning to use words. Our illustrations are divided into language objectives for improving receptive skills and those for improving expressive skills. At levels of early development the separation between these two aspects of language is a helpful reminder that a child must have a receptive understanding of a word before he can express or use it in a meaningful way.

Second, we discuss the choice of objectives for higher level children who already understand and use some language to communicate. Here we do not separate receptive and expressive objectives so sharply. The interaction between understanding and communicating is a normal part of conversation. Therefore language activities for higher level children will tend to include both aspects of language.

Receptive Language Objectives: Low Level

GOAL 1:   TO UNDERSTAND ACTION VERBS AND COMMANDS
Objective A: Appropriate response to "come" and "sit."
Materials: Favorite food or toy, used as a reward
Procedure: Approach child to within 2 feet and say, "Look." When he looks up, say "Come" and gesture for him to come. If he does not re-

spond to the initial gesture you may have to reach out and guide him toward you. When he responds he can be reinforced with a reward. For more detailed discussion of appropriate reinforcement, see Chapter 7. At first he may need to see the reward before he will come. Once he understands the routine, do not let him see any reward until he has moved to you. It often helps to give him a hug, pat, and a smile. When this is learned, delay the gesture and expect him to come because the word is spoken. Once learned, proceed to teach "sit" in similar manner. Finally, alternate your command: "Tommy come" or "Tommy sit."

Objective B: To understand "jump," "swing," "clap" (actions he enjoys).

Materials: None

Procedure: Take child's hands and start jumping with him. Begin to say, in rhythm with the jumps, "Jump...jump..." etc. Next hold out your hands and ask, "Jump?" and expect him to initiate the action. Finally, make no gesture but ask him "Jump?". If he takes your hands, or jumps himself, probably he understands the word. The second word, "swing," is taught in the same way, and then "clap." Finally, switch the words in random order to confirm his understanding of them without depending on situational cues or gestural directions.

Objective C: To understand word and sign for "swing" and "hug."

Materials: None

Procedure: Offer the child a swing and say "swing?" as you make the sign for swing. If he does not respond, repeat the word and sign, making sure he looks at you. Then swing him around. Do the same for "hug." If the child positions himself for the correct action, either swing or hug, he understands the message. Delay giving the sign occasionally to see if he understands the word alone.

Considerations in Selecting Objectives. Objective A introduces a child to the fact that a word spoken to him will have immediate consequences; if he hears and responds to "come" he will get something he likes. His awareness that words have some important reward for him is the first step in developing receptive language. At this stage the child may not know what the word "come" means, but he understands it is a signal for some kind of action. Next we ask him to learn a different action, to "sit." Once again, he can learn this response just from the experience of getting a reward after he has sat down. Finally we ask him to decide on the right action only on the basis of the word spoken. There is no reward unless he makes the right choice. As the child becomes aware of the need to discriminate between two words, "come" and "sit," his ability to listen becomes more important to him. The parent-teacher then delays giving the command word (come/sit) until the child is actually looking at the adult. Each step in this activity may take many days of repetition before the word is learned.

Objective B teaches the same beginning receptive vocabulary as the first activity. It illustrates words for actions children usually prefer to those in Objective A. Therefore external rewards are not usually needed. Instead, the parent-teacher joins the child in an action he enjoys and develops an interaction that requires parent-teacher participation, such as jumping together or swinging him around. While moving he hears the appropriate word repeated and can then associate this word to the movement. Once this is established, the parent-teacher can use this word as a question, "Jump?", thus suggesting a fun game to the child. In addition to providing motivation to the child for developing his listening and word discrimination skills, the parent-teacher is also teaching him words that he will want to use expressively. "Come" and "sit" are not likely to be the first words a child will want to use. He needs to understand them in order to fit into his home and school environment. The choice of vocabulary is based on two considerations: 1) those words that the child needs to understand in order to respond appropriately, and 2) those words he must understand in order to use them to communicate his own wants.

Objective C is planned for a child who makes no sounds approaching speech development and whose listening and word discrimination skills are extremely weak. We use signs in combination with the words "swing" and "hug" to add a visual mode of understanding our communication. We anticipate that with repetition he will be able to understand the word without also needing to see the sign. This can be checked from time to time by delaying the use of the sign. Meanwhile the sign helps to reduce the child's frustration over not understanding the word, and enables him to participate in a communicative interaction.

GOAL 2:   TO RECOGNIZE NOUN LABELS

Objective A: To match three objects to pictures (shoe, cup, spoon).

Materials: Shoe, cup, spoon, and simple pictures of each

Procedure: Place two pictures on the table. Hand child one object, for example, "shoe." Name it and ask him to put it on the picture of the shoe. You may need to give a hint by pushing the picture of the shoe slightly closer to him than the other pictures. Reverse the pictures and repeat the procedure. Avoid using the same position or order, since some children memorize a position on the table rather than deciding on the basis of the right match. Continue the same way for the other objects—spoon and cup. When this is learned without errors, proceed with variations.

Variations: 1) Place one picture on the table, giving the child a choice of two objects to make the match. 2) Show child the picture, name it, "cup," and tell him to find the cup, which is on a table across the room. 3) Show the child a picture, then ask him to get the object from another room. 4) Use this picture communication system during the daily routines, asking the child to get things to help with self-care or household tasks (shoes, pants, soap, towel, spoon, plate).

Objective B: To give object named (ball, car, spoon, shoe).

Materials: Small ball, toy car, spoon, child's shoe

Procedure: Place the ball on the table. Hold out your hand and say, "Give ball. . . ball." When child responds correctly, reward with food, praise, or a token (see Chapter 6). Next put down two objects, ball and car. Again ask for the ball and hold out your hand. Reward correct choice. Mark down his response on a chart so that you can see whether he is correct consistently or only by random chance. Child should give you the ball at least 8 out of 10 times. Continue procedure with the other objects.

Objective C: To understand three-word phrases: "ball to Daddy," "spoon to Mummy," "cup to Susie," etc.

Materials: Objects the child knows by name (spoon, cup, ball, car)

Procedure: Place all the objects in a box when the family is in the living room. Tell child to "come" and direct him to take one object to each person in turn, as you direct, e.g., "cup to Susie." At first point to the person he is to take the cup to, then withdraw these cues once he understands the task. It is helpful to emphasize the two key words, e.g., "CUP to SUSIE." If correct, praise and applaud. If he takes the wrong object or takes it to the wrong person, send him back to try again. Repeat the command "CUP to Susie" or "cup to SUSIE," depending on his error. Once this command is understood in the structured game situation, it should be generalized to home and school whenever possible.

Considerations in Selecting Objectives. Objective A is planned for a child who does not yet understand that a spoken word symbolizes a concrete object. We are teaching him first that a two-dimensional picture symbolizes a three-dimensional object. Although he is hearing the spoken word "shoe," he first will be matching the object to the picture. Once this connection is understood we then ask him to practice with the other variations. We ask him to look at the picture while we tell him the word, before he gets the objects from across the room. For this step he must rely on memory traces because the picture will no longer be visible.

Objective B uses no pictures. Here the child is taught to match the word directly to the object. Since children with a very small receptive vocabulary often have difficulty attending, or listening to words, this simple structure works best. The child has only to look and listen to the word before giving the object to the adult. Distractions to sidetrack his attention are avoided and rewards are immediate. Since the responses are recorded, the adult can keep track of his accuracy and will not be teaching new words too quickly.

Objective C requires the child to listen to two major words in a phrase, and to combine the meaning of both words to carry out directions. This activity is appropriate for a child who has learned a few labels for common objects and one or two names of family members. A child who impulsively moves the instant he gets an idea may have difficulty listening to a short phrase. Objective C teaches him that both words are important to the purpose of the communication, and it helps him develop his listening skills. This activity also trains for running errands and giving to people. Both can be used in the classroom and home to immediately generalize his beginning use of receptive vocabulary.

GOAL 3:   TO EXPRESS THE CHILD'S WANTS
Objective A: To say "wheee" for a swing, "bu" to get bubbles.
Materials: Jar of bubbles
Procedure: Sit child on your lap facing you. Bounce him four times, then swing him up and down while you happily say "wheee." Repeat several times. Then bounce him on your knees with the swing delayed, thus inviting him to say "wheee." Touching his mouth may serve as a helpful cue. When he makes the sound, swing him immediately again. A similar procedure is used for the "bu" sound. Blow the bubbles to the sound of "bu." Encourage the child to approximate the bubble sound by making it yourself ("bu-bu") before blowing more. Tasks involving bubble blowing or popping are of special interest to most children.
Objective B: To express the child's wishes with a sign.
Materials: Ball, book, chocolate milk
Procedure: Sit facing child, ball on your lap. Make the sign (hands clasped, fingers interwoven) for ball as you say "ball." Reach over and help child make this sign, then immediately play ball with him. Repeat procedure, each time prompting him to make the sign but giving less physical help as he begins to understand what you want. Once he learns this, expect him to make this sign each time before you play ball. Proceed in this way to teach a second sign, "book," indicating the special favorite book he likes. (Draw a picture of the sign you have taught him so that other adults will understand and use it with the child.)
Objective C: To label objects and pictures.
Materials: Cup, spoon, shoe, pants; pictures of same

Procedure: First check to be sure that the child has receptive under-standing of the words by asking him to touch each object as it is named. Then put all objects in a box. Ask him to pull out one from the box, any object he wants. Ask him, "What's that?" If he does not say the word, give him a clue by sounding the first letter: "it's a c____." If he still cannot remember, say the whole word "cup" and put the cup back into the box to be drawn out another time. Continue until all objects have been drawn out and named by the child. Record for each trial whether he knew it, needed a hint, or did not know it.

Variation: Place all objects the child has been learning on a table, and give him a paper bag. Tell him to name anything he knows, and if correct he can put this object into his "shopping bag." The objects he cannot name spontaneously are then given more drill during succeeding lessons.

Considerations in Selecting Objectives. Objective A is planned for a child who is already vocalizing—making vowel babble sounds with an occasional consonant. However, he is not using these sounds to communicate. The parent-teacher starts with a sound the child can make, "whee," and uses it in association with a fun game (swing or bubbles in this case). Once the child understands and expects the sound "wheee" to precede the swing, he is asked to make it in order to get the swing. He is not yet using a real word, but he is now using sound production to communicate his wants. The next step, "bu-bu," teaches him to make more than just a signal for action. He is now approximating the word "bubbles." This type of activity, appropriate for the beginning stages of expressive communication, is most successful when the vocabulary consists of one-syllable words that describe something the child really wants, such as foods, toys, actions.

Objective B is also appropriate for this beginning stage of expressive communication, but in this activity we teach the child to use a sign in addition to expecting a sound. For nonverbal children who do not echo words and sounds and do not experiment with sound production generally, the use of a sign is often their first experience with the power of communication. It may be the first time they have obtained what they wanted without having to move the adult's hand to the desired object. Here the child is started on three signs for things he really enjoys, things he would want to ask for frequently. The *Signed English Dictionary* (Hamilton et al., 1975; see Appendix B) shows the sign conventions. It is also necessary to check with all adults working with the child to assure consistent use of signs. Occasionally signs must be modified to fit the child's motor skills.

Objective C provides a structured activity with the repetition and drill necessary for developing expressive vocabulary. It requires the child's understanding of the need for communication. He wants to increase his vocabulary, but has difficulty either remembering a word or coming out with it. He will probably need frequent repetition over a period of many days. The child may recall the name of an object one day quite easily and have forgotten it the next. We therefore keep a chart so that we do not assume he has learned the word until he can recall it from his memory at least 8 out of 10 times for several days. This activity is also planned for a child who can sometimes remember a difficult word when he hears just the first sound, a cue that triggers his memory. The variation suggested in this activity is helpful for two reasons: 1) it gives additional practice to the same vocabulary, but in a new game, thus providing additional interest and a useful way of reviewing progress from time to time, and 2) it is helpful to the child who cannot remember a word when he is asked for it ("What's that?") but can remember a word when there is no demand or stress in the situation. This is the type of child who says nothing in class, but may repeat a song or a lesson when he is alone at home the next day. Some children may answer a question 5 minutes after it is asked, sometimes after the adult has forgotten what was asked. The "shopping bag" variation allows the child to ask his own question ("What's that?") and he picks the object he knows best, names it, and thus gains confidence in his skill. This confidence, in turn, helps him to remember more words as he scans the table of objects.

The preceding teaching objectives were intended for a child with low-level language development. They also illustrate some of the important principles we use for selecting all specific language activities. These principles are summarized as:

1. Receptive language precedes expressive language. The child must understand a word before he can use it meaningfully.

2. New words are learned more easily when they are taught singly or in short phrases.

3. The beginning vocabulary must consist of words the child has some motivation to learn; words about things he wants or actions that he enjoys.

4. Learning new words is facilitated when the child participates with movement or when he sees and feels an object as he listens to the symbolic representation (word). This simultaneous presentation of the word and the real experience helps him to understand and remember the meaning of the word.

5. When auditory attention and memory are weak, gestures or signs provide additional help for developing understanding and communication.
6. Since expressive language involves communicating intent, the first vocabulary taught should consist of words the child will have reason to use frequently.

Language Objectives: Higher Level   Higher level language goals, as discussed in Chapter 3, include a wide range of possibilities. These are narrowed down by focusing on meaningful communication of immediate importance to the child and his social situation. The selection of specific objectives has the same focus. This is illustrated with a hypothetical child for whom four typical language objectives and activities are presented.

John has a fair vocabulary for communicating his needs spontaneously. He understands some questions and sometimes takes part in a conversation. He seldom uses a complete sentence, preferring to speak in short phrases only. Our language goals for John were: 1) to increase his utterances to appropriate sentences, 2) to increase the variety of his grammatical structures, and 3) to increase appropriate use of pronouns, prepositions, and verb tenses. In order to decide on the specific objectives, John's mother made the following record of his language at home:

Situation: John comes home from school at 3 pm

Mother	John	Intent	Missing
"Hi."	—	?	"Hi."
"Did you hang up your coat?"	"On hook."	Affirmative	"Yes."
—	"For you?"	Points to cookie wanting it.	"For me?"
"What did you do in school?"	"Hot dogs, ice cream	Lunch menu.	"I ate ___." "We had ___."

This language record gives us three types of important information: 1) we know what John is saying, 2) we know why he is speaking, what he wants to say, and 3) we know what he is not saying, the words or grammatical structures he ought to be using to make his communication more effective. Our objectives are planned to improve this communication effectiveness.

Objective A: To answer questions with "yes" or "no."
Materials: Bell, car, ball, apple

Procedure: Hold up each object in turn, asking the question "Is this a ball?" (car, bell, etc.). Teach child to nod head and say, simply, "yes." Repeat the same procedure to practice the "no" response: "Is this a toothbrush?" (hold up the ball). When both responses are learned, begin to mix the questions to get "yes" or "no" responses. This activity can be used to practice receptive understanding of adjectives, e.g., "Is this a purple apple?" The more ridiculous the question, the more fun the child has in giving a "no" response.

Variation: This game is then used with verbs ("Am I throwing the bell?") (no) and with past tense ("Did I kick the ball?") (yes). Once learned, the appropriate answer to questions is expected in all real situations.

Objective B: To use pronouns (me, you, him, her).

Materials: Two dolls or toy animals, one of each sex; four plates and small food bits (raisins, nuts)

Procedure: Place the dolls to right and left of child and give a plate to each doll, your child, and yourself, simulating a tea party. Ask the child to give one peanut to the mother doll, then ask "Who is it for?" and teach the response, "It's for her." Repeat for other doll, then for you and the child, each time getting the response, "It's for him. . . for you. . . for me." Each time the child gets the peanut on his plate and says "It's for me," he can eat it.

Variations: Once the pronouns are understood, the dolls are used to develop a pretend conversation. Doll asks, "Is this for me?" Child answers, "Yes, it's for you" or "No, it's for him," depending on his wishes. The next time you hand out the peanuts and the child asks the question "Is this for me?"—speaking either for the dolls or for himself. Finally this language structure is expected in daily routines; he must ask "Is this for me?" before grabbing food. This activity can also be transferred to the dinner table at home while passing food between members of the family.

Objective C: To use the past tense of common verbs.

Materials: Pictures of sequences of actions, for example, child getting dressed, going to school

Procedure: Show the child the pictures, one at a time, and ask "What is he doing?" Child answers, "He is getting up. . . he is putting on pants. . . he is putting on shoes. . ." Now have the child lay out the pictures in sequential order, and ask him to tell the story: "What happened?" The child now uses the past tense, "First he got up, then he put on his pants," and so on.

Variations: Once the child is familiar with answering the question "What happened?" it is asked throughout the day, first about things the child has just seen happen, for example, "You tied my shoe" or "I threw the ball." Later the question is asked about things that happened in the past, for example, "I ate lunch," "I made a picture," or "I fell down." When the adult knows about special events that happened to the child at home or at school he can ask for a report in this format: "What happened at school?"

Objective D: To make social responses ("Hi," "Bye," "Thank you").

Materials: Toy telephones, some raisins, or other treat

Procedure: Pick up your phone, make a ringing sound. When the child picks up his phone, say "Hi." Point to child and indicate that you want him to respond with "Hi." Make another statement, or ask the child an easy question. Then say "Bye" and wait for him to respond "Bye" before you both hang up. Now give the child one treat, and coach him to say "Thank you." Repeat this game as long as it is enjoyable.

Variation: Once the child catches on to the need for social responses, they are elicited in varied order, and new, useful ones are added. These might include: "hello," "fine," "please," and responses to questions like "What's your name?" "Where do you live?" "How old are you?" When the responses are learned in this structured game, they are then expected from the child in real situations. When the child comes home from school, for example, he is expected to say "Hi" in response to his mother's greeting.

Considerations in Selecting Objectives. We chose the objectives by first observing the language the child was currently using, his emerging skills, and his language deficits. We then decided on the next step to improve this communication. In each of the sample activities we first taught the new language in a structured game format. We made it fun and enjoyable through the use of humor with Objective A, edible treats with Objectives B and D, and by talking about the child and his own experience in Objective C. The variations to each objective (A–D) illustrate the application of newly learned language skills to a real situation. The objective is not achieved in full until the child uses the appropriate language in his own spontaneous communication. Periodic observations and written reports of a spontaneous language are therefore important for evaluating and modifying new objectives in the child's language program.

INTERRELATIONSHIP BETWEEN FUNCTION AREAS

You will have noticed in the preceding examples of activities from the seven function areas that all the tasks involve more than one skill. Even language games will require the child to touch a picture or pick up an object. Gross motor games require visual attention, sequential memory, and imitation skills. As parent-teachers invent an activity to meet one specific goal, they must think about the other skills that the child must have to complete a task successfully. Since the child will have an uneven development of abilities (i.e., be very good at some things but delayed in other areas), parent-teachers will need to keep his level of ability in all areas in mind, to imagine this particular child doing each step of the activity as they plan it out. For example, a child with a poor ability to draw a circle would not be asked to draw a picture in a language activity; a child with awkward movements and poor balance would not be taught the word "over" by crawling over a table; a child who is highly distracted by smells would not be given felt markers for drawing. The most successful teaching activities are those that are individually planned to be appropriate to the child's functioning as a whole, rather than to only one aspect of his skills.

This overlap of skills in any teaching activity can be used to advantage when the following considerations are kept in mind:

1. The child has a need for success. It is enjoyable to the child to be asked to do activities that he knows he can do. An active and agile child likes to be asked to move around; a child who has good manual skills likes to arrange objects. The more difficult and therefore frustrating aspects of a task are tolerated by the child when he can also use his strong skills as well.

2. The parent-teacher can give help in weak areas. When a teaching task must involve a skill that the child does not yet have, the parent-teacher can support him with extra help, or can actually do this part of the task himself. For example, if a color matching or sequencing task involves threading beads, a difficult action for this child, the parent-teacher can ask the child to only grasp the correct bead while the parent pushes the thread through the hole. The awareness of specific difficulties that await the child and the readiness to give help at this point are particularly important when several children are being given the same activity in a group lesson. In this way a child can gain from watching and imitating his peers without experiencing failure and becoming upset.

3. One activity can meet several goals. When the parent-teacher knows where the child needs help in each of the function areas, the adult can often accomplish several goals at once by varying the routines or the materials of the activity. For example, objects used in language stimulation tasks can be hidden around the room for a child who needs to develop his visual tracking skills; sorting or matching tasks can be put into a "turn-taking" format for the child who needs to learn to control impulses and become more aware of the adult's presence.

It is helpful to arrange teaching activities in a balanced session. This means alternating different types of activities. For example, language activities are alternated with ones that do not require language skills, quiet table tasks are alternated with active gross motor games. Once the child understands the sequence of activities, the parent-teacher arranges the session so that a favorite activity follows a more difficult, stressful one. This helps the child tolerate the hard task because he sees that he will have an enjoyable one next.

The duration of a teaching session will vary according to the child's age, level of ability, and behavioral characteristics. Each activity in the daily program should be matched to the length of time the child can maintain organized attention. For example, one child might be able to sort 20 objects with good attention, whereas a younger child might only sort six objects before becoming restless and distracted. Maintaining organized attention is often difficult for developmentally disordered children. They will be more cooperative and will enjoy the activities most when they can complete them within the already established span of attention. If the parent-teacher finds it necessary to use punitive measures or excessive rewards, he must consider shortening the tasks to fit the child's attentional abilities more closely. Several short but completed activities are more productive than one long one.

An example of the several activities used in one teaching session is given in Chapter 10. This contains an entire program for a higher level older child. This program also illustrates the interrelationship of the various function areas, the use of strong skills to supplement weak areas, and the considerations of balance in type of activity and durations of teaching session.

Figure 13 shows Tommy's teaching objectives for the higher level functions discussed in this chapter. See Figure 6 in Chapter 4 for a blank Objectives Form.

Child: Tommy D. _____   Date: 10/1/78 _____

GOAL 1: CONTROL OF LINES WITH CRAYON
Objective: To keep scribble marks within a broad outline.
Materials: Crayons, paper, felt markers, glue
Procedure: Make a large circle on paper with black felt marker; line should be ½ " thick. Make a line of glue along the middle of the outline. Let it dry so it makes a hard ridge. Help T. scribble, guiding his hand lightly to demonstrate staying within the circle. Withdraw help, but remind him to go slowly if he speeds up. Next give him the same outline without the glue barrier. As he gains skill, gradually make the outline narrower.

GOAL 2: COORDINATE THE USE OF BOTH HANDS IN BEAD AND PUZZLE TASKS
Objective: To thread large beads independently.
Materials: Five large colored beads, shoelace
Procedure: Hold the bead yourself. Have T. push the shoelace in with one hand, release, then pull it out the other side. Repeat, this time helping him hold the bead, and you pull the shoelace out. Finally, coach him to do the entire procedure by himself, without help. Remind him of the need to let go of the shoelace in order to pull it out the other side.

GOAL 3: TO MATCH OR SORT BY COLOR, SHAPE, AND SIZE
Objective: To sort shapes (circle, square, triangle).
Materials: Five of each shape, cut out of heavy paper or thin cardboard
Procedure: Start with the circle and triangles. Place two sheets of paper on the table, teaching T. to place each shape on the paper with the ones that match. Repeat this procedure with two more shapes—square and circle. When this is achieved, ask him to sort all three shapes. Work until he can do this task independently.

GOAL 4: TO SORT DISSIMILAR OBJECTS OF THE SAME NAME
Objective: To put all cups, spoons, and socks together.
Materials: Four each of cups, spoons, and socks of different sizes and colors
Procedure: Place two trays on the table. Hold up one cup, name it, and put it on one tray. Hold up another cup, name it, and have T. put it with the first cup. Repeat with all cups. Do same procedure with all spoons. Start over, now asking T. to decide which tray to choose after you name each object. Finally, ask him to complete the sorting without hearing the object named.

GOAL 5: RECEPTIVE UNDERSTANDING OF OBJECTS, FAMILY MEMBERS, BODY PARTS
Objective: To point to family members when named.
Materials: Edible treats, small bag for each person
Procedures: While the family is still seated at the table (after supper) say to T., "Show me Daddy," and help him point. Praise him and tell him to "Go to Daddy," and get a candy ready for him. Repeat this with other family members (e.g., "Go to Granny"). Withdraw help with his pointing once he understands the game. Repeat the game several days until he is consistently correct.

Figure 13.   Objectives Form for Tommy.

GOAL 6: TO DEVELOP EXPRESSIVE LANGUAGE
Objective: To name common foods (juice, nut, grape, bread)
Materials: Small glass for juice, three saucers, nuts, bread, grapes
Procedure: Place the glass and one saucer on the table. Pour some juice into the glass and ask, "What's this?" If T. does not speak, name it yourself: "Juice." Ask again, "What's this?" and give him a drink when he responds (i.e., echoes you). Repeat this procedure with a grape. Then put down both grape and juice and ask, "What do you want?" Give him whichever one he names, accepting even a rough approximation of the word. Repeat the word again—"Juice"—as you hand it to him. When both words are learned, introduce a new one, e.g., "nut" or "bread."

Chapter 6.
Behavior Management

Principles of behavior management are part of any teaching situation, whether it involves normal or exceptional children. The adult rewards, approves of, and encourages desirable behavior and punishes, disapproves of, or discourages undesirable behavior. A large literature of such behavioral techniques has accumulated in recent years and pre-packaged educational systems have been developed. Our experience has taught us that it is a mistake to confuse operant conditioning techniques for changing behavior with programmng special education for autistic and similar children. When this technology is used instead of sound educational and developmental principles, thoughtful and individualized interaction between adult and child is too often sacrificed for pseudo-scientific techniques. For this reason we are confining our discussion of behavior management to one section or aspect of constructing an individualized educational program.

Many of the behavior management procedures used spontaneously by parents and teachers with normal children can be adapted to the special group of children we are concerned with. When we interact with an autistic or developmentally handicapped child, most of us give both positive and negative responses to that child. If we like what he is doing we give him a hug, a pat, a "good boy," a nod, a reward, or some kind of signal that he senses as approval. When he does something we do not like we correct him in some way, give him a "no," a negative feeling to redirect him. Teaching and child-rearing are most effective when our positive signals are greater and more frequent than our negative ones. However, both are necessary for guiding and teaching a child. When the child understands our signals and shows some appropriate responses, the interaction is spontaneous and requires no further special concern.

Most of our children have difficulties in understanding and expressing normal communication. They also show some peculiar and puzzling behaviors, which can interfere with their learning or getting along at school, at home, and in the community. When these behaviors persist and when they interfere with the child's learning, some special procedures are needed. It is helpful to distinguish procedures for mildly difficult behavior from those used for severely difficult behavior, procedures that often include a risk to the child's well-being.

Our major objective is to plan and carry out an individualized program that will optimize the child's adaptation in the best and least restrictive environment possible. With most developmentally disabled children there are times when unusual behaviors crop up with persistency and when unusual responses are considered by the adult. These interactions often involve some risk in the procedure used to benefit the child. In evaluating this risk-benefit ratio we aim at optimum treatment benefit at minimum risks. This requires treatment decisions based on evaluating the child's behavior as presenting a mild or severe risk. Since it is impossible to list all behavior difficulties, we will use four major categories. The first two refer to mild risks and the next two encompass more severe dangers:

1. *Risks to the child's learning.* Some behaviors may interfere with learning a task. For example, if the child persists in tapping the table with his fingers, he cannot use those fingers for holding a crayon. He may be taught to stop his tapping, or the crayon task may be postponed. On the other hand, if he taps the table only while learning to say a new word, the finger tapping may be ignored without interfering with language acquisition. In either case, the behavior represents only a mild interference with the child's learning.

2. *Risks to the child's home adjustment.* There are as many different behaviors stressful to a particular home environment as there are families and children. For example, one mother may become quite upset because the child makes a grunting sound with increasing frequency. It is not clear why he grunts nor has he responded to any spontaneous efforts to change this habit. Like the first category, this kind of behavior usually represents a mild risk to the child's home adjustment. Less frequently, but too often, we must deal with behavior that is severely risky to the child and his environment.

3. *Risks to the child's life and well-being.* This kind of behavior is shown only occasionally by most children. It may include running away into traffic or eating toxic substances, both without an awareness of the danger. It may also include self-injurious behavior, such as excessive self-biting, hitting, or head banging. However, self-injurious behav-

ior is more common with institutionalized children than with those living at home and in the community. Severely dangerous behavior usually requires immediate attention and needs to be controlled aside from other educational considerations.

4. *Risks to the life and well-being of others.* This category includes behavior threatening to the welfare of siblings, peers, parents, and teachers. It includes many forms of aggression, such as persistent hitting, fire setting, breaking equipment, windows, and furniture, generally endangering and disrupting the well-being of others. Sometimes this kind of behavior can be confined to the mild risk range, but, like the third category, it requires intervention priority before any other educational objective.

Any procedures we may choose for changing any one of these four types of behavior problems has a potential for misuse or for being ineffective under some circumstances and therefore could present some risk to the child. We discuss this potential for misuse as each procedure is described.

BEHAVIORAL INTERVENTIONS

Many types of behavioral interventions have been used successfully with autistic children. The choice of which one to use depends on the child's ability to learn the relationship between behavior and reinforcer, availability of intervention, and the severity of the problem. The parent-teacher will want to choose a management technique that will be both effective and the least restrictive one possible. By "least restrictive" we refer to a management intervention that matches the highest level of social and emotional development of which the child is capable. We do not want to reward a child with an immediate edible when he is capable of postponing gratification for a period of time in order to gain a later privilege. We would not spank a child who can be controlled by social disapproval or a short "cooling off" period in his room.

The following interventions are divided into three sections: positive reinforcement, mild punishment, and severe punishment. Positive responses are continually used and should be the major type of adult response with all children. Any negative intervention will be directed toward a specific "target" behavior and is most effective when the adult also gives positive attention to the child when he is *not* showing the behavior problem.

Positive Reinforcement

The following positive interventions are listed in developmental order; i.e., the youngest or most handicapped child will need immediate concrete rewards in order to understand the positive approval of the adult, whereas an older or more highly developed child will understand social approval and delayed privileges and will be able to control his behavior in order to get them.

Concrete Rewards   When the child's understanding of an interaction is at a low level, concrete or edible reinforcers are often the most effective. These may include raisins, nuts, cereal bits, or other food the child particularly likes. At first they are given immediately following each desired behavior, e.g., every time the child looks, comes, sits, gives. Gradually they are given less frequently as the child begins to understand social praise and can tolerate waiting for the rewards. Misuse can occur if the child is given foods that are incompatible with special diets or otherwise detrimental to his health. Care should also be taken that edible reinforcers are not used too frequently or for longer than effective. An edible treat is no longer a reward if the child does not want or does not enjoy eating it. Concrete rewards are always combined with social praise. As the child is given an edible, he is also praised, touched, and smiled at. This makes it possible to gradually decrease the concrete rewards as the social praise becomes important and meaningful to the child.

Social Reinforcement   Social reinforcement refers to some form of social interaction that causes the child to continue with the desired behavior. It can be in the form of an approving pat, an expression of "good," a nod of the head, or a smile. This form of reward is most frequently used and is appreciated at all ages. Each family has its own style of giving social approval, and the child's parents can be helpful in suggesting meaningful social praise that their child will understand. Social rewards can be misused if they do not match the child's understanding and therefore do not reinforce the desired behavior. A child may dislike being touched and find a pat on the head unpleasant. Some children find noise, particularly speech, unpleasant and do not respond well to constantly hearing such phrases as "good boy." One child, for example, worked best when the adult simply applauded and smiled without speaking.

Token Rewards   Token rewards are objects given to the child that represent the adult's approval. At the same time these objects tell the child how long he will have to wait for a desired privilege or consequence of good behavior. A paper star or smile face tells the child he has gained approval. A stated number of these tokens might result in gaining a special treat or privilege. Token rewards are particularly helpful in encouraging a child to carry out an independent task or routine, whether it be schoolwork or independent dressing. By giving one token at a time, until all the tokens are used, the child is encouraged to continue with the task without depending on constant social interactions. Token rewards systems that we have found effective include pegs in a small pegboard, checkers placed in a cup, beads on a necklace, and puzzle pieces that form a puzzle the child particularly likes. Misuse of token systems occurs when they are continued beyond the time the child needs them. Token rewards systems can become distracting both to the child and to the adult. When the giving and taking of token rewards consume time and divert attention from the ongoing activity, they are no longer helpful.

Competence Reinforcement For tasks the child understands and learns to enjoy, social and token rewards may be faded out for the positive reinforcement the child gets from succeeding with the task itself. The pleasure that comes from experiencing himself as competent is an inner reward and the most effective reinforcer. It is especially important for increasing the child's independent work activity and should be watched for carefully. Many children will choose in their free time an activity that they can do easily, such as a puzzle, and will work it repeatedly because they enjoy the sense of mastery. The use of external reinforcers at this stage of development may actually interfere with the learning process. The highest form of praise is the recognition that the child is competent, that he can make good choices, and can control his behavior to meet adult expectations.

Punishment

The mildest forms of punishment occur spontaneously and are necessary to the development of appropriate behavior. We refer to such adult responses as shaking the head, saying "No," scowling, removing a toy or misused utensil, leading a child away by the hand, and mild, brief scolding. These mildest forms of negative response present little risk to the child's well-being, nor do the following mildly restrictive procedures.

The distinction between mildly and severely restrictive procedures is not always clear-cut. It may vary for a particular child and particular situation. For example, temporarily withholding food from a child who can be expected to name the food is mild. However, withholding lunch when the child's eating habits are disruptive may be severely restrictive. The severity of any procedure can only be judged by the individual child's perception of the experience. Our labels for these procedures therefore must be adjusted by you to match your knowledge of a particular child. In addition, states and agencies are increasingly regulating all procedures used with handicapped children, so one should become familiar with local rules before implementing any of the following procedures.

Mild Restrictive Procedures *Extinction* is a technical term from the operant conditioning literature. It simply refers to ignoring or disregarding a behavior. Used with mildly annoying, nondangerous behaviors it is not a risky procedure. Extinction does not work unless it is applied consistently. For this reason it is important to obtain cooperation from teachers and parents involved. Care should be taken that extinction does not fade into ignoring the child beyond the targeted behavior. While intentionally ignoring an undesirable behavior, the parent-teacher must be alert to the child's actions and be ready to immediately reward good behavior when it occurs.

Time out from positive reinforcement refers to the interruption of an ongoing schedule of positive reinforcement for a desirable response. It includes turning away from the child and putting the rewards out of reach. By definition this procedure is only useful in situations that include positive reinforcement from others. Typically this would occur during a teaching session when the adult is actively attending and interacting with the child. The misbehavior causes a temporary interruption in this attention and interaction. It can be misused when the child enjoys this interruption and actually misbehaves in order to obtain it. Since this is one of the most widely used behavioral interventions, the reader may want more detailed information (Sulzer-Azaroff and Mayer, 1977; Vargas, 1977).

Social disapproval refers to the common practice of informing a child that his behavior is unacceptable. Disapproval should be in a form that is communicated to a child (from a shake of the head to a loud "No"). Care must be taken to see that the social disapproval does not strengthen the very behavior one is attempting to stop. Many children will prefer negative attention to no attention. Therefore, the balance between positive and negative social attention should be overwhelmingly positive.

Deprivation includes withholding from a child his own property or regularly scheduled events or privileges available to peers. This is generally effective for higher level and/or older children, who are capable of understanding the procedure. Its effectiveness decreases when it is used too frequently. If deprivation is being used as often as once a week, the adult should reconsider the technique and begin systematic documentation in order to judge its effectiveness. Methods for judging effectiveness of a procedure are discussed at the end of this chapter.

Overcorrection is a procedure to reduce the frequency of specific behaviors. It can take the form of positive practice or intensively performing an alternate behavior for a brief period (15–30 minutes). In the former, if a child spills milk repeatedly or intentionally, he may be required to clean the entire floor. In the latter case, a child who continues to tear up papers may be required to tear up cards into small pieces that fit into a slotted can. Overcorrection is generally used for fairly disruptive behavior. It is not used spontaneously, but should be planned, recorded, and documented. Care must be taken that it is not administered in an abusive manner, which may inadvertently reinforce the undesirable behavior. It is also difficult to implement without sufficient staff (Foxx and Azrin, 1973; Harris and Ersner-Hershfield, 1978).

Meal deprivation may be either a mild or severely restrictive procedure. It would be considered severe if it included denial of access to food during regular mealtimes. Brief meal interruptions for training in table skills would fall into the mild category. Any systematic meal deprivation technique should be pre-planned and not spontaneous. This requires consultation between parents and teachers, documentation, and reevaluation of effectiveness within a specific time limit.

Physical contact in the form of slaps or spanks on the child's bottom or hand is often used spontaneously in normal parent-child interactions. With parental agreement, and within school regulations, it may also be used in the classroom. It is sometimes useful to gain wandering attention and control, and it may prevent the need for more restrictive procedures. Care must be taken to use this procedure only when predominantly positive reinforcers are also used in the interactions. Slaps should not be used without warning or without trying less controversial consequences first. They should not be used without first obtaining agreement from all responsible adults, both parents and principals. When used inappropriately this procedure may reinforce the undesirable targeted behavior. In no case should a child be slapped on the face or with severity since it is too difficult to quantify and measure the effect.

Severely Restrictive or Risk Procedures   The following procedures should only be used when a behavior causes risks to the child and/or his environment as discussed earlier. The less restrictive procedures should have been tried first. When these severe procedures are judged to be necessary, a treatment plan must be made, one that involves all responsible adults. The behavior modification plan should be time limited and should consider the effects and risks of the procedure and the effects and risks of not using the procedure. Documentation and assessment of effectiveness are necessary.

Seclusion or *isolation* refers to the placement of a child in a locked or otherwise isolated space. This procedure should only be used when the child's behavior would be likely to cause physical damage to himself or others. It is not to be used, however, for self-injurious behavior since such behavior may continue in seclusion. Seclusion should follow a specific and well-defined behavior (i.e., "biting," "screaming") and be time limited (i.e., 1 to 5 minutes depending on the child's ability to remember the cause of the experience). The space for seclusion must be free of hazards, adequately ventilated, lit, and temperature controlled. There should be provision for observation through a space or window. Indirect consequences of isolation should be considered and direct consequences observed and recorded, even during isolation. For many children, isolation reduces the stimulus and enables them to reorganize their behavior. For some it may cause unreasonable fears or be an enjoyable time to indulge in self-stimulatory behaviors. Isolation should not result in the child's avoidance of a request. After isolation, the child should be required to complete the task or series of activities he was engaged in before isolation. As with all severely restrictive procedures, it is necessary to obtain agreement from all responsible adults. These precautions are not necessary for the commonly used mild form of isolation, such as placing the child in a secluded corner or in a chair facing the wall for short periods. Most parents have asked children to go to their bedrooms following a tantrum or fight to "cool off." Documentation of these mild types of isolation is not necessary, particularly when the desired effect is quickly obvious.

At-risk extinction refers to extinction, as previously defined, when it is used with potentially dangerous behavior, such as aggression, self-injurious behavior, and running away. At-risk extinction can be extremely dangerous because of the tendency of behaviors targeted for extinction to intensify before decreasing. The danger of using extinction on a child who is threatening to run into the street is obvious. For these reasons, at-risk extinction must be considered carefully before implementation. Every precaution must be taken to minimize injury, for example, protective devices for self-injurious behavior. This procedure should be planned in coordination with all responsible adults.

Aversive stimulation is the delivery of a physically painful or uncomfortable stimulus contingent upon a response (e.g., electric shock, unpleasant tasting or smelling substances, cold showers). The use of aversive stimulation is a serious matter. Sentiments against it are often stronger than against the use of drugs with known deleterious side effects. For these reasons it should only be considered as a last resort for potentially dangerous behaviors, not responsive to less aversive procedures. Because aversive stimulation can be very rapidly effective in suppressing a response (Azrin and Holtz, 1966; Lichstein and Schreibman, 1976), it cannot be responsibly ruled out for extreme cases. Should such a severe procedure be necessary, the following precautions are required: the procedure must be carried out by an adult trained in its use; the stimulus used for aversive stimulation must be specific and quantifiable; and the behavior to be decreased must be specifically defined, and the aversive stimulation used with that behavior only. Since aversive stimulation usually has situation-specific effects, i.e., the child may only learn to inhibit his behavior in the same situation with which the procedure was used, the program should contain some plan for generalization of the effects. The procedure should be preceded by a verbal command, e.g., "no hitting," so that this verbal command can replace the aversive stimulation as soon as possible; the procedure should have prior approval of parents and other adults. Every instance of the target behavior and consequence should be recorded daily. Progress must be summarized or documented weekly, with continuation dependent on the proved effectiveness of the program.

Psychoactive drug therapy is considered severely risky because over extended periods of time it produces harmful side effects, such as tardive dyskinesia, and potential risks to the child's health, as yet unknown. Drug therapy is often effective for hyperactive behavior and for decreasing arousal. It should be conducted under the supervision of a physician. The targeted behavior to be changed by the drug should be clearly defined and changes from observed baseline behavior recorded. A description of the possible side effects to be expected should be given to all responsible adults in contact with the child. These adults should then report behavioral changes back to the supervisory physician so that rational plans can be made for changes in dosage or type of medication. Physicians, parents, and teachers all bear the responsibility for knowing what physical checkups are required (such as blood tests) and making sure that the child is checked at required intervals. Drug effects should be monitored regularly. No drug regime of psychoactive agents should be carried out without clear time limits for review and termination. Drug holidays and drug termination can result in a withdrawal flare-up of the targeted behavior for a brief time period, and should be considered only in light of the treatment plan. Considerable individual variation in drug effects can occur in different children on the same day. Drug trials should be time limited and the effects and side effects should be charted and recorded.

SELECTING A TARGET BEHAVIOR

The behavioral management procedures we have described are used by the adult to change a specific targeted behavior in the child. It is easy to label a child disruptive, unmanageable, or hyperactive. It is more difficult to decide where to begin training him for more appropriate behavior. Behavior management techniques work most effectively when one or two target behaviors are taken at a time, in a step-by-step sequence. The selection of the appropriate objective or target behavior should be determined by the following considerations.

Change Potential
The child's developmental level of abilities will place some limits on the type of behavior he is able to organize and control. It will place limits on

how long he can sit still, how long he can attend and respond to language, how much he can inhibit his impulses, how long he can postpone gratification (or wait for what he wants), and how clearly he can understand "if-then" consequences. Expectations for behavioral change must be within reasonable developmental limits. The adult can make appropriate judgments by observing the child throughout the day. For example, if a child can sit still and attend to a favorite TV program for 5 minutes, then it is within his ability to do the same during a teaching session or at mealtimes. If, during his free play, he attends to nothing for longer than 2 minutes, it would be a mistake to attempt to use behavior modification to train him to sit still for 10 minutes doing the same task. There are also natural limits to a child's ability to inhibit or stop some behaviors. For example, it is difficult for many autistic and developmentally handicapped children to control their perseverative language or thinking, their ritualistic mannerisms, their unreasonable fears, and to some extent their self-stimulatory behaviors. When adults attempt to modify a behavior that is not really within the child's ability to control, they may be temporarily successful, but usually new aggressive or self-destructive behaviors will develop. We find that many of the autistic behaviors diminish naturally as the child develops new skills and alternative behavioral responses.

Priorities for Selection

The management program should focus on those behaviors that are the most important in terms of the child's successful adaptation to his environment. The hierarchy of risk behaviors was discussed in Chapter 1, pp. 10–12, and that discussion should be used as a guide to selecting priorities. Actions that cause physical danger to the child or others are easy to spot as appropriate targets for behavior management. It is more difficult to select the best target when efforts are made to improve the child's learning skills. For example, "eye contact" is often chosen as a target for behavior management. In some cases, however, this is trained into a child who is already using his eyes effectively to perceive what is happening with the adult and the materials. The child may be using quick glances or peripheral vision, but the adult decides that the child should stare directly at him. This can be achieved through training, but it results in an "empty" glazed stare, the expectation of a reward, and no increase in perception or understanding of communication. Important responses, such as "look, copy, point, say, give, put, come, stop, get, wait," are appropriate targets when they are necessary to the improvement in learning skills.

Frequency of Behavior

Behavior management techniques are most successful when the target behavior occurs frequently. This means that the child will get repeated experiences with the consequences and, therefore, learn the new rules more quickly. Some dangerous actions only occur rarely, such as throwing glass jars to watch them break. However, the behavior of throwing objects that do not break probably occurs frequently. It is appropriate then to designate "throwing" as the target behavior to decrease in the child. The behavior program would focus on modifying all inappropriate throwing behavior, regardless of whether the object might or might not cause danger.

Whenever a risky problem behavior is chosen as a target for change, the behavior program must also include plans for rewarding the increase of an alternate behavior. The majority of adult-child interactions must be positive ones. Therefore, every negative target (the behavior to be decreased) will have an opposite positive target (an alternate behavior to be increased). If, for example, we choose to decrease "throwing" behavior, we will need to reward the child for "putting down (in, on, away)" behavior. The way we choose to describe the target to the child will influence the success of the program.

Descriptive Praise and Reprimands

Behavior targeted for change should be clearly defined for all adults and the child. Behavior management techniques work best when they are used consistently by all the adults in contact with the child. Rules are learned more quickly by all of us when they are always true than when they are only sometimes true. Even a single adult may have difficulty in being consistent if the target behavior is not clearly defined in his own mind. If we expect a child to come when called, we need to know whether this means he must come after the first call, the second call, the fifth call, or just when. When decisions are left vague, they are made on the basis of the adult's mood. Such decisions are less consistent and therefore more difficult to learn. If, on the other hand, we decide he must come by the count of three, there is no question about the exact definition of what we mean by "come."

It is equally important to make clear to the child exactly what you want or do not want him to do. The phrase "good" or "good boy" may be pleasant to hear but it tells the child little about a specific behavior. The phrase "good sitting" or "thank you for giving" tells the child exactly what he did to please the adult. Undesirable behaviors should be clearly specified for the child; for example, "no biting." A child with little language skill will need a gesture or sign in addition to the words in order to understand the specific behaviors you refer to. The language used in describing a target behavior to the child should always be within his ability to understand. Special caution is needed for explaining a positive reward in terms of something the child did not do; for example, "good for not throwing." When a child lacks a concept of "not" he will be confused by this description and wonder why the word "throwing" was used.

SELECTING THE INTERVENTION PROGRAM

Once the target behavior has been clearly defined, all adults in contact with the child need to discuss the goal for change and select a management procedure that is mutually acceptable and practical. Positive consequences are tried first before the least restrictive or negative consequences are considered. It is important to have a consistent response to the target behavior at home and in school. It is obviously confusing to a child if a behavior is ignored at school (using extinction) and punished at home (using isolation). Parents and teachers must discuss the plan, clearly state the target behavior, describe the management technique to be used, and agree on a trial period after which they will evaluate the effectiveness of the intervention.

Evaluating Effectiveness

All behavior management programs must be judged on the basis of a change in the child's observable behavior. As we have stated earlier in this chapter, it is harmful to continue with a behavioral program when it is not working or when it is no longer necessary. We would not want a child to be still expecting an edible reward when he could be equally well motivated by social praise or inner satisfaction of competence. We would not want a child to be punished when he could not understand the reason, could not control the behavior, or did not find that particular procedure unpleasant. Intuitive impressions ("I have a feeling that...," "Something tells me that...") are not an accurate measure of change. Autistic and developmentally handicapped children often lead adults to form incorrect intuitive impressions. Their sparkling eyes give the impression of understanding what is being said or wanted. Their laughter gives the impression of joy or pleasure related to the real situation. These impressions cannot be used in judging the results of a management program. The child's actual behavior in very concrete terms must be the basis for this judgment. We need to know if the child actually carries out the command to sit, look, come, give. We need to know how soon and for how long (in minutes and seconds) he maintains a behavior. We need to know how often a behavior occurs within a specified time period. Only by documenting these observable facts both before and during a management program can we draw objective conclusions about the results of our management plan.

Charting Behavior

The need for objective and factual observations has been referred to. Although charts are not always necessary, especially when the effect is immediately obvious, they have some distinct advantages in some instances and are necessary in others. Charting has the following advantages:

1. The very act of counting and charting undesirable behavior often has the effect of decreasing the frequency of such behavior.
2. When the effect of the intervention is only partial and unclear to the adult, charting the behavior count provides an objective measure of the change, which may escape subjective, casual observations.
3. Charts are helpful for communicating with others concerned.
4. When the behavior or the treatment procedure presents an unusual risk for the child or his environment, charting is necessary to minimize risks and to maximize accountability.

When mild procedures are used to change mild behavior problems this factual documentation may not be necessary. For example, one parent wished to stop her child from eating with his fingers long after he was already able to use a spoon. She decided to remove his plate for 10 seconds every time he used finger feeding. There was no need to keep charts on this technique because he learned the rule rapidly and it was obvious to the parent that the procedure was working. Another parent, whose child was a slower learner, did need to keep a chart for the same behavior target. She disliked being punitive, was fearful that her child might not get enough to eat, and found it more comfortable to simply nag. However, she agreed to the procedure. She counted the frequency of his finger-eating behavior before starting the procedure (taking a base line), and she then charted his behavior during each meal for 5 days. Without this chart and the contract to continue for 5 days, this parent would have become discouraged and not given the procedure a fair trial. Since children's initial reaction to a new rule is often to increase the unwanted behavior, it is necessary to continue with a management procedure for several days before deciding that it is not effective. The behavior charts should provide space for noting any side effects that may develop. A judgment must be made between what is a ''fair trial'' and what may be causing harmful side effects.

Charts are only helpful when they are practical and possible for the adult to use. For this reason, charts must be individualized to fit the ability and time the adult has available for the purpose. The charts in this chapter are examples taken from our clinical experience, presented here to illustrate the aspect of individualization that is necessary if accurate observations are to be collected. Parents or teachers need to understand the purpose of the observations they will make — how the data collected will help them select and use the best behavior management technique. Each of the three examples illustrates a different type of goal: 1) goal to promote a desired behavior, 2) goal to decrease a mild problem behavior, and 3) goal to decrease a severe problem behavior. A brief description of the problem is given followed by an explanation of how the chart was helpful in evaluating effectiveness.

EXAMPLE 1:   INTERVENTION TO PROMOTE A DESIRED BEHAVIOR

Problem

John, a developmentally handicapped 6-year-old, had been fully toilet trained 1 year before, and was able to dress and undress himself easily. At the time of this charting procedure, he had been mildly soiling his underpants at frequent intervals during the day. Scolding and mild punishment, a natural response from his parents and teachers, had proved ineffective. Overcorrection in the form of lengthy cleaning-up procedures had been tried, but it was too difficult for the adults to take time to supervise. The following positive reinforcement intervention was discussed and agreed upon by all concerned. Both his parents and teachers charted his behavior and shared the results.

GOAL: TEACH JOHN TO KEEP HIS PANTS CLEAN

Purpose of Chart: In order to decide if this technique will help to motivate John to take responsibility for his own cleanliness, we need to know exactly how often he is now having accidents (baseline data). Then, as we begin to reward him for "clean pants," we can see if there is a change. In 2 weeks these data will give us clear evidence of our effectiveness.

Technique:
1. Place chart (see Figure 14) on bathroom wall. Have rewards (peanuts) nearby.
2. Every hour call John to the bathroom. Tell him to "take down his pants" and "look — are pants clean?" If so reward him and praise him. If not, state the fact, "Pants dirty." Quickly give him clean underpants, say nothing, and leave the bathroom.

Goal: To increase responsibility for cleanliness.
Objective target: To keep pants clean.
Child: John

Date	Soiled	Clean	Rewards
Fri.	IIII	I	O
Sat.	IIII I	II	O
Sun.	IIII	III	O
Mon.	II	II	O
Tue.	III	I	O
Wed.	III	II	II
Thu.	II	III	III
Fri.	I	IIII	IIII
Sat.	IIII	IIII	IIII
Sun.	II	IIII I	IIII I
Mon.		IIII	IIII
Tue.	II	II	II
Wed.		IIII	IIII
Thu.	I	IIII	IIII
Fri.		IIII	IIII
Sat.	I	IIII II	IIII II
Sun.		IIII III	IIII II
Mon.		IIII	IIII
Tue.		IIII	IIII
Wed.			

base line { brackets Fri. through Tue. (first five rows) }

Figure 14.   Chart kept for the objective-target of keeping John's pants clean. (Data are hypothetical.)

Conclusions. The technique was effective. Trips to the bathroom were reduced to three times a day. Every 1–2 hours John was praised and hugged, and told he was a "nice, clean boy."

EXAMPLE 2:   DECREASE A MILD BEHAVIOR PROBLEM

Problem

Jenny, a 5-year-old autistic girl, made mealtimes at home and at school unpleasant by continually eating with her fingers. Her primary interest was food, and Jenny ate all she could get extremely rapidly and messily. Her mother had nagged and scolded to no avail. Jenny had little understanding of language and was not consistently attentive to sounds. She had the skill to use a spoon.

GOAL: DECREASE USE OF FINGERS IN EATING

Purpose of Chart: Since you are making a new rule for Jenny, one you cannot explain to her in words, it may take a little time for her to catch on to what you want her to do. You need to continue the program for at least a week at every meal before you decide it won't work. Don't be discouraged if her first response is to increase the behavior. Be patient for this 1 week.

Technique:
1.   Take a base line. Mark on the chart (see Figure 15) every time she uses her fingers but do not start the procedure for 2 days.
2.   Remove her plate for 10 seconds *every* time she uses her fingers. Give no other attention to the behavior. Mark on the chart, then return her plate. Point to the spoon or put it in her hand.

Conclusions. Jenny quickly learned the new rule. The chart was discontinued, but her mother continued to use the "removal" procedure when the behavior recurred.

EXAMPLE 3:   DECREASE SEVERE BEHAVIOR PROBLEM

Problem

Jimmy, a hyperactive, agile 4-year-old autistic boy, was impulsively driven to tear up any paper he found within reach. Functioning generally at a 2-year-old level, but with little receptive language, Jimmy was unresponsive to verbal commands and laughed when he was spanked. He required constant adult attention and all books, newspapers, letters, and other paper materials had to be kept out of reach.

Goal: To improve eating habits.
Objective target: To decrease eating with fingers.
Child: Jenny

	Date	Breakfast	Lunch	Dinner	Total
base line	9/4	卌 III (8)	卌 I (6)	卌 卌 I (11)	25
base line	9/5	卌 I (6)	IIII (4)	卌 IIII (9)	19
	9/6	III (3)	卌 (5)	卌 I (6)	14
	9/7	II (2)	III (3)	卌卌 II (12)	17
	9/8	I (1)	卌 (5)	卌 II (7)	13
	9/9	(0)	II (2)	III (3)	5
	9/10	II (2)	I (1)	II (2)	5
	9/11	(0)	I (1)	(0)	1
	9/12				
	9/13				

Figure 15. Chart kept for the objective-target of decreasing Jenny's eating with her fingers. (Data are hypothetical.)

GOAL: DECREASE TEARING PAPER

Purpose of Chart: This chart will help us get answers to the following questions:

1. Does Jimmy know he should not tear paper (anticipate your response)?
2. Is he able to inhibit (stop himself for a brief time)?
3. Does he dislike the isolation procedure (cry, pull back)?
4. Does he have something else to do (alternate activity available)?

We can get these answers by closely watching his behavior and recording it. After a 2-week trial, we should be able to better understand what we can expect from Jimmy in terms of decreasing this habit.

Technique: As soon as he tears paper, immediately go to him, and say loudly, "No tearing," with an angry expression. Place him quickly in the isolation spot. Mark the event on the chart (see Figure 16) and count 1 minute. Open the door, lead him out, and direct him to an alternate ac-

Goal: To decrease impulsivity.
Objective: Eliminate tearing paper.
Child: Jimmy

		Did child anticipate?		Did he inhibit?		Dislike booth?		Next activity
Date	Time	Yes	No	Yes	No	Yes	No	
9-4	3:00		✓		✓	✓		blocks
9-4	3:40		✓		✓		✓	— .
9-4	3:42		✓		✓	✓		— .
9-4	3:43	✓		✓		✓		car
9-5	4:20		✓		✓	✓		TV
9-5	4:50		✓	✓				
9-5	4:52	✓		✓		✓		outside
9-6	4:50	✓		✓		✓		blocks
9-8	5:15		✓		✓	✓		ring stack
9-8	5:30	✓		✓		✓		
9-8	5:32	✓		✓		✓		supper
9-11	5:30	✓		✓		✓		supper

Figure 16.   Chart kept for the objective-target of decreasing Jimmy's impulsivity. (Data are hypothetical.)

tivity. Praise him when he begins appropriate play. If he screams or tears again, repeat the procedure. (Leave a newspaper or magazine on the table, but be sure his toys are also available, ones you know he can use easily.)

Conclusions. The data suggested the following pattern:

1. Jimmy disliked isolation.
2. Anticipation increased, showing he knew the consequence of tearing.
3. He began to inhibit, still an emerging skill.
4. The problem seemed to be worse just before supper time.

His mother decided to continue charting and she made two changes:

1. Removed all paper 1 hour before supper time.
2. Gave him a structured activity to do at this time.

Figure 17 shows a completed behavior management plan for Tommy, and Figure 18 provides a blank form for a behavior management plan.

Child: Tommy D.   Date: 9/10/78

1. **Current behavior problem:** Parents report that Tommy has a
strong attachment to "sticks" (twigs found on the ground) and to
his toy cars. He lines these up in rows, the sticks on the kitchen
floor, the cars in front of the doorway or on the stairs. If one of
these is moved, either accidentally or on purpose, he screams in
a tantrum response, sometimes lasting for ½ hour. He bites his
hand frequently during these rages. Since it is almost impossible
for the family, including 3-year-old brother John, to avoid
touching Tommy's sticks/cars as they move about the small kitchen, these tantrums occur several times a day. Father reports
having frequent disagreements with his mother-in-law about how
to handle this behavior, and Mother feels caught in the middle
and generally discouraged.

2. **History of problem:** Since 2 years of age Tommy has always
carried a stick in his right hand, becoming upset if anyone took it
from him. Over a year ago he began collecting sticks and lining
them up in a long row in the yard. At about this time he became
interested in toy cars also, and lined these up in a row at the
front door. At first his parents were pleased that Tommy could
occupy himself happily in this play activity. They felt it was quite
clever and tried not to interrupt or disturb him. Even when he
brought the sticks and cars into the house they continued to
cater to him until it became increasingly difficult and irritating to
step over or around them. Tommy's rigid need for sameness frequently interrupted the few hours his parents had together with
screaming tantrums and hand biting. Gradually his threatened
tantrums made his parents fearful of disciplining him for any
misbehavior.

3. **Past efforts to manage behavior:** Both Mr. and Mrs. D. have tried
moving the cars and sticks to Tommy's room and, when he threw
a tantrum, Father tried spanking. This increased his screams, so
he was allowed to continue his play. Grandmother has been sym-
pathetic. She claims she can prevent his tantrum by rearranging
the toys with him. Mrs. D. has shut Tommy in his room to "cool
off." Although this has quieted him down, she thought he continued to bite his hand while in the room, and he started to
scream again when let out if his toys were not where he wanted.

4. **Goals and rationale**
    A. *To increase an appropriate alternate behavior:* Train more
    acceptance of change in his play rituals.
    B. *To decrease an inappropriate behavior:* Reduce the amount
    of screaming when a tantrum does occur.
    C. *Reasons for goal selection:* Although Mr. and Mrs. D. dis-
    cussed problems of bowel accidents and tantrum scream-
    ing, the latter is the most disturbing to the whole family at
    this time. Their fear of starting a tantrum has inhibited all
    disciplinary efforts and caused conflict between family
    members. Tantrums occur daily, often when John ap-
    proaches his cars and whenever the sticks and cars are
    moved. His long history of special attachment to these toys
    makes it unlikely that tantrums will be reduced without also

Figure 17.   Behavior management plan for Tommy.

modifying his play rituals. If not modified, his insistence on keeping these rows intact is likely also to cause difficulties when he starts school.

5. **Procedure**
   A. *Who:* Mother, Father, and Grandmother will all need to carry out the management plan because each is in charge of Tommy at various times. Mother believes Grandmother will cooperate because she is eager to help Tommy make a good adjustment to school.
   B. *Where:* All three adults will come with Tommy to the clinic to observe the management procedures and agree on techniques. Mother plans to work with Tommy during the week. Father will take over on weekends. Grandmother will be available when needed.
   C. *When:* Parents will take baseline data for 1 week, and start procedures following the clinic visit. Baseline data will contain a daily record of each tantrum: when it occured and how long the screaming lasted.

GOAL 1:   INCREASE TOLERANCE OF CHANGE IN PLAY RITUALS
Objective-Target: To give stick or car to adult without fussing.
Materials: Two shoe boxes, five sticks, five cars, raisins, and nuts
Procedure: Step 1:   Use the cars and sticks in the structured sorting activity as specified in your Home Program [see Chapter 8]. When completed, have T. put each set of objects back in the shoe box and reward him with a raisin and praise. Step 2:   When he can do this without fussing, use the same task during nonstructured times, when T. is playing on the floor. Take the boxes over to him, put them on the floor, ask him to hand you one stick, show him a raisin, and give it to him as soon as he gives you one stick. Praise and reward for each action. Continue until you have three to five sticks or cars in the boxes. Use verbal praise for each helping action ("Thank you," "Good helping") and give pats and smiles also. When complete, give him a swing and a favorite edible (perhaps peanuts). If this can be completed without tantrums, an important precipitating cause for them will have been removed.

GOAL 2.   REDUCE AMOUNT OF SCREAMING WHEN TANTRUM DOES OCCUR
Objective-Target: To stop screaming within 1 minute.
Procedure: Step 1:   As soon as Tommy starts to scream, look at him and say firmly, "No screaming," then turn away, thus ignoring or "timing out" the behavior. If he stops, immediately turn back to him, smile, give him a pat, say "Good—quiet," and place your finger on your lips. Put the stick or car in the box and give him a raisin or nut. If the screaming does not stop by the time you count slowly to 10, proceed to Step 2. Step 2:   Repeat the loud and firm command, "No screaming," and move him quickly to the chair, sitting him down. Stand behind him to prevent him from leaving the chair, holding his shoulder if necessary. Keep him in the chair 1 minute, say nothing, then let him up. If scream-

ing continues, put him back again in the chair, again for 1 minute. Repeat this "benching" procedure until he calms down, counting how many repetitions he needed. If Tommy struggles to leave, use a cloth or belt as a loose seat belt to remind him to stay. Avoid physical wrestling or any interactions with him during this time. Post the following chart on the wall near the chair so you can record what happened.

6. Evaluation of progress

A. *Baseline data:*   Keep for 1 week before starting procedures.

date	time of tantrum	duration (in minutes)

B. *Chart of Goal 2:*   Record for 2 weeks, then reevaluate.

date	time of tantrum	duration (minutes)	type of restraint

(*Note:* This behavior management plan is presented as an illustration for you to use in developing a similar one for your own child.)

Child: _____   Date: _____

1. **Current behavior problem:** (Describe behavior concretely, telling where and under what circumstances it occurs.)

2. **History of problem:** (When did it start and how did it develop?)

3. **Past efforts to manage behavior:** (State the various techniques used in the past, who used them, and how the child responded.)

4. **Goals and rationale**
    A. To increase an appropriate alternate behavior:
    B. To decrease an inappropriate behavior:
    C. Reasons for goal selection: (Importance of changed behavior to child and to parent-teachers; priority.)

5. **Procedure**
    A. *Who:*
    B. *Where:*
    C. *When:*
    GOAL 1:   To increase...
      Objective-Target:
        Materials:
        Procedure:

    GOAL 2:   To decrease...
      Objective-Target:
        Materials:
        Procedure:

6. **Evaluation of progress**
    A. *Baseline data:* (How long, what facts are needed).
    B. *Chart:* (How long, what facts are needed).

Figure 18.   Blank form for behavior management plan.

Chapter 7.
Teaching Strategies and Techniques

We have discussed the selection of teaching goals and objectives within seven areas of mental functioning in Chapters 3–5 and behavior management in Chapter 6. Each of these topics included some references to the strategies of teaching methods and structures. In fact, it was virtually impossible to illustrate these topics without reference to teaching structures and methods. Because they form an integral part of every teaching program, in this chapter we discuss them in more detail. When we are talking about teaching structures, we refer to the conditions of time, place, and materials that we have prepared for the child before our teaching session begins. Methods, on the other hand, refer to the parent-teacher's side of the interaction aimed at facilitating the child's learning.

TEACHING STRUCTURE

Less than a decade ago it was widely believed that autistic and developmentally disordered children suffered from repressed feelings and wishes. Accordingly it was believed that they should be taught in an unstructured situation allowing them free self-expression. Our own experience and research (Schopler et al., 1971) agreed with those of others, who found this belief to be erroneous. Lack of structure, in fact, tended to increase our children's aimless and psychotic behavior when contrasted with structured situations for the same children. We also found considerable variation in the children's response to structure. Children at lower levels of development needed more structure and were more disorganized by relative freedom than children at higher levels of development, who already had skills to use in an unstructured situation.

For these reasons it is well worth the parent-teacher's extra effort in carefully planning where, when, how, and with what the lessons will be taught. Parents at home and teachers in the classroom will have limitations of choice dictated by their situation and other responsibilities. However, the best solution will be found when the following points are considered:

1. *Space*   The space chosen for teaching should be comfortable and free from distractions of noise and movement. At home this may mean a separate room away from the television noise. At school this may mean a dividing screen preventing the child from watching other children in motion. The same space should be used routinely so that it becomes associated with the behaviors expected from the child when he is working. If keeping the child still is particularly difficult, placing a table diagonally across a corner and sitting the child inside the confined space may help.

2. *Time*   The time of day chosen for lessons should be one that can become part of a daily routine. At home this might be always after supper. At school it might be always after morning circle. It is often helpful to schedule teaching sessions to precede a desired activity (just before a favorite television show, just before snack time). This gives the child motivation to cooperate during sessions since he has something to look forward to when he is finished. Children adjust better to short, daily sessions at home than to longer, less predictable ones. Once a child gets used to a routine lesson period he will often get his materials spontaneously and show that he wants to have a lesson when that time comes.

3. *Duration*   The length of each teaching session should be planned on the basis of the child's ability to sustain attention and on the pressures of the parent-teacher's schedule. Sessions may vary from 10 minutes to 1 hour, depending on the child. Each teaching session will contain several different activities. The length of each activity and the pace of movement from one activity to the next may vary from day to day, since these children are often inconsistent in their ability to attend and in their speed of working. Although it is important to note the child's fluctuating attentiveness and tolerance for frustration, it is not helpful to allow him to leave an activity at the first moment he wishes. Attention and organization tend to increase rapidly when the child is expected to "finish" or to do "one more" step. When the child wants to leave an unfinished task, it is important to understand the reason for his disinterest. Although there are many possible reasons, they usually fall into two most important categories. Either the task has been

unpleasantly difficult, or the ability for completing the task has been well established but the child is uncooperative. How the parent-teacher responds depends on which of these two alternatives is motivating the child's disinterest. If the task has been difficult, the adult can get the child to finish with a little extra help. If, on the other hand, the task has been consistently completed in the past, and the child is uncooperative for other reasons, he should be required to complete it without extra help. However, caution is advised against prolonging the sessions whenever the child is working well, unless he is given the choice to stop at the expected time. Otherwise he may learn that disruption and uncooperative behavior are the most efficient way to terminate a teaching session.

When moving from step to step within a task, or from task to task within a session, the parent-teacher should maintain a pace that is neither too slow nor too fast. Signals from the child (e.g., idleness, self-stimulation, increased excitability) help the parent-teacher to adjust the pace accordingly.

SELECTION OF MATERIALS

When choosing the materials to be used, careful consideration should be given to the child's preference for color, shapes, textures, and objects. Strong preferences and attachments, for example, cars, catalogs, strong smells, red objects, can often be observed during the initial assessment. They may also form strong dislikes, for example, puppets, loud noises, sticky materials. These strong responses are often seen as undesirable. However, they can also be used to help the child learn. Some children are so distracted by certain materials (shiny surfaces, sticks, glue, objects that roll) that they cannot attend to a lesson with that material in an appropriate way. These should usually be replaced by materials that the child enjoys handling, but that he is not driven to use in perseverative and self-stimulatory ways.

The materials should be easy to obtain. The most common items likely to be found in the home are preferable. Few parents or teachers can afford to buy expensive commercial educational materials. If they do make this investment, there is a temptation to continue using these materials long beyond the time when they are still appropriate for the child. In addition to the expense involved, commercial "teaching programs" cannot always be individualized for a specific child. These children should be taught a language vocabulary that is immediately usable in their daily experience, that can be used to describe and request what they want. Pictures of city life and farmyard scenes may not both be appropriate for the same child. The child who does not recognize the names for his own clothing does not need to learn the names of zoo animals. Clearly some of the materials can be more easily bought than made at home (puzzles, blocks, pegboards, beads, assembly toys). However, these can also be used in a variety of ways. Generally we have found it more satisfactory to make our own materials.

Further guidelines for selecting materials are that they should be:

a. *Safe* Avoid poisonous and dangerous materials that require constant supervision when the child handles them.

b. *Plain* Use materials that have simple shapes and single colors. Avoid irrelevant, complicated designs, frills, wiggling parts, and shiny surfaces. These tend to distract and confuse the child who may overattend to small details.

c. *Common* Use materials that are familiar at home or at school, materials whose names are often heard in everyday conversation. Avoid overly imaginative pictures, such as funny animals dressed in human clothes. The children think concretely and are often confused by pretend or imaginary ideas.

d. *Easy* Use materials that are easy to hold, lift, and manipulate; use materials that are easy to see (bright colors, large shapes, simple, undetailed pictures with no confusing background details). Many developmentally handicapped children have poorly developed fine motor skills and they are frustrated by tasks that require manual strength and precise manipulation of small items.

e. *Appropriate* Use materials characteristic of the child's developmental age, modified to take advantage of his particular preferences and interests (e.g., a ring-stack toy that when assembled becomes a top the child can spin).

f. *Containers* The parent-teacher will also need to collect various containers to keep the teaching materials in, containers for storage and for use during the presentation of the task. Useful containers are coffee cans, shoe boxes, vegetables trays, envelopes, plastic bags, wash basins. A list of materials we have found helpful is provided on page 240 of this manual.

PRESENTATION OF MATERIALS

The organization of materials and the orderly sequence of presentation during the session are critical to effective teaching. Putting the materials for each activity into a container prevents items from falling, slipping, or rolling away. Containing the materials prevents the confusion and over-

Task: child picks up crayon on his left, marks on the paper, puts crayon on his right, then picks another from the left pile, continues until finished.

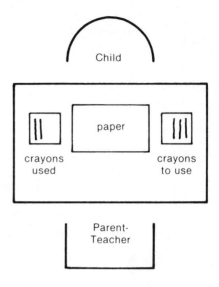

Figure 19.   Arrangement of materials for coloring task.

stimulation caused by clutter. Only the materials needed for the activity at hand should be visible to the child. When materials are placed on the table, they should be arranged in such a way as to clarify visually the organization of the task presented. He should be able to see clearly what materials he is to use first, where they should be placed, and where to put them when the task is finished. Little sorting trays, shallow bowls, or colored paper squares help the child see where things belong. Tasks that require the child to make gestures or speak can also be clarified visually by the use of tokens. (For example, the child is asked to touch parts of his body on command. A cup and 10 checkers are placed on the table. Each time the child touches a body part, a checker is placed in the cup. The child can see that this represents a completion of a part of the task, and he can see how many more times he will be asked to touch his body.) When some children understand visually exactly what and how much they should do in a task, they are more willing to continue working until they have completed the task. Figures 19–21 illustrate how to structure a task through the arrangement and presentation of the materials.

TEACHING METHODS

To help a child learn we observe him carefully so that we can learn how to help him best. We have to let him know what we expect him to do, and

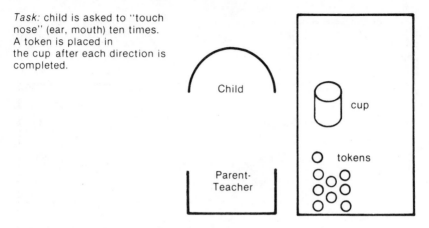

Task: child is asked to "touch nose" (ear, mouth) ten times. A token is placed in the cup after each direction is completed.

Child

cup

tokens

Parent-Teacher

Figure 20.   Arrangement of materials for token task.

must show him in various ways until he can do it independently. How to accomplish this teaching aim depends on the child's motivation and level of skills as shown by his responses. Some children have little difficulty working alone on a task they understand, but have great difficulty attending to new materials. For other children the reverse is true. They will attend to new tasks but will not work independently on familiar activities without continued attention and encouragement. Since the aim of teaching is to enable each child to attain skills for his own use, we have identified different methods by which to fulfill this aim.

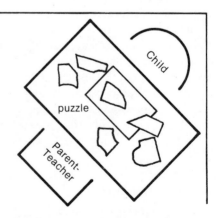

Task: child is told to complete the puzzle before leaving his seat. When finished, the table is moved to allow the child to leave area.

Child

puzzle

Parent-Teacher

Figure 21.   Arrangement of materials for puzzle task.

We have discussed teaching as an interaction with a child in which we provide different amounts and degrees of help. The methods we use with any child are therefore not readily prescribed independent of the child's response to the interaction. However, for the sake of clarity we list some of the teaching methods we have found most useful with our children. They are listed roughly in order of providing from the most to the least help to the child. They are intended to show some of the choices open to the parent-teacher but not to prescribe the order of use with a particular child.

Manipulation   Manipulation involves physically taking the child's body and guiding him through the motions necessary for task completion. Sometimes the parent-teacher may just begin the activity with manipulation in order to get him started on the task. At times, manipulation is a useful technique for bringing the child's attention back to the task, making him aware both that the parent-teacher wants him to act and what the task is at the same time. This technique requires little effort from the child and can be particularly useful when error-free learning is needed to get the child started on a new activity, or when one part of the task presents particular difficulty for the child.

Direct Assistance   Direct assistance is provided to the child when the parent-teacher hands him the materials to use or adds finishing touches to the child's product. Assistance may be in the form of placing teaching material in the child's hand or pulling child and chair closer to the table.

Demonstration   In demonstration the parent-teacher performs the task himself as the child watches. After the demonstration, the child is asked to do the same activity himself. If the task is difficult, the demonstration may have to be repeated and gradually modified to taking turns with the child (e.g., first the parent-teacher places a puzzle piece, then hands the next one to the child, then takes another turn, etc.).

Routines   Routines can also be used as a teaching method. By having a child repeat a procedure like sorting, threading, or stacking until it becomes a routine, the parent-teacher can help him master the skill so that he can then carry it out without further instruction. While the child is repetitively doing the task, the parent-teacher monitors his work and provides rewards and corrections as needed. This technique is particularly helpful to children who naturally enjoy repetition. New concepts and skills can be presented in the same familiar procedures, and the child can attend to the new element in the lesson because the procedure of the task is familiar to him.

Cues   A cue is a signal that offers and encourages part of the response required from the child by a task. This signal may be a nod of the head, a touch to the body, a point to an object. It may be an encouraging inflection, telling the child he's on the right track, or the beginning sound of the necessary word response. The *cue* hints at the answer and is often sufficient for the child to complete the task by himself. Cues may be either faint or strong. For example, a child who is told to "go to the door" and does not move may respond to a slight head gesture in the direction of the door, a slight touch, or a firmer push. If he is asked to name a jar of bubbles, he may recall the word when he only hears the first sound, or he may need to hear the entire first syllable. The parent-teacher may need to give a visual and an auditory cue simultaneously. For example, the child who looks at a picture of a boy eating and is asked "What is the boy doing?" may need two cues: a gesture of eating and the first sound, "eee--." In order to use cues effectively it is important for the parent-teacher to cue the child no more than necessary and to discontinue or fade the cues as the child is able to respond correctly without them.

Pantomime   Pantomime means going through the motions involved in doing the task without actually using the materials, for example, motions of rolling clay without clay in the hands. Pantomime does not always mean going through a complete task. It includes any "sign" used to describe a shape or motion to be carried out (e.g., making a circle with one's hands). This will supply sufficient clues to the child to enable him to complete the task.

Verbal Directions   Verbal directions refer to spoken language, but they may be supplemented with signed language. Directions give information through the use of vocabulary and syntax. A parent-teacher will use verbal directions simultaneously with other teaching methods, but he needs to know how much the child's comprehension comes from the verbal directions and how much he is relying on gestural cues as well. The selection of appropriate teaching methods depends on an accurate assessment of how the child comprehends the directions. In the long run it will be more efficient for the child to respond to verbal directions, as signs and gestural cues are then reduced or faded.

Every teaching method involves both observation and language. A good part of each teaching session will be spent in just watching the child's attempts to perform a task. There is no need to be actively directing a child if he already understands a task. Since the ultimate goal is for the child to work independently, to experiment and to be able to learn from his errors, this must be encouraged whenever possible. Passive observation enables the parent-teacher to be aware of what the child has learned and where he still needs help. Overly intrusive and active teaching is not only tiring for the child, but tends to foster overdependence on the teacher and reduces the child's willingness to try things on his own.

Verbal language accompanies all teaching techniques. Even with the child who has no understanding of language, the teaching sessions are not conducted in silence. Communication is enhanced when the complexity of the language used is appropriate to the child's level of understanding. So, for example, the parent-teacher may say any of the following to encourage the child to put the block on the table: "block...table," "put block on table," "put the red block over on the table." In general, we have found that in working with more impaired children, parent-teachers need to speak less, make their sentences shorter, use simpler words, and talk more slowly than they do habitually.

We have discussed several teaching techniques that we use frequently. However, the most exciting and effective ones are those developed by individual parent-teachers based on their best understanding of their child's unique learning patterns.

Chapter 8.
Implementation
at Home and School

By now the reader without previous experience with developmentally disabled children should be aware of some important differences between the implementation of a teaching program for normal children and one for the special children we are concerned with in this volume. Individualized teaching efforts are a desirable aspect of any high quality educational program. Nevertheless, it is relatively easy for the educator to predict normal responses to a specific curriculum. For example, the driver's education curriculum is quite similar from one high school to the next. This similarity of curriculum is not the case for our group of children. For them individualization is not merely associated with educational quality, it is actually a necessity.

When a normal child learns a new word or new arithmetic function, we expect him to use this new information not only in school, but also at home and in the community. For autistic and developmentally disordered children, on the other hand, such transfer of knowledge cannot be taken for granted. For example, an autistic child may learn to identify his teacher's green sweater. However, he may have to be taught separately that grass is also green, and that a green sweater may be worn by his sister instead of his teacher and still be green. There is a tendency for our group of children to be excessively concrete, to overselect irrelevant details, and to have trouble understanding the rules by which facts can be generalized from one situation to another. For these reasons teaching is much more situation-specific than it is with normal children. In order to facilitate generalization of a learned event from one situation to another, individualized collaboration and carryover between teacher and parent are essential.

The school and the home are the child's two primary learning sites. No matter how experienced the teacher or how well informed the parent, there are different teaching or learning problems for the child at home and at school. Many of these differences are valid and real. Too often they are ignored and misunderstood by both parents and teachers.

COMPARISON OF SCHOOL AND HOME TEACHING

Both parents and teachers share the general educational objective of helping the child to attain optimum independence and adaptation in the least restrictive environment. However, what they can do toward that end should differ in some respects but also be complementary.

The home environment is relatively free to accommodate the different needs of each family member. They live together more weekly hours and for many more weeks than do teacher and child. Family relationships tend to be more intense and restricted to fewer individuals than relationships between teacher and students. One or both parents may have a job to maintain their families. Extra efforts with the developmentally disabled child require energies from parents in addition to what they expend during their working day, whereas teachers are with the child during a specific number of hours daily. Parents are involved with the child's sleeping problems, and the necessity for every family member to get a night's sleep. Teachers, on the other hand, are expected to maintain a safe and productive learning environment for a group of children. They give individual attention and help to the children as needed without ignoring the rest of the class they are responsible for. Parents deal more frequently with cooking, feeding, dressing, and toileting problems, and teachers are involved with the special curriculum for speech and other survival skills defined by their educational program. Many specific differences between individual families and classrooms could be itemized. Rather than listing them, however, it may be more useful to consider the differences between the social roles of parents and teachers.

Social Role of Parent and Teacher

Parents have both the right and the obligation within broad limits to decide questions affecting their family life-style. They also help their child to adapt to the family's way of life. Because they live with their child from the moment of birth, parents have unique experience and knowledge of their own child's special needs. This intense experience is not readily shared by teachers or professionals. Unless there is clear and explicit evidence to the contrary, parents should be recognized as the foremost experts on their own child. Usually they have the most consistent motivation for helping their child to learn and adapt. To the extent that this broad goal is achieved, they are also most consistently reinforced by the child's successful steps in that direction.

However, autistic and similar children have unusual difficulties in learning and adaptation. For this reason parents are more dependent on the expertise and support of professionals and teachers than they are with their other children. The teachers' social role requires that they convey certain skills and social behaviors to the child. They have training and experience with special teaching procedures. They are also exposed to many more children than are parents. The special learning needs of these handicapped children require close coordination between parent and teacher roles. In the past, differences between teachers' and parents' roles went unrecognized too often, leading to unnecessary hostility, disagreement, and poor communication between teacher and parent.

To carry out an effective individualized educational program, valid differences between school and home must be understood. Collaborative home-school teaching integration would appear to require extra effort from overtaxed parents and teachers. However, such extra effort is only burdensome at first. In our experience, the resulting improvement in the child is a source of pride and gratification for both parents and teachers. If that is not enough, Public Law 94-142 also mandates this collaboration.

Parent-Teacher Collaboration

The most effective collaboration between parent and teacher can be achieved by regular personal contact. These face-to-face meetings can take different forms, depending on the time and resources available to the parents. Currently, mothers are more often able to be directly involved than fathers. At the most intense level the parent spends regular periods in the classroom each week, perhaps working on certain tasks with the parent's own child or other children. This is done under the teacher's guidance, although some parents learn to function effectively as assistant teachers. They carry some of the teaching responsibilities, and in the process learn more about their own child.

A second form of coordination involves the parents' observation of classroom activities. This is useful when parents' direct work in the classroom is not feasible, or when it is confined to special events or holidays. A parent may make cookies for birthdays or help out during special classroom trips.

A third way of integrating school and home teaching can occur when parents demonstrate home training activities to the teacher. For example, a mother may demonstrate how she has trained her child to clear the table or bring familiar objects. Such demonstration may help the teacher to incorporate such a teaching activity in the school curriculum; it may also enable the teacher to show the mother why it cannot be done. More often a teacher may demonstrate to the mother learning activities she can use with her child at home. For a child with unusual language handicaps, such a demonstration can show the use of sign language.

Some parents are not able to be involved in their child's school program either by participating or by observing in the classroom. This fourth kind of home-school integration can be achieved by regular parent-teacher conferences. These are usually held at monthly intervals. The teacher reviews the child's progress and difficulties since the last conference, and the parent reports her observation from the home. These conferences are especially helpful for reviewing consistent behavior management procedures between parent and teacher, along with home-school teaching programs.

Although the child's teaching program is best implemented through parental involvement with the teacher and classroom, it is equally important for the teacher to make occasional home visits. These serve the very useful purpose of observing the child and his family on their own terrain. Home visits often result in showing the teacher unknown aspects of the child's behavior. These may include either unsuspected skills in adjustment to home routines or behavior problems not apparent in the classroom. Such visits often lead to improved integration between school and home teaching; they virtually always result in better understanding. Many of our teachers have developed a meaningful social relationship with their children's parents. They may be invited to the home for supper, to help out with baby sitting, or otherwise enter into a close and positive personal relationship of mutual support. As the teacher obtains better knowledge of the parents' home situation and specific problems with the child, this information can be worked into the child's educational program. Although good parent-teacher relationships are helpful to most children, they are especially important with developmentally handicapped children. For them, the teaching program is not so easily separated between school and home. It must include structured plans for both social adjustment and skill acquisition in order to achieve the child's best adaptation, and that includes both home and school.

CHILD AND SCHOOL COMMUNITY

By now you will have noted that our teaching emphasis is on the interaction between the child and his environment. Education progresses as the child changes with his newly learned skills. However, many of our children continue to have some form of handicap. Their adaptation will also be improved as others in the community can understand and accommodate to the handicap. Next we discuss ways in which broader adaptation can be achieved in the school.

Normal children may be invited into the special education classroom. They may work on remedial activities with the handicapped children. They may also participate in social play structured by the teacher. The right form of the interaction between normal and special children is decided by the teacher on the basis of developmentally appropriate social or educational activities. We have found that this kind of interaction is most helpful to both groups of children. Normal children learn to understand and accept developmentally handicapped children. They also feel the pride and satisfaction of taking a helping role with the handicapped child. Conversely, the handicapped child has a positive experience in playing and interacting with normal children.

At a more advanced stage in the child's education, he may join the normal group's class with decreased special structuring of the learning situation. At first this may be done only for brief periods or for special activities, such as lunch, recreation, music, and art. For some children this mainstreaming can then be increased in time and subjects until the child is assimilated into the regular school program. For other children, mainstreaming may not be advisable. For children whose language and learning rates are too impaired to benefit from a regular classroom experience, a self-contained class experience will be more adaptive.

Exposure between other school personnel and the handicapped children often promotes improved adjustment. The principal, secretary, janitor, and lunchroom personnel all can play a vital part in contributing to the child's learning. However, to make these interactions productive, the teacher needs to supply the school personnel with information about the child's limits of communication, understanding, and special problems.

The special education teacher can promote understanding between school personnel and developmentally disabled children in other ways; for example, by having the children's work represented on bulletin board exhibits or having the children participate in gymnastics and school programs, as in Christmas performances and making Christmas cards. Teachers can also give workshops during teacher meetings that explain the special group and their educational activities.

A structured learning interaction between handicapped children and the community can be fostered by classroom field trips. Children may be taken to grocery stores, restaurants, on buses, and to the zoo. Such trips not only broaden the child's experience, but also help the community to overcome irrational expectations and fears of these children.

The individual educational program for a child may call for special visits with other professionals, such as physicians, psychologists, speech therapists, occupational therapists. In each case, as in the interaction with parents, the teacher both learns from the specialists and offers them important information from her unique expertise with the child. This mutual collaboration is not only essential for implementing the child's individual educational program, but it also enables the community to learn that it is providing reasonable education and treatment for autistic and communication-handicapped children.

COMMUNICATION AND RECORDING

Collaboration between parents, teachers, and other professionals can be no more effective than is the communication between them. It often depends on the availability of accurate records and reports.

Some form of recording the child's progress is an essential part of any teaching or treatment program. It provides the parent and professional with information necessary to the ongoing process of change in content and technique as the child moves ahead. Some programs place rather rigid requirements on parents for recording in detail their observations of the child's responses. We have found such inflexible requirements to be impractical and sometimes potentially harmful to the parent's effective teaching and enjoyment of the teaching process. Plans for keeping records are made instead on an individual basis depending on the following conditions:

1. *The parents' needs and abilities*   Some parents find it helpful to keep charts, record language samples, or write descriptive paragraphs of typical or unusual episodes of their child's behavior. They find that it increases their interest, improves their observations, and gives them a sense of accomplishment. Such records are extremely helpful in deciding when to move on to the next specific objective or when to start on a new goal. Other parents have neither the time nor ability to record such observations. When pushed by the professional to do so, they become confused and distracted during the teaching session, and even feel that they have failed to help their own child. The needed information must then be obtained through frequent discussion in person or over the phone.

2. *Professionals' need for information*   Parent and professional will be exchanging information and observations during their regular meetings. However, the professional may need specific information that cannot be obtained in this way; for example, how often the child wets

himself, what time he fell asleep, what words he used spontaneously. Such information cannot be given accurately from memory. The professional will have to obtain it through written records or phone conversations, depending on the parents' abilities. Success in getting this information will depend on how the professional explains the task and helps the parent with it. Our experience has included the following techniques, in order of their difficulty:

a. Simply tell the parents what you need and why you need it. ("Please write down every spontaneous utterance you hear until you have recorded 50. This will tell us what language structures he is ready to learn next.")

b. Tell the parents why you need the information and discuss with them what time would be the easiest for them to record it. If necessary, give them a chart with the date and time written down. Use an example of behavior from the classroom to illustrate how to fill out the chart.

c. For those parents who cannot keep or return charts, telephone calls are arranged. ("May I call you at 4:00 pm? I would like to have you tell me what words you have heard John say during the day.")

d. Whenever possible, a home visit is helpful. It enables the therapist to be specific and concrete in suggestions, to demonstrate techniques for observing and recording home behavior, and to be more understanding and supportive of the parents' life-style.

An example for recording the child's progress at home follows. This weekly home log is useful in enabling parents to keep track of progress in their home teaching and also for sharing such information with the professionals involved with their child. Although the format does not cover all of the special recording needs discussed previously, we have found it especially useful for tracking progress in a new program or with parents first beginning their systematic special education efforts.

Example of Weekly Home Log

Format   The following questions are written on three pages, with space below each question to be filled in by the parent. These logs are returned to the professional each week.

Note to Parent   This record is to help your teacher or therapist know how your child is doing at home. Please fill it out with this idea in mind. Most of the questions can be answered at the end of the week, but daily notes will be useful if you have the time. Be sure to jot down any question or concerns as they occur to you.

PAGE 1:   HOME TEACHING

How much time did you spend on the Home Teaching Program each day this week?

Monday — 45 minutes
Wednesday — 1 hour
Sunday — 1 hour

What were your goals?

Goals: To get Robin to spell simple words using sounds of letters. To help Robin understand the concept "more" and "one more."

What progress?

Progress: He understands the first and last sound, but I have to emphasize the sounds much of the time. I'm not sure about "more." Sometimes he does OK and not so good another time.

Any problems? (What have you tried? What worked? Describe child's response.)

Problems: He still gets silly, laughs a lot when a task is hard for him. He usually calms down if I give more help, but not if I scold him.

Do you want some new activities to teach?

New activities: None yet. I'm not sure how fussy to be about his writing.

PAGE 2:   SELF-HELP SKILLS (Eating, dressing, toileting, etc.)

What are you working on?

Goals: Asking for more, not grabbing food. Learning to wipe and flush toilet.

What progress?

Progress: So-so. He can ask for more but forgets. Toileting depends on his mood, and how soon I get to him. A little progress, I think.

Any problems? (What have you tried? What worked? Describe child's response.)

Problems: I'm trying moving the serving dishes out of reach so I don't have to prompt him to ask or scold grabbing behavior. Don't know if this will help but it makes meals a bit pleasanter.

Are your goals too difficult? Is he ready for new goals?

New goals: No, two at a time is plenty.

PAGE 3:   GENERAL BEHAVIOR (tantrum, sleeping, discipline, medica-tion, mood)

Have you seen problem behaviors this week? How often?

Problem behavior: Silly laughing and very restless two nights this week.

What did you try? Describe the child's response.

What tried/child's response: One tantrum when I scolded him for playing with the TV knobs. I put him in the corner for 5 minutes. He settled down once I got the other children out of the room.

Are you using any medications? What ones? Any problems?

Medication: The doctor lowered the dosage (Mellaril); so far so good. Appetite remains good, still not hitting out at people. The laughing spells seem to come when he is confused, or doesn't want to do something.

Any unusual events? (new skills seen, new concerns, unusual family events)

Unusual events: Took the family to Hardees this week — Robin sur-prised us; he did really well. I'd like to take him to our family reunion next month. How can I prepare him for this? Any ideas?

How does your child feel about school? Do you want a conference or home visits?

Response to school: He is eager to go, gets dressed quickly. This week he repeated some school phrases: "sit down." Some days he is really silly when he gets home. Do you know what the supervision on the bus is like?

Example of Parent-Teacher Notebook

The following Parent-Teacher Notebook is an excellent format for main-taining continuing communication between teacher and parent, not read-ily achieved by monthly parent-teacher conferences. The teacher sends home a summary of her school observations, and the parent responds with observations from home. This is especially useful when collabora-tion between school and home is primarily positive. Serious differences and problems are best resolved in personal conferences and specially designed charts, as in Chapter 6.

This log was kept in a spiral-bound notebook and sent home on Fri-day, and was returned to the teacher the following week. Six-year-old Jamie had no speech but could use about 10 meaningful signs. He func-tioned generally at a 2½- to 3-year level. Excerpts were taken from the beginning of his second year in the classroom. There had been many contacts between teacher and parent, both at home and in the classroom.

TEACHER REPORT — 9/20

General. This has been a good week. Jamie is much calmer and has had only four temper outbursts. We think he is settling down into the classroom routines again after the summer vacation. He is beginning to seek our attention and tell us what he wants; he's used "ball," "tickle," and "bathroom" signs spontaneously this week. On 3 days he let Tony play next to him at the sand table without pushing or hitting. He is taking one small taste of every food at lunch now, and, believe it or not, he tried a piece of lettuce without any prompt.

Lessons. The color sorting is really solid now and we are moving on to a new task — matching a row of alternating colored pegs. Jamie is working on sorting pictures of food versus clothing. I am using the chart I showed you of pictures illustrating classroom events. Jamie goes and points to the picture of what he wants to do next (bathroom, water fountain, sand table, etc.). This is making sense to him. Can you come in next week one afternoon? I would like to show you this chart and how he uses it. I think it might be useful for you at home. I also have two new signs to show you: "outside" and "open."

Home suggestions. I agree with your idea for controlling his behavior when you have company (i.e., giving him a special activity to *do* while you are talking). Why not put some of these in shoe boxes so they will be ready when you need them. Activities we have used at school that he likes are: cutting strips of paper, threading beads, coloring within a stencil, and using Lego blocks. You might also try play-do and a plastic knife. It will probably work better if the shoe box games are only used for these special "company" times. He is more interested in materials that are a bit new, not always available.

MOTHER'S REPORT — 9/24

I couldn't write this until Monday because we had a busy weekend. On Saturday I took Jamie to my neighbor's and for the first time he went upstairs with the 3-year-old and played in her room for 10 minutes! *No trouble.* Sunday they invited him over, and this time I left him there for half an hour. My neighbor said it went OK. Now I have a new problem. Jamie has started to open the door, and he wants to leave without waiting for me. I have to watch him very closely. I spanked him once, but I don't think he understood why. I have noticed recently that he is looking at the labels on cans and boxes. I'd like to teach him to read. What do you think? Yes, I can get over to the classroom on Thursday, about 1:00. See you then.

Professionals' Communication with Parents

The implementation of teaching programs can best be achieved when certain principles for parent communication are kept in mind.

Supporting Parents   Parents, like everyone else, including professionals, need support and positive feedback in order to maintain their investment and efforts in a very difficult task. Indeed, love is not enough. Professionals easily slip into the error of perceiving the parents' failure at providing adequately for the child. Even with the well-meaning and positively disposed professional, this frequently occurs by implication when discussions with the parents are focused on what went wrong and what does not work. Although some information on major difficulties is necessary, it is most important to find out what does work, even if only partially. Parents after all know their children very well. Often their failures consist not in choosing the wrong things, but, out of uncertainty or insecurity, giving up too soon on successful approaches. The professional who fails to explore the parents' successful efforts carefully will miss out on useful information and will have to flounder in re-inventing everything from the beginning.

Acceptance of Individual Differences   Although many general principles are useful for thinking about the problems of children and their families (allowing authors to write books like this), individual differences among the values and life-styles of families must be respected. The individualized functional assessment of the child helps in this. However, it is intended to help the child's adaptation at home. This can only be achieved when parents' needs, values, and aspirations can be understood and accepted.

Appropriate and Practical Advice   Professionals are often able to generate many "good" interventions for a particular problem or task. These are based on formal learning, professional theories and knowledge, and experience with children. Parents of autistic and developmentally disordered children have tried a great many different interventions with their children and their experience will provide much clarification. It is an easy and common pitfall for professionals to formulate "solutions" to problems based on their knowledge and expertise and assume that they are inherently correct. When such interventions fail, it is too easy to identify the parents' implementation as the cause of failure. However, the only "correct solution" to any problem is one that works. Often the best intervention is found only by trial and error, and requires tolerance of failure on the part of the professional.

A useful principle, which is built into our clinical program, is based on this golden rule of programming: "Never ask someone else to do something you haven't tried first yourself." This practice protects parents from well-meaning but erroneous advice. Allowing parents to "try it out" allows for further modification of the program to their individual styles and needs.

Parents' Need for Information   The more relevant information parents have on the nature of their child's problem and the basis for the program, the more cooperatively and effectively they will implement the program. Many parents, despite multiple evaluations and much advice, are surprisingly uninformed about the professional findings on their children. Parent activist efforts have fortunately decreased this somewhat. Information on how and why goals and specific objectives were selected, why particular behavioral techniques work, and any additional relevant information will enhance the parents' self-image and sense of full participation, increase trust between therapist and parent, and encourage parents' efforts and initiative. The educational program is often most effectively communicated to parents by demonstration. It should also always be written down for the parent in specific and clearly understandable terms. Jargon should be reserved for interactions between professionals trying to impress one another. It has no place in communication with parents. Formats for communicating goals and writing the individualized educational program are provided in Chapters 3, 4, and 5. Additional sample programs are provided in Chapters 9 and 12.

REVISING THE TEACHING PROGRAM

Once the teaching program has begun it also needs to be assessed and changed in subsequent programs. The curriculum planner needs to keep track of the changes occurring in the child, the home, and the classroom. We review progress in each case about once a month, and administer a formal diagnostic reevaluation at the end of the year. This ensures that teaching programs remain appropriate to the changing situation, and makes use of new information as it develops. The question of what and when to write a new teaching program is asked with every evaluation. Some children achieve at a fairly consistent pace from day to day. Skills that they begin to learn one day are maintained and increased at succeeding lessons. They settle into the routine of the sessions with predictable consistent behavior. There is less need for detailed records on such children. Others, however, are quite the opposite. They may do extraordinarily well one day and have apparently forgotten everything on another day. Their moods are unpredictable, and their performance at the clinic or in the classroom may be widely different from time at home. These children may make sudden jumps forward or remain at a plateau with no progress for weeks at a time.

It is difficult to make objective judgments on such children unless records are kept. Parents and therapists form strong emotional impressions, depending on what they remember most vividly ("he was impossible, no attention to the task, no understanding of the concept, he's got it, we're going too slowly, let's move ahead fast," and so on). The decision to move ahead or change directions must be based on the overall level of progress, including both good and bad sessions. For these children, keeping concrete objective data is important. When behavior management techniques are used to improve disruptive behaviors or to implement new growth in self-help skills, charts of the child's responses to these management techniques are necessary in order to accurately evaluate their effectiveness.

Sometimes difficult changes have to be made. A child may be showing new behavior problems at home but not at school. A difficult task without much past success may need to be continued a while longer. Any change in curriculum, family pressures, or classroom needs can threaten constructive collaboration between parents and professionals. When communication is open and continuous such difficulties can usually be resolved while maintaining the best interest of child and family.

FORMAL AGREEMENT

We have now discussed the individualized assessment of the child, his family's needs, and his classroom's requirements. We have formulated appropriate expectations, goals, and teaching objectives in the major function areas. We have considered behavior management procedures and have reviewed methods of teaching and developing communication between school, home, or other sectors of the community.

PL 94-142 now requires that we use the information gathered from all available sources to formulate an individualized education program (IEP) endorsed by the schools and parents. The IEP is intended to cover a school year. As with many laws it is possible to meet the letter of the law and still avoid the spirit. However, if we have done a thorough job with the issues discussed in this manual, the IEP becomes primarily a formality that includes the following points, listed in the Federal Register (1977) and elaborated in Turnbull, Strickland, and Brantley (1978):

1. The child's current level of functioning is documented.
2. Annual goals are formulated.
3. Short-term teaching objectives are identified.
4. Special services to be provided are named.
5. Participation in a regular classroom is identified, as appropriate.

6. Dates for initiating services and their duration must be listed.
7. Evaluation procedures, objective criteria, and schedules for reassessment are stated.

We have been discussing how a child's IEP is dependent on the best obtainable understanding of him, using both formal and informal evaluation procedures. Appropriate teaching goals and objectives are derived from the evaluation and implemented both at school and at home, with good communication between teacher and parent. This forms a sound basis for the IEP.

The three final steps for completing Tommy's IEP contract are presented in Figure 22. First is his initial home program used by his parents during the summer before he entered school. Second is the classroom report prepared by his teacher. This lists the teaching objectives and her rating of progress during the first month of school. Third is the IEP, developed by his parents and teachers based on both classroom and home observations of Tommy's current skills and his rate of learning.

A blank IEP form is provided in Figure 23. If the child we have asked you to keep in mind while reading this manual will be needing an IEP, it will be helpful for you to sketch your expectation for how it will be formulated.

INITIAL HOME PROGRAM

Child: Tommy D.   Date: July 15

Note to parents: You can help Tommy prepare for school by introducing him to the teaching structure: sitting, attending to directions,
cooperating, recognizing the sequence of tasks, knowing he will get
a reward when he is finished. The following activities use skills
Tommy has already developed so they should not be difficult for him.
Spend about 15 minutes at the same time each day, and choose a
time when you will not be interrupted by John, TV noise, or people
moving through the room. It will help if the "work time" is followed by
something he really enjoys, like a snack or outdoor play.

GOALS: 1. To sit down for 2 minutes without getting up.
2. To "wait" for 5 seconds without grabbing materials.
3. To "give" any object when you hold out your hand.
4. To understand "finished" and cooperate in putting the
materials away.

Activity 1: Stacking blocks
Materials: Tin can large enough to hold six blocks, six blocks
Procedure: Place the blocks inside the can, put it on the table,
and call to Tommy, "Come...time to work." Guide him if
necessary. When he is sitting down, push the can to him and let
him dump out the blocks, and then stack them up in a tower,
which he enjoys. When stacked, praise him, then hold up your
hand and say "Wait" and prevent him from knocking over the
tower. Count to five, then say, "O.K....push," letting him push
them down. Now tell him to "put the blocks away" and help if
needed. When done, say "Finished...good work," smile, get up,
and give him a swing.

Activity 2: Crayon lines
Materials: Five crayons in a box; large piece of paper
Procedure: Place the box of crayons on his left, the paper in
front of him, and the lid of the box on his right side. Call Tommy
to "Come work," leading him if necessary. Take one crayon,
make a long line (from his left to right). Hand him the crayon and
help him make the same mark. Point to the box lid and say, "Put
crayon in." Praise and smile. Repeat with next crayon, and continue until all crayons have been used. Then say "Finished" and
ask him to help "put crayons away." When the lid is on the box,
say "Give me the crayons," then let him get up and give him
praise and a swing.

Activity 3: Stepping over blocks and boxes laid on floor
Materials: Three blocks of wood (approximately $2'' \times 4'' \times 12''$),
three boxes (4" tall)
Procedure: First demonstrate the activity. Walk to the first
block, stop, carefully step up and over it, then go on to the next,
and so on, until all three blocks are passed. Now tell Tommy,
"You do it," and take his hand to guide him. When he has finished the "trip" praise and reward. Give less and less physical
help until he can step over the blocks independently without
touching. When this becomes easy, use the taller boxes in the
same way.

Figure 22.   Initial home program, classroom report, and IEP for Tommy.

Activity 4:   Sorting two sets of objects
   Materials: Five sticks, five cars (taken from the ones he plays with), two shallow vegetable trays, two shoe boxes; raisins
   Procedure: Put the two trays on the table, and keep the sticks and cars in your lap out of his sight. Hand him one car, point to a tray, and say "Put it there." Give physical assistance, and the moment he releases the car into the tray, praise and give him a raisin. Now hand him one stick, point to the other tray, give physical help, and again reward with a raisin as soon as he drops the stick into the tray. Continue to give the cars and sticks one at a time, and point to the correct tray if he begins to make an error in sorting. Praise and reward all cooperation and prevent errors. Do not let him take out the sticks and cars until all have been sorted. Say "Finished" and tell him to "Put them away," each set into a separate shoe box. Now say "All finished," let him get up, give a swing, a pat, and then give him a snack.

MONTHLY CLASSROOM REPORT

Child: <u>Tommy D.</u>   Date: <u>October 2</u>
Classroom: <u>Special I—Self-contained</u>   Teacher: <u>Ms. Cooper</u>

Area		Objective	Activity	Skill rating
SH[1]	1.	Urine training	Remain dry, go when told	E + [2]
	2.	Bowel training	BM only on toilet	E
	3.	Undressing—pants	Pull down, step out, unaided	E +
	4.	Carry tray	Hold tray without spilling food	E −
B[2]	1.	Decrease screaming	Put behind screen, within 5 min	E
	2.	Decrease hand biting	Turn away for 20 sec	NS[3]
	3.	Respond to "wait"	Wait 2 sec before drinking juice	E +
	4.	Stay in chair	No prompts, for 2 min during task	C[1]
VM[3]	1.	Work buttons	Pull out large button, no help	C
	2.	Buttons	Push in, pull through, with help	E
	3.	Crayons	Color within wide outline	E
	4.	Handle scissors	Open and shut, no help	E +
M[4]	1.	Climb steps	One foot per tread, no help	E
	2.	Throw large ball	To child or adult from 3 feet	C
	3.	Strengthen pincer	Pinch clothespins onto box	E
	4.	Make gestures in songs	Clap, open/shut fists	E −

Co[5]	1.	Match shapes	Sort circle/square/triangle	E +
	2.	Size discrimination	Stack nesting cups	E
	3.	Sort pictures by function	Clothes/food/cars	E −
	4.	Associate objects by use	Shoe/socks, cup/plates, toothbrush/toothpaste	E
L[6]	1.	Express wants	"Juice, cookie, bubbles" (snack time)	E
	2.	State actions	"Jump, run, swing" during	E −
	3.	Respond to commands	play "Come, sit, stop, touch, give"	E +
	4.	Touch pictures	Shoe, pants, shirt, cup, spoon, car	C
S[7]	1.	Respond to "wait"	Wait 5 min before touching blocks	E +
	2.	Parallel play	Plays next to child with cars for 2 min	E
	3.	Inititate contact	Asks for jump or swing (gestures)	E +
	4.	Accept physical contact	Sits on lap for 30 sec	E

Function code: [1]Self-Help; [2]Behavior; [3]Visual Motor; [4]Motor; [5]Cognitive; [6]Language; [7]Social. *Rating code:* [1]Completed; [2]Emerging; [3]No skill; [4]Temporarily discontinued.

Parent Contacts
One home visit and weekly phone calls. Mrs. D. has observed classroom twice. She plans to come on Tuesday mornings regularly and will demonstrate her home teaching activities. Tantrum screaming now occurs rarely, usually on weekends. Tommy now keeps his cars and sticks in his bedroom. Dressing skills have improved; Mrs. D. reports he is more motivated to dress himself on school mornings. Very tired after school, he usually plays in his room for an hour.

Individual Education Program (IEP)

Name: Tommy D.   Date: October 1
Birth date: 12/6

SUMMARY OF CURRENT LEVEL OF PERFORMANCE

Language: Expressive—1 year echoes single words, not communicative. Receptive—Three to 5 verbs, 5 to 10 nouns; responds to common commands with situational cues.

Motor: Gross motor—very active; runs, jumps with both feet; climbs, but balance poor. Fine motor—holds crayon, closes scissors, pincer grasp weak. Visual motor—inset puzzles and threading emerging, circular scribble.

Cognitive: Matches objects, matches pictures to objects.
Self-help: Toilet skills; urine with prompts, bowel accidents frequent.
Dressing; takes off socks and shoes, coat. Pulls down shirt.

Social/Emotional: Plays alone, tantrum when interrupted; does not
seek help or physical contact; no response to "wait/stop"; attention
to task is 1–2 minutes.

LONG-TERM GOALS
Improve expressive and receptive language skills
Increase social relatedness, acceptance, and inititation of contact
Improve self-help and motor skills (dressing and toileting)

Goals for the year	Criteria	Evaluation date	Percent of time in regular class	Special services	Percent of time in special services
1. Language, expressive Answer "what" questions			K-1	a	
15–20 nouns (common objects)	100%	June	0%		100%
5–10 verbs (swing, tickle, run, go, jump, push, play, want)	100%	June	0%		100%
2. Language, receptive Respond to commands (jump, run, sit, touch, give, go get, put push)	100%	June	0%		100%
Touch body parts (eyes, ears, nose, mouth, hair, feet, stomach)	50%	June	0%		100%
Identify family members, teachers	100%	June	0%		100%
Touch pictures named (20-30 common objects, clothes, food)	80%	June	0%		100%
3. Social relatedness Respond to "wait" for 5 sec	100%	March	10%		90%
Respond to "wait" for 10 sec	100%	June	10%		90%
Respond to "stop"	80%	June	10%		90%
Tolerate parallel play, 3 min	100%	March	10%		90%
Give toy to another child without fussing	50%	June	10%		90%
Initiate contact for help	80%	June	10%		90%
Accept hug, lap, no fussing	100%	March	0%		100%

Goals for the year	Criteria	Evaluation date	Percent of time in regular class	Special services	Percent of time in special services
4 . Self-help					
Put on, take off pants and coat	100%	June	0%		100%
Work zipper and large buttons	100%	March	0%		100%
Urine control, no accidents	80%	March	0%		100%
Bowel training, on toilet, prompted	100%	June	0%		100%
Carry tray and cup unaided	100%	June	0%		100%
Put away own toys, prompted	80%	June	0%		100%
5. Behavior					
Decrease tantrum to less than 2 min	80%	March	0%		100%
Decrease hand biting, less than two episodes daily	100%	June	0%		100%
Walk in line, holding child's hand, prompted	50%	June	10%		90%
6. Motor skills (fine, gross/visual motor)					
Climb steps unaided	100%	March	10%		90%
Throw/catch ball with others	80%	June	10%		90%
Ride tricycle unaided	100%	June	0%		100%
Use scissors to cut on line	80%	June	0%		100%
Color within line	70%	June	0%		100%
Use playground equipment	80%	June	50%		50%
7. Concepts					
Match by shape (circle, square, triangle)	100%	June	0%		100%
Discriminate size (nesting toys)	100%	March	0%		100%
Sort by color (blue, red, yellow, green)	80%	June	0%		100%

a   Special self-contained

Date of reevaluation:	**Procedures:**
March (special self-contained)	Teacher observation checklist
June (regular, K 1)	Teacher observation checklist
June (special ed. services)	Psychoeducational Profile

Individual Education Program (IEP)

Name: _____   Date: _____

Birth date:_____

SUMMARY OF CURRENT LEVEL OF PERFORMANCE

Language: Expressive—
                    Receptive—

Motor: Gross motor—
                Fine motor—
                Visual motor—

Cognitive:

Self-Help:

Social/Emotional:

LONG-TERM GOALS

Goals for the year	Criteria	Evaluation date	Percent of time in regular class	Special services	Percent of time in special services
1. Language, expressive					
2. Language, receptive					
3. Social relatedness					
4. Self-help					
5. Behavior					
6. Motor skills (fine, gross, visual motor)					
7. Concepts					

Date of reevaluation: **Procedures:**

Figure 23.   Blank IEP form.

Part II.
Illustrations
of Issues
in Programming

In this part of the manual we have included examples of four major issues in working out individualized teaching programs: 1) a home teaching program for parents, 2) a sequence of programs modified over time, 3) adaptation of teaching activities to meet behavior problems, and 4) teaching objectives at different developmental levels in nine teaching areas. Although you may find some activities for a particular child you are working with, it is unlikely that a program can be transferred to another child without modification. Over 2,500 individual home programs have been developed for 850 families in our TEACCH program. Although there are similarities between some teaching programs, none of these has been identical to another.

Chapter 9 illustrates a home teaching program for a higher level boy. Brief case material from the center and home is included in order to provide the necessary context for illustrating individualized programming.

Chapter 10 includes a series of teaching activities changed over time for two children. For the sake of clarity only one primary area of programming was selected for each child. The first is to illustrate changes in language objectives, both receptive and expressive. The second is an example of programming changes in the cognitive performance area. Both these cases show the child's development of skills over time and the resulting change in structure and teaching techniques. The frequency and degree of change in each teaching program depend, of course, on the child's rate of learning.

Chapter 11 provides examples of variations in similar teaching activities for the purpose of accommodating to three kinds of behavior problems: extremes of activity level, distractibility, and peculiarity of interest. These are by no means the only behavior problems for which special programming is needed, but we have found them to be especially common. Variation in teaching structure is shown for the same teaching activity in order to clearly illustrate how individualization of structure helps behavior management.

Chapter 12 illustrates the variety of teaching activities that may be formulated in nine teaching areas. Those from the PEP are also discussed in Chapters 4 and 5. We selected examples, arranged by developmental level of difficulty, for each of the nine areas. These developmental levels are approximations and cannot be expected to suggest the same sequence for each child.

Chapter 9.
A Home Teaching Program

Name: Dick B.

Description

Dick is a healthy, attractive 4-year, 9-month-old boy, the only child of a happily married couple in their late 30s. A responsive and cuddly child, Dick has no disruptive behaviors and is a great source of happiness to his close-knit family. His parents had become aware of abnormal development when he was about 2½ years old. Pronounced echolalia, aloofness from other children, and peculiar "toe dancing" behavior began at that time. Their concern increased as he entered nursery school and did not participate in social or structured play with other children. He seemed unusually bright in developing reading, spelling, and counting skills by age 4. However, Dick became overly absorbed by numbers and letters and would play with little else. Although he spoke easily, the content of his talking was predominantly immediate or delayed echolalia.

Assessment

On standardized nonlanguage tests, Dick did show an above average intelligence. His language skills were estimated to be 1½ to 3 years below this level, however, and language demands were clearly stressful to him. Although Dick was able to follow directions at a 4-year level, he could not express his ideas beyond a 2-year level, and used very short phrases with confused grammar. More commonly he moved the adult's hand to indicate what he wanted. When asked a question, e.g., "What is it?" he would repeat the question. His only initiation of social interactions consisted of a few repetitive questions — "What's this?" "What time is it?" — used out of context with the situation. Dick was often responsive to the adult's approach, but rarely initiated or took turns in any social play.

169

Parent Priorities

Dick's parents wanted him to be able to talk to them, to tell them what he had done in school, to tell them how he felt and what he was thinking. They wanted him to be able to play with other children, to make friends and not always play alone with letters and numbers. They observed at home that he avoided exercise, and they were bothered by the peculiar "dancing" behaviors that came when he had nothing definite to do.

Therapist Priorities

The therapist observed that Dick enjoyed interactions but had very limited and inefficient ways of initiating contact with others. His language handicap interfered with any continuation of social play even when it was structured by another person. The ability to take turns and share materials was poorly developed. In addition, he lacked the fine and gross motor skills necessary for normal peer play and classroom activities.

Beginning Program

Both of Dick's parents were interested in actively teaching him at home. They had not done this before, but they had an accurate understanding of his handicap and level of ability. An intelligent and well-organized couple, they were able to use a broad, flexible first program, one that provided many possible variations and encouraged them to use their own judgment. The goals were discussed verbally before the program was given; language, taking turns, and physical exercise predominated.

DICK'S FIRST HOME PROGRAM

Dick seems very comfortable working and playing games with both of you. You have done such a good job of encouraging and supporting him that he seems to be willing to try even difficult tasks. Our best approach may be to intersperse difficult tasks with easier ones, and to incorporate activities he likes with harder skills (e.g., using the lotto game or beads for language tasks).

Since Dick seems better able to concentrate when there is a clear routine and he knows what is expected, it's important to set up activities clearly and let him know when it's time to work and when he can take a break or choose a play activity.

Here are a few beginning activities for you and Dick to try — I mentioned them at our last meeting. They may be quickly learned and outgrown, or they may need repetition. We all need to be aware of which skills Dick learns easily and which ones need practice and clarification.

GOAL: TO INCREASE DICK'S ABILITY TO LABEL NOUNS RECEP-TIVELY AND EXPRESSIVELY AND HIS RECEPTIVE UNDERSTANDING OF DESCRIPTIVE PHRASES

Objective: To name and/or identify common objects (food, clothing, toys, furniture, animals, vehicles) and color and function descriptions.

Materials and Procedures: You can make or buy lotto sets of clear, simple pictures of common objects and actions. It would be best to have several categories (e.g., food, clothing, vehicles, toys, furniture, animals, flowers) with several examples of each, and also pictures of people performing specific actions (e.g., eating, running, drawing, swimming, climbing, throwing, sleeping). Using the lotto cards may be more fun for Dick than a picture book, which has no games to play with cards.

For now, let's try one expressive and one receptive activity.
Expressive:
1. Put out the board. Take one card and ask, "What is it?" Let Dick name it, or if he can't, have him repeat your label. Try to use, and get him to use, complete sentences (e.g., "It's a plate").

    You can also try "What color is it?" — Let's not use more than those two for right now.
    Receptive:
1. Put all the cards out. Ask Dick to put in a certain card by name, description, or use. Try these forms:
    Put in the (name). (e.g., cup)
    Put in the (color) one. (e.g., green)
    Put in the one you (function) (e.g., eat with, ride on)

GOAL: TO DEVELOP ASSOCIATION AND CATEGORIZING SKILLS

Objective: To match pictures of similar objects (spoons, balls, keys) and sort by categories of function (eat, wear, wash with).

Materials and Procedures: Cut out several pictures of similar objects (e.g., several kinds of spoons, balls, cups, keys, shoes, boys, trees). Put out all of one kind (e.g., spoons) among several other pictures. Ask Dick to give you (or put in a box) all the spoons.

The next step in this activity, which we can begin as Dick is ready for it, is to put out pictures that all belong to a certain category (plus others that do not) and ask Dick to give you all of one category (e.g., all the things that you wear, all the toys, all the things you eat with, all the things you use to take a bath — the last example might be soap, towel, bath tub, and wash cloth).

GOAL: TO INCREASE UNDERSTANDING AND USE OF DESCRIPTIVE PHRASES AND TO DEVELOP COOPERATIVE GAME SKILLS

Objective: To take turns threading beads and pasting pictures using descriptive phrases.

Materials and Procedures: Using beads or paper cut-outs of various sizes, shapes, and colors, take turns making strings of beads, paper collages, etc., by asking for and giving each other a "big green block," "little yellow ball," "biggest blue triangle," etc.

You can also adapt this to other descriptive words and materials that match them. For example:

a. Wood — "hard," cloth — "soft," sandpaper — "rough," fur — "fuzzy."

b. Pictures of people — tall, short, thin, blond (you could make a picture of a crowd together).

GOAL: TO INCREASE COORDINATION, BALANCE, AND PHYSICAL STRENGTH AND TO INCREASE SOCIAL INTERACTION IN PHYSICAL PLAY

Objective: To hop, jump, kick, catch, throw. To "compete against himself," and to follow a demonstration.

Activities:

1. Individual exercises in which Dick can "compete against himself," seeing how many he can do. Example:

    hop on one foot

    jump on two feet

    kick ball against wall

    catch ball

    throw ball from line into container (you can have him stand behind a drawn or taped line or a low table)

    jumping jacks (may need to break this down into arm and leg movements at first)

2. Cooperative games that involve a pattern of motion (e.g., London Bridge, catch, dodge ball, catching a bounced ball).

    Try variations that involve Dick with other players: e.g., play a game of catch in which you call out a name and throw to that person.

3. Follow the Leader: Ask Dick to watch and follow you, doing what you do. Since simple, one-step imitation is easy for him, you can try a series of several actions (e.g., jump up and down, crawl under a table, open the door).

You can also use actions that may be a challenge to Dick motorically (e.g., hit a target with a bean bag; hop on one foot, stand on one foot for several seconds, walk along a line drawn on the floor or a balance beam). Get Dick to take turns with you being "leader."

Chapter 10.
Progression of
Teaching Objectives
Over Time

The following two cases illustrate changes in a child's teaching objectives as new skills and behaviors are acquired. The child's entire teaching program designed for all his current goals is not reproduced here. For the sake of clarity only the objectives for one area are presented along with the attending behavior problems. For the first child, Wendy, the language objectives of her teaching programs are included along with techniques for managing her disruptive and provocative behavior. Objectives for improving cognitive skills and social behavior are described for the second child, Scot.

A brief description of each child provides the context for our selection of program goals. Following each set of teaching activities is a progress evaluation. This summarizes the child's progress in each activity and discusses the reasons for making appropriate curriculum changes, illustrated in the subsequent set of activities. Program evaluations and changes were made at approximately 4- to 6-week intervals, but this schedule was adjusted to meet individual needs.

CASE 1 — WENDY

Four language programs over a 7-month period
Description: Wendy was a 4-year, 9 month-old girl with handsome, large brown eyes, a frequent broad and "teasing" smile, and a strong well-coordinated body. She was extremely active and restless with fast and impulsive movements. Wendy had no prior school experience and was scheduled for a classroom placement in September.
Concerns: 1) *Language:* Wendy used some poorly articulated echolalic speech, such as single-word echoes and two repetitive, meaningless

phrases: "How-r-you" and "yah-yah." She did not use words or gestures to ask for what she wanted but did climb up to cabinets, open doors, or simply grab what she wanted. Her parents stated that "she never listens." At the assessment Wendy's receptive language was at a 1-year level. 2) *Behavior:* Wendy's behavior was disruptive and provocative. She grabbed objects from others and would run off laughing. When scolded, chased, or spanked she only laughed more. Her most frequent "tease" game was to offer an object to her mother and then pull it back out of reach as soon as her mother reached out. Although Wendy could control her behavior for her father, her mother was unable to get her to follow gestural cues or listen to verbal directions.

GOALS: 1) *Receptive language* — To increase her understanding of nouns and verbs, i.e., names of common household objects and actions that are part of her daily routines.

2) *Expressive language* — To increase her motivation to communicate her wishes and to teach new communicative gestures.

3 *Behavior* — To decrease the disruptive "tease" game and to increase cooperative responses, i.e., give an object, wait, listen, touch, sit.

FIRST PROGRAM — FEBRUARY 17 — (ONE ACTIVITY)

Objectives: *Behavior:* To give an object, to look and listen, to sit briefly. *Language:* To select object indicated by point and word.
Materials: Spoon, cup, sock, toy car, toothbrush, comb, soap, shoe, potato chips (used as a reward).
Procedure: Call Wendy to the table, showing her the chips. As soon as she is seated give her one. Then place four of the objects on the table, say "listen...," and then *point* to one object, naming it — "cup." Now hold out your open hand, palm up, saying, "give me cup." Hold a chip in the other hand ready to give to Wendy *as soon as* she places the cup in your palm. Do not try to reach out to take the cup. You want Wendy to *voluntarily* give it up. When all four objects have been given in this "swap" game, praise her, applaud, and let her get up.

Progress evaluation: It took quite a long time to change Wendy's grabbing and running off behaviors, but she really wanted the chips and your patience has been worthwhile. She now comes easily to the table when she sees the chips and the materials. She has stopped the "tease" games because she saw you wouldn't play it; i.e., you just waited for her to voluntarily "give." Now that she is handing you objects without teasing you can use this open-palm gesture throughout the day when you want something from her. We need to reduce her dependence on food rewards next. She still needs to see the chips on the table, but she can wait a short time before getting them. We can also expect her to remain seated for longer, 2–3 minutes, without getting up. *Language objectives.* Wendy is clearly understanding what object to select from your point cue and recently from just the words (without a point): spoon, cup, toothbrush, shoe, and car. We can now use pictures of objects to increase her receptive vocabulary. We'll also teach her to "touch" rather than "give" in response to your directions. Wendy also needs an appropriate way to tell us what she wants.

SECOND PROGRAM — MARCH 30 — (TWO ACTIVITIES)

Objectives: *Behavior:* To increase sitting time to 2–3 minutes. *Language:* To touch a picture of an object named, no cues.

Materials: Pictures of familiar objects cut from magazines or catalogs, i.e., spoons, cups, shoes, cars, socks, soap, dish; edible treat.

Procedure: *Behavior management:* Place the "treat" on one side of the table, where she can see it but it is out of reach. Give her one piece after every three or four responses. Praise each response, using words, smiles, and applause. As soon as you think it possible, delay giving the edible reward until the end of the activity (task). Place two or three pictures on the table; name one picture and hold out your hand, asking her to "give" it to you. When this is established, you need to teach her to simply "touch" the picture you name. You will need to guide her hand at first, showing her what you mean by the verb "touch." If she gets disruptive when you introduce this *new* response, you may need to back down and give more frequent edible rewards until she gets used to it.

Objective: To express her preference by giving a picture.

Materials: Three toys she likes, pictures of these toys, three foods she likes with pictures to match

Procedure: Place the three toys on the table near you, out of Wendy's reach. Place the three matching pictures in front of her. Ask her "What do you want?" and gesture to the three toys. If she reaches out to take one, stop her and direct her hand to the picture of that toy. Tell her to "give" you the picture, and hold out your hand for it. Then swap the picture for the toy. Whatever picture she hands you, take it from her and give her back the matching object. Name her choice, "Car. . . you want car." Give her a few moments to enjoy playing with the toy. Then repeat the game. Next use the same procedure with the three foods. Be sure you give her the food that matches the picture she hands you. Let her eat a piece. This way Wendy will begin to realize the power of being able to communicate her preferences.

Progress evaluation: Objective 1. Wendy is now able to make four to six responses before needing an edible reward, and she has become much more aware of your praise. She looks at your face with curiosity, watching for your smiles, and she now smiles when you praise and applaud her correct responses. You can continue to add new nouns, pictures of clothing, and common utensils that she uses. We will go on to teaching her the meaning of verbs. *Objective 2.* She particularly enjoyed choosing the food she wanted in this activity. You can start using this picture system in the kitchen. Tape up pictures of her favorite food on the refrigerator and let her point to what she wants you to get for her: juice, milk, cake. The next activities will focus on understanding verbs and copying your actions. We will be introducing not only new vocabulary, but also a new structure in the Simon Says game. This structure is similar to group lessons she may have in her future classroom, and she will have to control her restlessness sitting in a chair without having a table in front of her. Keep the activities short (2–3 minutes) until she can complete them comfortably without fussing or needing edible rewards. Continue giving smiles, praise, pats, and applause.

THIRD PROGRAM — MAY 10 — (TWO ACTIVITIES)

Objective 1: To listen to directions using action words (verbs). To increase ability to copy (imitate) what you do. To stay in her chair without table barrier.
Materials: None
Procedure: Sit across from Wendy and play Simon Says making very simple motions for her to copy, e.g., raise hands, clap hands, touch nose, stamp feet, pat tummy, touch toes. Say each direction as you do the action. Give her a few moments to think about what she should do since this is new and perhaps difficult. You may need to guide her hands to cue the correct response. Give her a hug after each one.
Objective 2: To understand action words and do them without copying.
Materials: Hairbrush, toothbrush, cup, spoon, washcloth, pillow
Procedure: Place the objects on the table. Tell Wendy, "Show me eating." Help her select the spoon and pretend to eat with it. Praise her, i.e., "That's right...you are eating." Then put the spoon away and ask for another action, "Show me brushing." When *all* the objects have been used, give her a hug, applause, and a treat. Words to teach: brushing, drinking, washing, sleeping, eating.

Progress evaluation: Objective 1. Wendy was quick to copy your actions and this will be a help to her in school. She does have difficulty stopping the actions, however, and tends to get overly excited and silly with some of them, i.e., clapping hands, stamping feet, patting tummy. Continue with this game from time to time, but *wait* until she stops each action before you reward her with your smiles and praise. The next step will be to ask her to carry out action directions without seeing a demonstration or having a concrete object to use. With her improved understanding of both nouns and verbs, we can now ask her to listen to a two-word phrase attending to both the verb and the noun, and carry out the direction. We will use pictures again since this will enable us to teach a much wider vocabulary. Her behavioral control is much improved, providing she clearly understands what she is supposed to do. The minute she gets confused you see the old "teasing" habits return. You can start to expect her to sit at a task for up to 10 minutes without getting up. She will need some concrete rewards during this time, but, rather than continue to use edibles, let's introduce a token reward system. These tokens will let her see how much she has to do, how long the activity will last, and they will reassure her that she is doing a good job and will succeed. Her expressive use of communicative gestures has increased. You can ask her to name what she wants, but be careful not to tell her the word, i.e., "Do you want juice?" It would be easy for Wendy to simply echo your last word "juice," and we want her to spontaneously name her preferences. Ask her "What do you want?" and get her to point to a picture, and then name it. If she can't remember the word, cue her with the first sound, "j____."

FOURTH PROGRAM — AUGUST 1 — (TWO ACTIVITIES)

Token Reward System: Use five clothespins and a glass cup. After each response, or every three to four responses (depending on her need for rewards), place one pin in the cup. When all five are in the cup, the activity is "finished" and she then gets her treat. Give her a place to sit and eat her treat before starting the next activity. Take the pins out of the cup and start over. In this way you will be giving her a brief rest from working without letting her get up and move around. This will increase her ability to inhibit her restless activity, an important preparation for the coming school year.

>   **Objective 1:** To listen to directions and pantomime actions without using a real object.
>   **Materials:** None
>   **Procedure:** Sit across from Wendy as you did for the Simon Says game. Get her attention by saying "Listen...look at me" and then say "Show me washing face." At first you may need to start the ac-

tion yourself, but your goal is to get Wendy to be able to do the actions just from your words. Vary the noun and verb combinations so she has to listen to both key words, i.e., "washing face...washing hands" and "clapping hands...waving hands."

Objective 2: To scan the whole page to find the picture you name.

Materials: Picture book with pictures of real things she knows and with people doing common actions.

Procedure: Open the book to any page. Ask Wendy to "touch" one object in the picture (car, chair, Coke, banana). Help her search over the whole page by moving your finger around until she finds it. You may need to repeat the word while she is looking. Ask her to find the pictures of the nouns, verbs, and noun-verb phrases you have taught or would like her to learn next. Start the lesson with two or three easy directions to give her confidence and enable you to praise her right away. Keep your vocabulary limited but use these words in as many different combinations as possible, e.g., eating banana, eating ice cream, dog running, girl running. If Wendy makes a mistake, repeat the phrase giving extra emphasis to the word she missed, "girl RUNNING" or "GIRL running."

Progress note: In September Wendy entered a self-contained classroom for communication-handicapped children. The disruptive "teasing" behaviors recurred from time to time — her first contact with each new teacher, when tasks were confusing or language beyond her comprehension, and whenever she was not well (over-tired or had a cold). These behaviors did not last and gradually disappeared. Receptive language increased rapidly but she continued to need structure to organize her attention to this language. She began to use her vocabulary to express her preferences in one- or two-word phrases, such as "Go out," "Eat lunch," "Swing me," "Have bubbles." Her mother maintained control over her behavior at home and continued with structured teaching tasks for two reasons: first, they were enjoyed by Wendy and provided an opportunity for many positive interactions, and, second, she could often calm Wendy down by giving her an easy structured table task. Wendy's teacher provided suggestions for new materials and appropriate activities.

CASE 2 — SCOT

Five cognitive performance programs over a 6-month period
Description: Scot was an attractive 3-year-old boy whose solemn expression rarely changed, giving the impression of a serious little old man. He looked at others and understood some verbal directions, but he remained aloof, never smiled, and did not show pleasure in affectionate

contacts. Scot was content to play alone for long periods with one or two toys and was not a difficult child to manage. An only child, he had no experience with other children. His parents hoped to enroll him in a special classroom within a few months.

Concerns: 1) *Cognitive performance*   Scot's play consisted of looking closely at a few toys, picking them up, looking again, placing them on the table or floor, and peering down to look at them again, repetitively. His favorites were a toy red telephone with a curly cord; a toy radio with a little red knob on the end of its aerial, and a car with black wheels. He showed little curiosity for objects in the distance and was not experimental in his play. During the assessment evaluation, Scot showed a potential for age-appropriate skills in cognitive functions. 2) *Social interactions skills*   Scot did not understand imitation games and was not spontaneously watching his parents and trying to copy their actions. He did not like interruptions in his play and showed no pleasure when patted or praised. He did smile when he was swung around or jumped up and down, but he made no effort to initiate any contacts.

GOALS: 1)   *Social* — To watch adult, imitate actions, and take turns. To initiate social interactions.

2)   *Cognitive* — To sort by shape, color, size. To match on the basis of function and possession. To select the most appropriate category for the task.

FIRST PROGRAM — SEPTEMBER 21 — (TWO ACTIVITIES)

Note to parent: These first activities will be mostly to give Scot practice in sitting and doing tasks with direction from an adult. We should make them easy for him at first, so that he can accomplish them and get a swing or other reward.

Objective 1: To attend to a task, looking for objects in increasingly larger space. To understand the structure of completing the task before getting up.
Materials: Four to five blocks, a coffee can with plastic lid in which a hole has been cut for the blocks to go through, a shallow tray
Procedure: Put the blocks on the tray and the coffee can in front of Scot. Gesture for him to put the blocks into the can. Gradually move the tray of blocks farther away so he has to look around the table to see where to reach for the next block. When all are in, say "all finished" and let him get up. Go to him and give him a swing, praise him, and pat him.
Objective 2: To sort two sets of objects. To persevere through task until it is finished.

Materials: Two trays; 10 objects of two different shapes (five spoons and five spools; five blocks and five clothespins; five pencils and five beads)

Procedure: Place one object in each tray showing Scot how you want them sorted. Now hand him the other ones (four blocks and four pins) one at a time. Help him at first by guiding his hand or by pointing to the correct tray. Give less help as he catches on to the point of the game. If he makes a mistake, remove that object and hand it back to him, saying "try again." If he gets restless or fussy you may need to give more help, but try to encourage him to think out the solution himself.

Progress Evaluation: Activity 1. Scot now likes coming to the table and working with you and he understands the need to "finish." We can now lengthen the activity to 2–3 minutes by using more blocks and asking him to go farther afield to get them. At first he didn't like having you move the blocks around, but now he is used to this interference and is expecting to have to search to find them. We can now teach him to look away from the table, to the floor or across the room, to find the blocks. Because he likes to push them through the hole and hear them drop into the can, he will be motivated to search around the room. This gives us a good opportunity to teach him to follow a pointing gesture. *Activity 2.* Scot now understands sorting different objects into two sets and even made some self-corrections without needing your prompts. Your observation that he seems bored by this activity is probably correct. We can move ahead fairly rapidly to several new steps; sorting into three sets, sorting on the basis of color and size. We are not sure, at this point, which will be easy and which difficult for him. Therefore you need to continue careful observation of his ability to correct errors.

There is a potential drawback to these sorting tasks that Scot can do independently. He still prefers to be left alone, disliking interference from others. However, he needs to develop more skill in watching and copying others. This will be important to play interactions with other children. Therefore we will start a new activity with his favorite blocks, one that requires him to watch and copy what you do.

SECOND PROGRAM — OCTOBER 14 — (THREE ACTIVITIES)

Objective 1: To visually scan the distance for blocks. To understand a pointing gesture.

Materials: Coffee cans and 10 blocks

Procedure: Place the can in front of Scot and scatter the 10 blocks over the whole table area. Point to each block (nearly touching it) in the order you want it put into the can. Next put some of the blocks on the table, some on a chair, and some on the floor nearby. Continue to point to each block in order, but increase the distance between your finger and the block as Scot begins to understand the gesture. Gradually increase the distance Scot has to go to find the next block until he is able to look all around the room, follow your pointing gesture, and find a block from across the room.

Objective 2: To sort objects into three sets. To sort on the basis of color and size (e.g., big/little).

Materials: Three sorting trays; objects (keys, spools, spoons); objects in two colors (blocks, socks, pegs); objects in two sizes, i.e., big and little (spoons, balls, blocks, beads)

Procedure: Use the same procedure as before only put down three trays and provide three sets of objects. For the color and size sorting, you should use only two trays. Teach the color sorting in the same way you did the first program, but be prepared to give plenty of help at first since we are asking him to do it a *different* way. Use the words "blue" or "yellow" as you point to each tray. If this goes smoothly, you can introduce the concept of size: have Scot put the "big" objects in one tray and the "little" ones in the other. Be sure to use the words "big" and "little" as you point: "It's a *big* spoon . . . it goes with *big*. . yes, *big*."

Objective 3: To copy what you have just done (immediate imitation).

Materials: Shoe box; three pairs of objects (spoons, beads, crayons); three pairs of blocks (two red, two blue, two yellow)

Procedure: Place one spoon, one bead, one crayon in front of Scot, and the same three items in front of you. Put the box between you. Now pick up one item (spoon) and tell Scot to pick up the same one. Put yours in the box and tell him to do the same. Repeat this procedure with the other two items. Continue this game, varying the items or the order in which you pick them up. Use the colored blocks to get him to pick up the same color that you do. Be sure he copies each step correctly.

Progress evaluation: Scot is working well for 5 minutes now. He is consistently sorting the three colors correctly so you can start to use some different ones now. His understanding of "big/little" is emerging. Be sure you use objects that are very different in size, and use these words during everyday routines, i.e., "big glass of juice," "little cookie." Scot remains very solemn, but he does smile broadly when you swing him around. Although he does not come to you for it, preferring often to stay at the table playing with the materials, you need to give him this physical contact after each activity. Try giving him a mild tickle before the swing to see if he grows to enjoy this also.

The new activities work on concepts and social behaviors that will be helpful to Scot in school: 1) the concept of sequence, i.e., that there is an order of first-then-last to the activities; 2) the understanding of "taking turns," i.e., waiting for the other person, and knowing when it is his turn and when it is your turn. Although Scot did a good job in picking up the same object as you (Activity 3), he had trouble waiting for you and wanted to rush ahead.

THIRD PROGRAM — OCTOBER 29 — (TWO ACTIVITIES)

Objective 1: To organize tasks himself with a beginning, middle, and end.
Materials: Four-piece inset puzzle: pegboard, 10 pegs, box for the pegs
Procedure: First demonstrate the sequence to Scot; dump out all the pieces of the puzzle; put them back in; then put the puzzle on the toy shelf. Now ask him to complete this sequence himself. Demonstrate with the pegs: take them out of the box, put them in the pegboard, put them back in the box again. Once Scot knows what to do, sit back and watch him do it for himself, giving as few prompts as possible, but do not let him forget the sequence and start to use the materials repetitively.
Objective 2: To take turns.
Materials: Coffee can and 10 blocks suitable for stacking
Procedure: Take turns picking one block out of the can and putting on top of the one before, i.e., making one tower between you. Push the can to Scot when it is his turn and pull it back to you when it's your turn. Use the words "Scot's turn . . . Mummy's turn" as you move the can. Once he learns the game, begin to wait for him to push the can toward you, rather than pulling it away from him. Remind him if he starts to stack, forgetting your turn, by saying "Whose turn?" and help him touch you and say "Mummy."
Variation: If this game gets too easy for Scot, you can use different colored blocks and have him pick the same color you just stacked.

Progress evaluation: (Note to the reader: The following note to Scot's parents describes his *general* progress and explains the shift to more receptive language used in the next activities.) *Note to Parents.* I do not think I let you know strongly enough what a lovely job you are doing teaching Scot. The exciting progress we are seeing is the result of your hard work. His vocabulary of simple nouns and verbs has increased greatly, and he is understanding many adjectives as well. Let's try putting these words together into short phrases. By describing an object you want him to get from across the room, you will give him receptive language training as well as continue with the past goal of visually searching for objects in the distance. We can also use a past activity — sorting into trays — to increase his ability to organize words into a new category, same function. In the next program you will find an activity that uses the beads you gave Scot for Christmas. It is always a good idea to use new and different materials when you teach attributes of color, size, and shape. Scot now has a good ability to carry out the orderly routine of getting out and putting away his materials. You can add one more step to this routine; teach him to bring the finished materials over to you, hand them to you, and get a big swing in return. This will encourage the habit of coming to you, and, in this sense, initiating social contact.

FOURTH PROGRAM — DECEMBER 30 — (THREE ACTIVITIES)

Objective 1: Visually searching for objects described by adjective phrases.
Materials: Familiar objects, a large box
Procedure: Place the objects around the room while Scot watches. Then sit next to him holding the box. Tell him what to get ("Get the little car") and when he does have him put it into the box. Use the adjectives you have worked on in the sorting tasks: "Get the red block... Get Mummy's shoe... Get the big glass."
Objective 2: To sort pictures of objects by name and by function (all cars, shoes, cups; things to eat, wear, play with).
Materials: Pictures from magazines/catalogs, cut out and pasted onto index cards (be sure they are things he has seen and will recognize, like food he eats, clothes he wears, toys he has used)
Procedure: Teach him to sort these pictures in the same way you taught the sorting before, using two or three trays. Use your judgment on how fast to progress, being sure Scot can self-correct before you move to a new task. Try the following: 1) sort shoes, cars, houses; 2) sort food, toys; 3) sort clothes, food, cars.
Objective 3: To take turns stringing beads, imitating Mother's choice.
Materials: Set of beads (different colors and shapes), one string
Procedure: Put several beads in the can in front of Scot. Hand him the string and let him put one bead on. Then take it back and you put one on. Gradually give him more responsibility for remembering to give you the string for your turn. Name the bead that he puts on, "little red," "blue square," etc. When this is easy for Scot, you can begin to tell him to "do one like Mummy" and ask him to state what that will be. Vary this game by putting on "*all* the red ones" or "*all* the little ones," changing the category from day to day, so that Scot gets used to following your organization.

Progress evaluation: Activity 1. This task was successful when Scot watched you place the objects around the room, but he had more difficulty getting objects he did not see you place, when he was not paying attention. Now that Scot is in school and you are not teaching him as often, I suggest you continue working on this skill during daily routines. Make a point of asking Scot to get you an object from across the room, e.g., "Get Daddy's paper," "Get me the wastebasket," and use a clear pointing gesture if he needs help. *Activities 2 and 3.* Scot's progress in organizing materials into categories and in following your directions is good. The most important improvement is his increased enjoyment in sharing materials with you, and he is no longer aloof and overly serious. Because these structured games help Scot to increase his social interactions with you, it would be a good idea to continue with them, even though Scot is now getting a good educational experience in school. The following suggestions are for you to choose from, using your own good judgment about which will be most helpful and how to structure the activities.

FIFTH PROGRAM — FEBRUARY 16 — (SIX OBJECTIVES)

Objective 1: To use possessives to describe clothing and objects ("Mummy's shoes...Daddy's hat...Scot's shoes...Mummy's bag").

Objective 2: To place possessions appropriately ("Where do Daddy's shirts go? Where do Scot's shirts go?").

Objective 3: To identify people in photographs and in the mirror.

Objective 4: To give directions to others (being the leader in Simon Says).

Objective 5: To identify mistakes made by others. Let Scot discover your mistakes to see if he can use the concept of nonsense or incongruity to make him more aware of logic and order. For example, in sorting tasks, what will he do if you stick in one or two objects that don't belong in any category?

Objective 6: Think back over all the games you have played and see how many of them could be used for giving Scot a turn to be "teacher."

Progress Note: In February, Scot entered a classroom for communication-handicapped preschool children. At the age of 5 years, 6 months he made a successful transition to a normal kindergarten classroom.

Chapter 11.
Teaching Structures
for Behavior Problems

We have chosen three major behavioral difficulties that can be disruptive to successful teaching of developmentally handicapped children: 1) extremes of activity level, hyperactive speed, or lethargic, hypoactive movements; 2) distractibility (the child who is not observant or is highly distractible); 3) peculiarities of interest (children who have either little interest in materials or who are overselective and perseverative in their play with materials). In order to illustrate how the structure of the activity facilitates behavioral control, we have used the same basic activity for each extreme of the three behavior difficulties, varying only the structure of the activity.

A simple activity requiring the child to put blocks through a square hole has been structured differently for the hyperactive and hypoactive child. A task requiring the child to select the object named by the teacher is structured differently for each child with visual attention difficulties. Three types of sorting tasks illustrate variations in structure for children with problems of interest in materials. Following each activity is a note to the parent-teacher explaining why the activity was chosen for the child, how it will help the behavior difficulty, and how the parent-teacher should adjust teaching style.

CASE 1, ACTIVITY LEVEL: 3-YEAR-OLD HYPERACTIVE BOY

BLOCKS IN CAN

Objectives: To grasp block and release it *into* the can. To sit in chair for 1 minute. To return to chair when called.
Materials: Ten blocks, can, raisins in a small box

Procedure: Put the blocks in a box next to you and the can in front of Johnny. As soon as he sits down hand him the first block. Say "Put in." (You may need to hold your hand just above his to prevent throwing.) As soon as he drops it, praise him and hand him the next block; repeat until finished. Praise him, say "Finished," and move the table out, saying "Go play." After 1 minute, call him to "Come." Hold up a raisin for him to see, then place it on the table in front of his chair. Let him pick it up only when he is sitting down. Praise, smile, and proceed to next task.

Note: Johnny needs to slow down, but he has to learn this gradually. He wants to be doing something all the time, so if you keep him waiting too long he will try to leave the table. You want to go only a little bit slower than Johnny. This may mean hurrying a bit yourself. You should place his chair against a wall and the table close up in front of him (see Figure 24A). Then it will be more difficult for him to dart off, and it will be clear to him that you expect him to stay seated. Once Johnny gets used to this structure and does not try to leave before all the blocks are in the can, then you can place the table and chair away from the wall (see Figure 24B) and lengthen the task by giving him more blocks until he is working for a full minute without trying to leave.

CASE 2, ACTIVITY LEVEL: HYPOACTIVE CHILD

BLOCKS IN CAN

Objectives: To grasp and hold a block. To initiate the next movement. To increase motor activity.

Materials: Five blocks, can, paper, raisins

Procedure: Place the can on Billy's left and the colored paper on his right. Put the five blocks, separated, on the paper. Tap on the table to get his attention, point to a block, and say "Put in." Wait about 5 seconds. If he has not moved, repeat the direction and gently lift his hand and move it to the block. Help him grasp it. Guide his arm until it is over the can. Then let him release the block. Praise him after each block drops. He also likes to have his neck or hand tickled and can be motivated with this reinforcement. Continue this way. Each time you help him try to give less and less assistance, only what he needs. When all are in, say "Finished" and stand up. Lead him to the window (or where you put the raisins). Show him the raisin, but put it where he has to reach up or stoop way down to get it. Before returning to the table, play some gross motor games like swinging, jumping, climbing up steps.

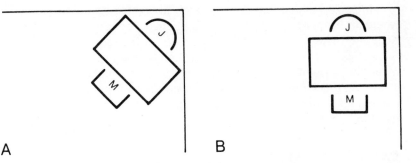

Figure 24.   A, Table used as barrier. B, No barrier needed.

Note: Billy is naturally slow in his movements and he will let you do everything for him unless you are careful. You need to keep his attention organized to the activity, but at the same time you will need to give him time to initiate actions. Try to count slowly to five before you give him help. Gradually he is helped and motivated to increase his pace because he knows a reward will come and knows that you will *not* do the task for him. The physical exercise after the task is finished will help to give him more energy for the next activity in the lesson.

CASE 3, VISUAL ATTENTION AND DISTRACTIBILITY: HIGHLY DISTRACTIBLE CHILD

TOUCHING OBJECTS NAMED

Objectives: To look at adult when told to "look...listen." To inhibit touching objects until told to "touch." To keep attention focused on the table area.

Materials: Common objects he uses (spoon, cup, soap, crayon, shoe)

Procedure: Place all five objects in a box in your lap or on the floor out of Tony's sight. Tell him to "sit down" and then push the table up close to him. Say "hands down" and show him that you want his hands under the table, in his lap. Now place three objects on the table, saying "Look...listen." As soon as you get eye contact, tell him what to touch: "Shoe...touch shoe." Praise him for "good touching" and, if he is correct, confirm this by saying "Yes...shoe." Mark his response on a chart. Now again tell him to put his hands down and wait until they are under the table before placing the next three objects on the table. Continue until you have asked him to touch all five objects at least once. When finished, praise him for "good working" and let him get up for a reward.

Note: Remember that Tony is easily distracted so you need to work where there are no noises and no other objects nearby for him to touch. Keep the TV off and the other children out of the room while you work. Keep all other toys out of sight so he won't be distracted by them either. By giving Tony only three objects to look at and by marking on your chart after each touch response, you are showing him a very clear organization and repetitive routine, one that will help Tony maintain organized attention throughout the task.

CASE 4, VISUAL ATTENTION AND DISTRACTIBILITY: NON-OBSERVANT CHILD

GETTING OBJECT NAMED

Objectives: To look at adult when told, "Listen. . . get shoe." To scan whole table searching for object named. To look around room for object named. To go and bring back this object.

Materials: Common objects (spoon, toothbrush, crayon, Teddy bear, cup, shoe)

Procedure: Take three objects and show them to Bill one at a time. Be sure he looks at each one, holds it, and then puts it on the table. Then place the three objects on the table, separated widely to encourage visual scanning. Say "Look. . . listen. . . get shoe." If he does not look around, move his hand in the direction of the object to help cue his visual attention. When Bill gets used to this game, begin to place some objects on the floor near him. As he improves in scanning for the object, you can begin to move them farther off.

Note: Bill seldom notices objects or things that are going on around him. He needs your help in looking at and listening to things that are at a little distance away from him. In addition to this game, you can also help by the following: Leave some toys in sight and ask him to get one of the toys named. Ask him to help you carry objects to their special place (magazines, towels, shoes). This will help him become more aware that objects stay in a certain place. When the telephone or doorbell sounds, tell Bill, "Listen. . . the telephone" and take him with you to point to the phone or to open the door. Ask him to carry packages for you or move objects as you tidy up the house.

CASE 5, SPECIAL INTERESTS: PASSIVE GIRL

Note: Child has few play skills; her main interests are watching TV and handling jewelry.

Objectives: To associate jewelry with body parts (neck, arm, finger). To give single-word responses without prompts. To give short phrases with prompts ("on arm," "it's a ring").

Materials: Collect your old jewelry and Jan's so that you have four each of rings, bracelets, necklaces, earrings; four sorting trays in the bottom of which you paste a picture of a specific body part (neck, ear, finger, arm)

Procedure: Place the trays in front of Jan and ask her to name each picture as you point to it. (Help her if needed.) Hand her one piece of jewelry and ask, "What is this?" Tell her to "show me where it goes" in the tray. After the sorting is finished, take out each piece of jewelry, asking "Whose?" Help her learn to say "Mummy's ring," "Jan's bracelet," etc.

Note: Jan's interest in jewelry is a good way to introduce the new concepts of body parts and possession. Once this is understood and she can use the language for these concepts, we will generalize to more important clothing. This will help her improve self-help skills and respect other's property at home and at school. As she watches TV you can point out the jewelry she can see, e.g., "pretty necklace." Our next objective will be to use paper dolls and cut-out clothes in the same type of sorting structure. We can then generalize this interest to develop play activities with real dolls.

CASE 6, SPECIAL INTERESTS: CHILD WHO REPETITIVELY STACKS TIN CANS

Note: Child dislikes interference in stacking play, and has no imitation skills.

Objectives: To look at what you do, imitate this action, and accept the different arrangements you create.

Materials: Twelve cans (four each of soup, tomato paste, small juice); 5″ × 8″ colored paper (one each of red, blue, yellow); a shallow box

Procedure: Place all the cans in the box, to be passed back and forth. Take turns with Doug picking up one can and placing it on one of the colored papers. You go first. Place a soup can on the red paper. Then hand the box to Doug and ask him to do the same thing — place another soup can next to yours. Each type of can should be placed on the same color, e.g., soup on red, juice on blue. Be sure that Doug places each can correctly and does *not* stack them. He should follow the arrangement you have established (see Figure 25). Once the routine is understood, you can begin to vary the activity in the follow-

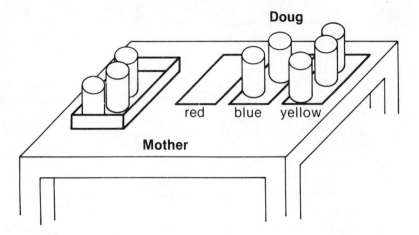

Figure 25.   Imitation and arrangement task, matching cans to colored paper.

ing ways: 1) line the cans in vertical or horizontal rows, 2) put them ly-
ing down side by side or end to end, 3) change the type of cans or the
number to be used.

Note: We know that Doug is good at stacking cans, but the point of
this activity is to teach him to accept new ways of using these cans. We
want him to be more aware of your actions, to look at what you do and to
take turns following your example. Imitation and taking turns will be an
important ability for teaching Doug new skills with different materials.
We chose this activity because it is repetitious and the structure is visually clear. Since Doug likes repetition and a precise order in his own play,
he will be comfortable when this new arrangement is also predictable and
clearly organized.

Chapter 12.
Teaching Objectives in
Nine Function Areas

In this chapter, teaching activities are illustrated for nine important function areas, most of which are evaluated directly by the Psychoeducational Profile (Volume I). All of the activities have been used effectively in our program. Many of the teaching procedures overlap with more than one of the function areas. For example, the imitation activity that follows involves imitating the behavior of animals. The same activity could be used for teaching social skills, i.e., taking turns. Nevertheless it is useful to maintain the identification of different area goals even in similar activities. This serves to remind the parent-teacher of the current teaching focus. If the teaching emphasis is on imitation toward verbal skill development, then the subsequent program would pursue emerging language skills. Imitation of animal behavior could be followed by imitation of animal sounds or names. On the other hand, if the primary goal is to develop better social skills, then the next program might move from taking turns with animal behaviors to taking turns with picking up food or with using toys.

DEVELOPMENTAL LEVEL

The teaching activities in each of the nine areas are arranged by developmental age, that is, the child with whom we used these activities was functioning at the age level designated for each activity in that area. Usually there is considerable variation of developmental age for the same child in different areas. Moreover, the chronological age of the child is usually higher, often ranging to twice his developmental age. The reader must not expect that the activity designated by a particular developmental age will fit all children of that same age. However, it is a most helpful clue in planning activities used by a beginning teacher or for a new child. Additional developmental sequences can be found in Appendix A.

COMPLEXITY OF TEACHING ACTIVITY

It is helpful to keep in mind that the activity specified in most areas can be readily altered to make it more complex or difficult. In other words, alterations of an activity can make it appropriate for children at quite different developmental levels. For example, the pictures used for receptive language training on p. 213 can be replaced by less familiar objects, by action verbs like "riding" or "gluing," going all the way to adolescent interests, e.g., making a wiring diagram, using a loom. These activities are not intended to be precise instructions of how and what to teach your child. Instead they are like an enlarged snapshot of an ongoing event. It becomes most useful when integrated into your own experience and is then applied to a particular child.

The examples are grouped in the following nine areas: 1) *Imitation* is especially useful for developing certain language skills and cooperation — which is important for other learning skills (see also Chapters 3 and 4). 2) *Gross motor* activities involve control of body and muscle groups (see Chapters 3 and 4). 3) *Fine motor* activities refer primarily to precise control of hands and fingers used in writing, self-help, and vocational skills (see Chapters 3 and 4). 4) *Eye-hand integration* includes the integration of perceptual and motor functions. It is involved in fine tuning of motor coordination needed for cognitive development (see Chapters 3 and 5). 5) *Cognitive performance* refers to matching, categorizing, and sequencing skills needed for organizing and understanding information from the environment (see Chapters 3 and 5). 6) *Receptive language* is the understanding of verbal, signed, and symbolic communication (see Chapters 3 and 5). 7) *Expressive language* includes the skills of using these same communication processes (see Chapters 3 and 5). 8) *Self-help* skills are the basic functions of eating, toileting, and dressing, needed for survival in the community. The overlap between this area and the others is illustrated in Tommy's case. Although it is a most important curriculum area for our children, we have not discussed teaching procedures in greater detail because several excellent self-help teaching guides are already available (see Appendix B). 9) *Social* skills refer to the knowledge needed for living with and interacting with another individual or group. They involve the integration of skills included in the other eight areas since every teaching interaction is also a social interaction, even at the simplest level. This area is directed at the most general and also the most important goals of this manual.

IMITATION

Objective 1: To encourage verbalization through imitation of sounds (developmental age is 6–18 months).

Materials: None

Procedure: Put your finger over your mouth and say "sh." Put your hand over your mouth, Indian style, and say "wah-wah." Play "This little piggy went to market" and let John have a turn to say "wee-wee-wee." Smack your lips as in kissing. Push a block off the table and say "uh-oh" as it falls.

For each of these actions, begin by demonstrating and then prompting John[1] to make the movement. Improvise any way that you want to in order to get him to do the actions. You will need to repeat one of these actions many times (perhaps 20 or more) before changing to a second one. After he has learned two actions you can begin to use them alternately.

John does not know what you want him to do at this point. Therefore, you will need to move his hand or touch his mouth to prompt him at first. Gradually you can give less and less help until he begins to imitate by himself.

Objective 2: To imitate doll play activities (developmental age is 1–2½ years).

Materials: A doll, small blanket, spoon, Kleenex, cup

Procedure: Sit with Jane at a table or on a rug or bed where she is comfortable. Give a doll, blanket, spoon, etc., to Jane and yourself, placing them in a pile or in a shoebox. Take out your doll and place it in front of *you*. Gesture for her to do the same. Take out a blanket and lay it over your doll (perhaps you would tuck it in or sing a lullaby). Gesture (or tell) her to do the same. Help her if needed. Repeat this with different actions. If she catches on to the game, have her do something and you copy her. *Suggested actions:* cover with a blanket, pat hair, feed with a spoon, wipe the nose, give the doll a drink, undress or dress, walk the doll, make it jump, sit, etc.

Objective 3: To imitate hand movements (developmental age is 2–3½ years).

Materials: Beads and string

Procedure: Give Tony the string. Give him a bead and let him put it on. For subsequent beads, have Tony clap his hands in imitation of you (you clap, he claps) before you give him the bead. When he has the

---

[1]Each activity in this chapter was designed for a specific child in our program. Hence we used different proper names in each of these illustrations.

idea of clapping and does it consistently after you, change the imitation activity to tapping the table or hitting it with your palms.

Note: The purpose of this activity is for Tony to copy you doing one of these things. He can learn this most easily when you make it part of a *routine.* Tony likes to string beads and this will motivate him to *do* what you do in order to get the next bead.

Objective 4: To imitate speed and volume using a soundmaker (developmental age is 3–4½ years).
Materials: Drum and stick or spoon and pan
Procedure: Demonstrate the meaning of each word separately — fast-slow, loud-soft. Beat the drum fast then give Jimmy a turn. Help him do it *fast.* Repeat this, beating *slow.* Do the same with loud, soft. Once he understands and can imitate these qualities, you can combine them — fast and loud, fast and soft, slow and loud, slow and soft.

Objective 5: To imitate animal movements (developmental age is 4–5½ years).
Materials: Pictures of animals (frog, rabbit, bird, duck, elephant, fish)
Procedure: Give Tim the book and have him find the animal as you direct him. Ask him, "What's that?" Have him answer. You tell Tim, "A bird flies." "What does a bird do?" Help him answer, "Flies." Do this for whatever animals you can. (Example: It's difficult to answer for elephant and duck, so skip this step for them.) You move like the animal while you say, "Look, Tim, I'm flying like a bird." Say, "Let's be birds" and lead him through the motions, if necessary. As Tim learns these, tell him "Fly like a bird" without you doing it first.

Objective 6: To imitate body movements and poses (developmental age is 4½–6 years).
Materials: Pictures from magazines of people in action
Procedure: Have Tom adopt different poses like those in the pictures and others you can devise. You can also do various "exercises" where Tom has to make his arms and legs work together, like arms up, feet apart; arms down, feet together; one hand on head, one hand on tummy; raise hands in air, stand on one foot.

Use games with a group of children:

a. Have the children dance around in a circle, using different body positions. When you clap your hands, the children should "freeze." Then have them imitate the position of one child.

b. Play "statues," where you spin one child, then let him run and fall down in a position and hold that position. Have the others imitate his position.

You balance on your tiptoes and have Tom do the same. Stay on your tiptoes until you count to 10.

You stand on one foot and have Tom do the same. Stand on one foot until you count to five, then change and stand on the other foot until you count to five.

Do the elephant walk: You and Tom bend forward from the waist allowing your arms to hang limply with hands clasped. Walk forward by taking big steps. Say, "Let's pretend to be elephants. Here's how to make his long nose."

These activities will be much more fun for Tom if you can make games out of them. Be sure to have someone *do* them with him. Remember how much Tom loves praise, so be sure to tell him "Good boy!" The real key to success here is to have fun and enjoy these exercises!

GROSS MOTOR

Objective 1: To throw in a specific direction (developmental age is 1–2 years).
Materials: Bean bag, cardboard box or trash can
Procedure: Have the box near Jimmy. Kneel beside Jimmy. You take the bean bag and drop it in the box. Get it, give it to Jimmy. Direct him, "Drop." Help him until he can go and do it himself. Get him to pick it back up and give it to you.

When he can drop it in, move the box 2 or 3 feet away. Get him to throw it in. Direct him, "Throw." You probably will have to move his arm in a throwing motion as you say "throw" to help him understand. When he can do this, stand, sit, or kneel behind the box and direct Jimmy to throw. As he does this, remove the box and get him to throw to you.

Objective 2: To develop leg muscles for squatting and bending (developmental age is 2–3 years).
Materials: Paper bag, large food boxes (empty or full)
Procedure: Place the bag with groceries on the table. Show Simon that the game is to take one box at a time and arrange it on the bottom shelf of your cupboard (he will need to squat down). After leading him through the action, begin to give less help. Encourage him to keep up the activity with praise or occasional help. You might repeat the words, "Finish it."

When the bag is empty, praise him, give him a tickle and a "jumping time," and then a food reward. You want him to know that he gets something good when the job is done.

Do this activity every day at the same time so he expects it and it becomes a routine.

Objective 3: To improve ability to climb steps, run, and go on tiptoe (developmental age is 2½–3½ years).
Materials: None
Procedure: Play the game "follow the leader," and include Susie's brother as well. Start the game by standing in line. Say, "Time for follow the leader." The first person goes around the room in various ways and the others follow. You will want to have Susie in the middle, so she can follow one of you while the other helps her from behind. Gradually you can give less help. Use running, walking, going up steps, jumping from the bottom step, turning around, falling down, jumping in place, clapping hands, walking with hands on your head, touching different places, squeezing through narrow openings.
Variation: If you play this game with her alone, it may be helpful to attach a rope from you to her until she learns the rules of the game.

Objective 4: To increase balancing ability (developmental age is 3–4 years).
Materials: $2'' \times 4''$ board, about 5' long; two small blocks to place under the board; two bean bags
Procedure: Place the board on the floor. Show Greg how to walk "on the board," then help him to do this (you may need to hold his hand). Gradually give less help. Let him hold on to your thumb but provide less and less support. This will teach him to begin to rely on his own balance.

When he gets good at this, put the board up on the small blocks. Praise him a lot when he crosses over without stepping off.
Variations: Ask him to carry a bean bag across and dump it in a bag or box at the other end. Ask him to carry a bean bag in each hand.

Objective 5: To improve hitting and kicking muscle control (developmental age is 3½–4½ years).
Materials: Large softball and bat, beach ball, and wastebasket
Procedure: Use a large, plastic lightweight bat and a large softball for batting the ball. Demonstrate how to hold the bat, including swinging at an imaginary ball. Allow Jim to practice swinging at an imaginary ball. Stand about 3 feet from him and throw an underhand ball to him. (*Note:* If this is hard for him you can hang a soft foam ball by a string and let him practice this way.)

To kick a ball into a basket, use a large lightweight ball about the size of a beach ball. Use an empty wastebasket that is big enough for the ball to fit into. Place the wastebasket on its side so that the ball, when kicked, can easily roll into it. Allow Jim to stand about 3 to 4 feet from the basket. Have him kick the ball into the basket. Allow him at least 10 attempts each time the activity is done. As he gains more skill, move the basket farther from him.

Objective 6: To strengthen muscles and their control (developmental age is 4–5½ years).

Materials: Jump rope, masking tape

Procedures: To play "wheelbarrow," ask Greg to get on the floor on his hands and knees, as if he were going to crawl. Tell him he is going to "walk with his hands." Stand behind him and pick up his legs with a firm grasp around the ankles. Have him place his entire forearm on the floor for support. As he gains more skill, have him use his hands alone. Tell him to "walk" and follow him, holding up his legs.

To play "scooting race," sit on the floor with legs extended forward. Have Greg sit beside you in the same position. Scoot across the floor by forcing one leg forward at a time with a pushing motion of the hip. It will seem as if you are walking with your buttocks. Race across the floor to some object or person as a goal. For now, he may need a third person to squat down facing him and help him move his legs one at a time by pulling forward on each one alternately.

To play "tug-of-war," place colored masking tape on the floor to mark a "line." Give Greg one end of the rope to hold and you take the other (or give it to another child to hold). Tell Greg to "pull" the person "over the line." At first you will need to make it easy for him to do this. Reward him. Gradually make it harder for him to "pull" so that he learns to use his muscles more.

Objective 7: To increase bilateral coordination, using a different movement for each side of the body (developmental age is 5–6 years).

Materials: Paper and pencil

Procedure: Have Mary do movements requiring knowledge of left and right. Stand side by side so you don't confuse her as to left and right. You can do songs like "Hokey Pokey" ("Put your right hand in and put your left hand out") or you can make up your own song or game. You could also do exercises like: "Put your right arm up," "Shake your left hand." The most important thing is that Mary not only hear the direction but also have you to imitate.

Have Mary touch or move parts of her body designated as right or left on command without having you to imitate.

Draw a hand. Have Mary put her hand on the picture and tell you which hand it is. Ask her, "Which hand is that, your right or left?" or "Is that your right hand or your left hand?" Do the same for her foot.

Objective 8: To coordinate jump to moving rope (developmental age is 5½–6½ years).

Materials: Piece of heavy rope for swinging

Procedure: If two people are available, each one can hold an end of the rope and turn. If only one person is available, then you can tie one end of the rope to something (chair, table leg, tree). Demonstrate how you jump rope. Have Tom stand in the middle of the rope and tell him to "jump" as the rope comes to his feet. Move it slowly back and forth, very slowly at first, and gradually make the swinging arc larger. Have him count each time he jumps. You might keep a "jump chart" and let him keep a record of how he does each day. Be sure to praise him.

FINE MOTOR

Objective 1: To improve grasp and release of objects (developmental age is 6–18 months).

Materials: Play-do; small blocks; nuts and raisins

Procedure: Have Tom sit at a table for this activity. First help him roll the clay into strands (about ½"–1" across). Have Tom pinch small pieces off the roll, while you hold it, and place the pieces in a cup or can. You may need to pull the coil apart yourself, at first, and simply have him put the pieces in a cup. Once this is easy for him, go ahead with teaching him to pull it apart also.

Note: It is often helpful to a child if you do the first part of a task and let him do the finishing part. Then you can gradually do less while he does more and more. This is encouragement to him because he *knows* he will be able to finish the task.

Collect various items such as blocks, raisins, nuts, etc. (small objects that require a pinching motion to pick up). Encourage Tom to pick up each item, using his thumb and fingers, and place each in the bowl. Do this for 5 minutes (unless Tom becomes frustrated — then work for short periods for several sessions).

Objective 2: To improve fine motor coordination of both hands (developmental age is 1–2½ years).

Materials: Large shoe box with lid; variety of smaller boxes and containers that open by different methods (matchbox, ring box)

Procedure: Fill the large cardboard box with the smaller container and place a very small food reward in each one. Have Tom open the lid of the large box. Help him to open each of the smaller boxes.

Note: He may continually come back to one particular container. If he does this, direct his attention to and help him to open another one. If Tom begins to move away from you with one of the small containers, simply take it away from him and put it back in the box with as little fuss as possible. Be *very* generous with verbal praise and try to make it a "fun game," where opening each new box will be an exciting surprise.

Objective 3: To handle a felt pen (developmental age is 2–3½ years).
Materials: Paper, four felt-tip colored pens (non-toxic watercolor)
Procedure: Place paper in front of Edie and all four pens on her left side. Show her how to take off top of pen. Make some marks on the paper. Then place the top back on the pen and put it in a box on her right. Repeat with all four pens. Watch as she uses these. Take turns with her and, by working at the same time, demonstrate some new strokes to her (dots, circular marks, solid coloring).

Objective 4: To use scissors for simple cutting (developmental age is 2½–3½ years).
Materials: Scissors, 1-inch strips of colored paper
Procedure: Help Louis place his thumb and fingers correctly. Help him open and shut the scissors by guiding this motion with your hand over his. Reduce your help as you feel his muscles beginning to initiate a cut movement. After this becomes easy, help Louis hold the paper strip in his other hand. When this is comfortable, you can mark dark lines at 2-inch intervals on the strips and ask him to cut "on the line." Accept an approximation at first and praise him.

Note: The cut pieces can be used to make a collage (design) using paste and plain paper.

Objective 5: To cut with a table knife (developmental age is 3–4 years).
Materials: Table knives; play-do or cookie dough
Procedure: Give Jane a piece of play-do and take one yourself. Roll it into a cord — help her do this. Cut yours into pieces — "make cookies." Get her to watch you. Ask her to "make cookies." If she has difficulty, stand behind her and help her hold knife and cut. Lessen the amount of help until she can manage alone. Ask her to place each piece on a plate.

Note: You may need to start with a little "butter knife" and then go to the heavier, larger table knife.

Objective 6: To develop muscles for grasping and rotating (developmental age is 4–5½ years).
Materials: One piece of wood, 1½ inches thick; stove bolts with large nuts, a short-handled screwdriver

Procedure: Drill holes into the wood. Glue the nuts over the holes in the wood. Have John screw each metal bolt into the nuts on the board with his screwdriver. Then have him remove the bolts. (While you're working on this, you might ask questions like, "What's this?")

EYE-HAND INTEGRATION

Objective 1: To develop pre-puzzle skills (developmental age is 6–18 months).
Materials: Egg carton; large beads or other objects that fit into the carton
Procedure: Place the carton on the table. Hand Tommy one bead and focus his attention on one indentation in the carton. Guide his hand to the indentation and help him release the bead into the hollow. Repeat until the carton is filled. Help him close the carton. Then dump out the beads and start again.

Note: Give him only enough help to focus his visual attention and aid him when he really needs help; reward the finished job.

Objective 2: To improve visual attention to play activity (developmental age is 1–2½ years).
Materials: Jack-in-the-box, ring stack, xylophone, busy-box, blocks, tin cup, sauce pan
Procedure: Put a jack-in-the-box, cash register, or busy box in front of Jimmy. (If possible, let Jimmy choose the toy.) Point to one of the "openers" and tell Jimmy to "Push" or "Turn" or whatever word is appropriate. If he doesn't respond, take his hand and help him.

Ring stacks can be made with jar rings and a paper towel cylinder. Hand Jimmy one ring at a time, tell him to look (hold the ring up near your eyes). Then give him the ring and tell him, "Put it on." Guide his hand as necessary.

Hit the xylophone yourself, then hand the stick to Jimmy. Tell him to hit it. Don't worry about him hitting the same key; you want him merely to hit the instrument after you.

Using about 2-inch cubes, like ABC blocks, stack blocks up into a tower and then get Jimmy to knock them down.

Have Jimmy scoop water from a large container of water to a smaller, empty container with a cup.

Note: If you are using a toy like rings, blocks, beads, or puzzle, hold up the piece and try to get Jimmy to look at it before he takes it. Move it as he reaches blindly so he has to glance to see where it is. Give him the piece and help him, if necessary, to do the task. If you are using things like water play, show him how to pour, taking his hand as necessary to help him. Withdraw and direct him with gestures.

Objective 3: To use two hands cooperatively for threading (developmental age is 1½–2½ years).
Materials: Beads, pipe cleaners; tinker toy spools, shoelaces
Procedure: Hold bead near your eyes. Say "Look" (showing hole). Hold bead and place pipe cleaner in Jane's hand. Move her hand to push pipe cleaner through hole. Move her other hand to pull it out. Help her hold bead herself and push in. Help her transfer bead and *pull* out.

Note: Help her as much as necessary until you can gradually withdraw help. Let her make a necklace (using shoelace) and wear it.

Objective 4: To improve placement of puzzle pieces (developmental age is 2–3 years).
Materials: Four-piece inset puzzle (using meaningful objects easily recognized, e.g., fruits)
Procedure: Place the puzzle in front of John and have him take the pieces out and give them to you. Just cue him with the command "Take them out" and, as he takes one out, hold out your hand and say, "Give it to me." You can name the piece to be taken out if he understands words. Hold one piece up near your face and tell John, "Look." When he looks, hand him the piece and say, "Put it in." When he has the piece in, praise him for his success. If he has trouble putting the piece in, guide his hand very slowly and deliberately, saying things like "turn," "put it here," "push" — whatever direction is appropriate. It is vital that your language be very simple. When John can put in two pieces as you direct, add a third and fourth.

Objective 5: To assemble a cut-up picture using visual cues (developmental age is 2½–3½ years).
Materials: From colored paper cut simple shapes that can be assembled to make a picture, i.e., house (rectangle, triangle, square) or car (rectangle, two circles)
Procedure: Draw an outline of assembled picture on paper for Frank to use as a guide. Place two pieces in front of Frank. Show him how to arrange them to make the picture, then disassemble. Give him one piece to place on the sheet. Help him then to put paste on the white paper and place the colored piece over the paste. As he gets good at this, you can ask him to assemble the pieces without having an outline to guide him.

Figure 26.   Simple picture of a car. The dotted lines indicate where the circle belongs.

Objective 6: To imitate drawing motions (up, down, around) (developmental age is 3–4 years).
Materials: Two crayons and paper or chalkboard and chalk
Procedure: Seat Kathy beside you. Have a piece of paper in front of you. Make a line. Say "Down" as you make it. Give the crayon to Kathy. Say, "You make one." Guide her hand and say "down" as she makes the line. Do the above saying "up," "across," "around."

Note: Guide Kathy's hand as much as necessary in this task. The purpose is that she copy the line or circle after you. Withdraw your hand periodically to see if she will do it herself. You can also do this task on a blackboard, where you have her copy whatever line you make. The directions "up" and "down" are better taught on a blackboard because it is a more true up/down motion.

Objective 7: To draw circles (developmental age is 3–4½ years).
Materials: Worksheets of simple pictures to be completed by drawing one or more circles (see Figure 26)
Procedure: Help Dave position the crayon in his hand. Guide his hand to trace the circle. Withdraw your help as he is able to trace on his own. On blank sheets of paper, let Dave practice the round-and-round motion of a circle. Note the size circle he naturally makes. Use this when you prepare your tracing papers.

You may want to staple these together as "Dave's own book" or hang them on the wall.

Objective 8: To change direction of line, when appropriate (developmental age is 4–5 years).
Materials: Worksheets (see Figure 27) made ahead of time, plastic covers so you can reuse them, felt tip marker or crayon

Figure 27.   These mazes require the child to change direction of the line. Covering the worksheets with plastic enables you to reuse them.

Procedure: Give Allen a worksheet with about three mazes on it. Use a green dot on the left to tell him where to start. A red dot on the right will remind him to stop. Help him with verbal cues, e.g., "Start here...," "Whoa...stop" ("Slowly...careful...").

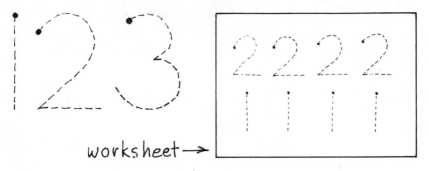

worksheet →

Figure 28. Dotted numbers. Colored dot indicates where to start writing.

Objective 9: To draw a house (developmental age is 4½–6 years).
Materials: Paper and crayons, Greg's doll house or picture of a house
Procedure: Show Greg the crayons and let him select the one he wants. Have him identify the color. Draw a square. You should guide Greg's hand at first. You might have to guide his hand for each item. Have him draw a roof, chimney, door, windows. After he finishes the picture, ask him to touch the various parts. Ask him "What's this?" and have him identify the parts of the picture. Have Greg touch the corresponding parts on his doll house.

Note: You could use Greg's doll house as a model for his picture. To do this, have the doll house next to you. Ask Greg to touch the roof of the doll house, then have him draw one on his picture.

Objective 10: To write the numbers 1–6 (developmental age is 5–6½ years).
Materials: Paper with numbers dotted out. Colored dot indicates where to start the line (see Figure 28)
Procedure: Teach one number at a time, being sure John feels confident with one before you start teaching the next one. Tell John to "make number 1." Point to where he should start. Guide his hand if needed, but encourage him to do it himself. As he makes the line, following the dots, state the direction of his stroke, e.g., "Down." This will help him when he goes ahead to making these numbers without dotted cues. Number 1="Down." Number 2="Around..down.. stop..over." Number 3="Around..stop..around." Number 4="Slant down..stop..over..down."

COGNITIVE PERFORMANCE

Objective 1: To increase visual attention and memory for object out of sight (developmental age is 6–12 months).
Materials: Cup, small edible rewards

Procedure: Sit across from Tony on the floor. Show him the edible. Move it up in front of your face and, when he looks at you, say "Good boy" and pop the food into his mouth. Repeat this three times.

Place an inverted cup close to Tony within easy reach. Show him a bit of food, put it under the cup while he is watching, and gesture for him to pick it up. When he recovers the food, pat or hug him and say, "Good boy." If he fails to go after it, take his hand to help him and reward him as if he had done it himself.

Gradually try to increase the distance between Tony and the cup without moving it so far away that he loses interest.

Objective 2: To track a moving object and look for it when it disappears (developmental age is 6–12 months).
Materials: A rolling toy car
Procedure: Roll the car slowly off the edge of the table. Draw Harry's attention to it if he doesn't look for it. Take turns retrieving the car. Give Harry a turn pushing it off the table, guiding his hand. Use lots of facial expressions of surprise and delight to make this game fun and increase his interest.

Objective 3: To point to indicate wants; reaching toward object (developmental age is 1–2 years).
Materials: Edible rewards or favorite toy
Procedure: Offer Mark the reward/toy. Get him to look at it. Then place it on the table. Help Mark point to it. Do this yourself; then guide his hand to point. When he has pointed, let him go get it. As you repeat this (many times throughout the day), gradually fade your help until he can point without help. Encourage him to point to many things he wants before you let him have them.

Objective 4: To stimulate picture recognition (developmental age is 1½–2½ years).
Materials: Six simple pictures of words that Ed knows well (spoon, shoe, soap) mounted on cardboard
Procedure: Place two pictures on the table with one pushed closer to Ed. Name the close one and ask him to give it to you ("Give me spoon"). Reverse the left-right position of the two cards and keep the same card (spoon) pushed forward. Ask again, "Give me spoon." Repeat this three times. Repeat with a second picture (shoe).

When Ed is consistently making correct choices, place the two cards in an equally close position so he no longer is getting position cues. Give help when it is needed. Do not let him fail more than two times before giving help. Continue in this way with all six pictures.

Objective 5: To teach shape recognition (developmental age is 2–3 years).

Materials: A lotto card, made of cardboard, divided into four sections by heavy black lines; cut-out shapes (two each of circle, square, triangle, rectangle) with one of each pasted in each square

Procedure: Give Jack a shape and tell him to "put it on." Get him to look at his shape (you name it), then touch the one like it on the lotto card.

Note: You may need to help him look at all four lotto shapes before he decides which one is the "same."

Variation: Place all four loose shapes on the table in front of Jack. Point to one lotto square (top left) and name it ("This is a circle"). Tell him to "find circle" from his row and "put it on."

Objective 6: To match identical pictures on lotto board (developmental age is 2½–3½ years).

Materials: Paste a set of identical pictures (drawn or cut from magazines) on a large lotto sheet divided into six squares and on individual cards

Procedure: Place lotto board in front of Jerry. Hand him one picture (one card) and help him find one "like it" on the lotto board. Show him how to place the card *on top of* the lotto picture. Proceed this way with each picture. As he understands the task, you can begin to give him two pictures at a time to place. Eventually you want him to draw a card from a box (of the cards) and place it correctly. This will then become a more independent task.

Variation: Similar procedure can be used with sets of actual objects, six objects to a set.

Objective 7: To understand "different," recognize dissimilarities (developmental age is 3–4 years).

Materials: Set of objects like blocks, shapes, cars

Procedure: Put three objects on the table—two same, one different. Have Jim look while you say, "This is a block, this is a block, but this is a car. These are the same [point to the two blocks]. This one is different [point to car]. Give me the one that is different."

Start with objects that are very clearly different, i.e., three blocks, one car or three cups, one block. Gradually make the differences more subtle, i.e., three red blocks, one yellow block (color difference only) or three triangles, one square (shape difference only).

Objective 8: To match and recognize colors (developmental age is 3½–4½ years).

Materials: Paper, crayons, picture book

Procedure: Draw simple outlines of common objects (apple, orange, banana, grapes, grass, sun, leaf). Show Brad the real object and name its color. Then ask him to choose the same color crayon. As he colors, repeat "Apple is red," etc. Ask him "What color is ____?" From time to time go through the picture book with him "finding things that are *red*." Try asking him, "I'm thinking of something red—what is it?"

Objective 9: To increase body concepts, expressed in drawing (developmental age is 3½–4½ years).
Materials: Paper, pencils/crayons
Procedures: (*Note:* Be sure Dick can locate on himself, you, and a picture the following parts: head—face parts; body—shoulders, arm, hands, legs, feet).

Draw a figure part by part, having Dick touch the part on himself and you and telling you what comes next. Say, for example, "Now I'm drawing a head. Touch your head. What comes next?" (Point to your neck, if necessary. Have Dick say "Neck.") "I'm drawing the neck under the head. Touch your neck. What comes next?"

Stand Dick opposite you and touch the body part on each other so Dick can see, as in a mirror, the ways in which the different parts of the body are related to each other. Draw a figure with one thing missing. Ask Dick, "What's missing?" After he tells you, have him draw the part in. Begin with an obvious part like an arm or head. As Dick gets better, make two things missing. Make the exercise progressively more difficult. Do the same for a face with one eye missing, and so on.

Objective 10: To learn time sequence (developmental age is 4–5 years)
Materials: Pictures that show a child doing routine things (from magazines, books, or stick figure drawings)
Procedure: Have Paul identify what's happening in each picture. Then lay the pictures out on the table (start with four—one for each time of day). Help Paul put them in sequence from morning to night. They might be: 1) get up, 2) go to school, 3) eat dinner, 4) go to bed. When they are in order, have Paul hand you the one you do in the morning, afternoon, evening, night. Increase the number of pictures so you have three or four activities for each time of day. When Paul can hand you each one on command, ask him "When do you get up?" as he hands you the picture. Have him answer "morning" or "in the morning."

Objective 11: To recognize and correct missing parts (developmental age is 4½–5½ years).
Materials: Worksheets (see Figure 29), pencil/crayon

A Make it the same.   B What's missing?

Figure 29.   Worksheets for correcting missing parts. A, Child looks at completed picture on left, then completes picture on right. B, Child locates missing part of each picture and fills it in.

Procedure: *Make it the Same.* Give John a worksheet. Have him identify the parts on the complete picture. Then have him look at the incomplete picture. Have him identify the parts on it. Then say, for example, "Look John, this one has windows. Make this one like it. Put in windows." Try to guide his attention so he looks at the finished one and then completes the unfinished one. You might try getting him to answer "What does this need?"

What's Missing? Show John a picture. Have him identify it and any parts he knows. Then ask him "What's missing?" and point to the missing part. After he answers, say "Fix it" and have him put in the missing part.

RECEPTIVE LANGUAGE

Objective 1: To increase awareness of sound differences (developmental age is 6–12 months).
Materials: None
Procedure: Choose three or four physical movements that Johnny enjoys, such as patting hands against another's, rocking in your lap, lifting up and down, swinging in the air, pushing back and forth in a cart or walker, bouncing him in your lap. While you are rocking or whatever, make playful sounds like you would while bouncing a small child on your lap, e.g., "ba ba ba," "weee," "da da," "ah ah," "yo yo yo," "ma ma, mmm, ooo." Include any sound Johnny is already making himself. You need not match up a specific movement with a specific sound, but do change movements when you change sounds.

Objective 2: To learn "coming" and "sitting" and to increase relating skills (developmental age is 6–18 months).

Materials: None

Procedure: Sit Jim in a chair facing one parent (6 feet away). Second parent should stand behind Jim, as a prompter. Gesture and say "Come." (Prompt may nudge him forward.) When he arrives at seated parent, praise him, hug him, and say "Good coming." Turn Jim around and tell him to "sit." Help him if needed. Work for 5–10 minutes, alternating "sit" and "come." You should change places so Jim will respond to both of you.

Note: At the beginning you will need to pair the spoken word with a very clear gesture. Gradually work toward moving the chairs farther apart, using fewer prompts or smaller gestures. Finally you will want Jim to come and sit from a distance without needing even the gestures to understand your meaning.

Objective 3: To learn family names (developmental age is 1–2 years).

Materials: Photographs of family

Procedure: Lay the photographs on the table. Point to one or hand it to David, saying "This is John. Take it *to* John." Do this for other family members. Ask David to take other things to people: "Give this cup to John" or "Give John a kiss." Do this throughout the day. Place the photos on the table and ask David to "touch" each of the people as you call their names.

Objective 4: To understand common nouns (developmental age is 1½–2½ years).

Materials: Three or four objects Ann uses (shoe, comb, brush, ball, truck, doll)

Procedure: Place about four objects on the floor a short distance from you both. Tell Ann to get one of the objects, pointing to it and getting her to look. Say, "Get the brush," for example. If Ann has trouble following your direction, bring her back, tell her again, and lead her to the object. Get her to pick it up and return with you. Direct her to give it to you. Say, for example, "Give me the brush." When you have the object, tell her to look and use it. Give it to Ann and tell her to do it. *Example:*

You: "Look, Ann. Brush hair" (acting it out as you say it).

You: "Here, Ann [handing brush], show me brushing hair."

Ann makes motion with you helping her as much as necessary.

Proceed this way for each object. Keep repeating until Ann can get each object and return it without getting confused. Play with or pantomime the function of *each* object. You can add objects as she learns the first group. Only add one at a time and never have more than eight for the task.

Objective 5: To learn to "stop" and "go" in response to commands (developmental age is 2–3 years).
Materials: A second child/adult to "help," a colored circle taped to the floor to make "home base"
Procedure: Have your helper stand on home base. You direct Jimmy to stand on a starting line several yards away. When the helper says "Go," you and Jimmy "stomp" (walk) toward him. When he says "Stop," you and Jimmy stop. Continue this way until you reach home base. Then both you and your helper give Jimmy a hug. Trade places with the helper while you give the command and he walks with Jimmy. Try to wait for Jimmy to initiate the "Go" or "Stop" response before helping him.

Objective 6: To learn a sequence of directions (developmental age is 2½–3½ years).
Materials: Common objects (spoon, car, box, cup, can) or small favorite toy
Procedure: Set up a routine seating where Jim can return after each direction or sequence of directions. Have a candy reward to give him when he returns. (*Note:* If Jim becomes distracted and can't complete the task, bring him back, sit him down, and re-give the same direction.)

Give Jim one direction (e.g., "Turn off the light and sit down," "Come back") and have him do it and return to you. (*Note:* If necessary, simplify the directions: "Turn off the light and jump up and down. Light and jump. Light and jump." If possible, get Jim to repeat the two words before he gets up to follow the direction, "Light then jump.") If Jim gets preoccupied, say something like "What's next?" to get him refocused. Give him a sound cue or gesture to the next action before you decide he is too distracted and needs to redo the whole task.

After a series of two-part directions, like the above, drop the "sit down" and substitute another action (e.g., "Turn off the light and jump up and down").
Variations: After Jim has begun to follow other directions, you can try directions like: "Get the cup and put it on the table." "Put the spoon in the cup and the cup on the table." "Put the car and the toy in the box."

Objective 7: To understand the prepositions "on" and "under" (developmental age is 3–4 years).

Materials: Several objects to hide (ones he can label easily: shoe, cup, car)

Procedure: Show Mike an object you are going to hide. Have him cover his eyes and place it either on or under something in the room. Tell Mike where it is, emphasizing the preposition—"It's UNDER the couch." Help him find it and repeat its position—"Right, it's UNDER the couch."

Repeat for a number of hiding places. Then if other members of the family are available, one can help Mike do the hiding and respond to the question "Where is it?" from the other.

If you wish you can teach these concepts in another way simply by asking Mike to place several objects on and under things in the room. When each is placed, ask him, "Where is it?" and help him with the response—ON the chair, UNDER the pillow, ON the window sill.

Objective 8: To understand labels for furnishings by function, room, and position (developmental age is 3½–4½ years).

Materials: Pictures mounted on cards of a kitchen, bathroom, bedroom, living room and things that go in each room (e.g., lamps, stove, sink, bed, table, refrigerator, toilet, bureau)

Procedure: Lay out the pictures of the rooms and have Jim hand them to you on command. Say, for example, "Give me the kitchen." When Jim knows the rooms, start using the pictures of things that go in the rooms. Use them as follows: Put two rooms on the table (kitchen and bedroom). Put out about five pictures for each room on the table. Have Jim hand you each picture on command ("Give me the sink, refrigerator, bed, etc."). You say "Bed goes in the bedroom" and put it on the pictures of the bedroom. Put the pictures out again and tell Jim to give you two (bed and bureau). Then give them back to him and say, "Put them in the bedroom."

Objective 9: To increase understanding and use of adjectives pertaining to nonvisual stimuli; to recognize opposites (developmental age is 3½–5 years).

Materials: A variety of things that taste sweet and a variety that taste sour (M&M's, raisin, banana; lemon, grapefruit, Sweet Tart) and a variety of things that feel hard and feel soft (metal, wood, nail; cotton, cloth, stuffed animal); words "sweet," "sour," "hard," and "soft" written on cards

Procedure: Put the labels "sweet" and "sour" on the table. Give Kenny a taste of something sweet. Tell him, "That's sweet." Have him put the rest or a like piece in the pile marked "sweet." Do the same for "sour."

Objective 10: To improve understanding and use of the prepositions in, on, under, on top of, next to, between, behind, and to improve understanding and use of questions that begin with "Where" (developmental age is 4½–5½ years).

Materials: About 6–10 small objects, such as a cup, paper clip, pencil, ink pen, fork, penny, piece of string, ball

Procedure: Sit facing Doug with the objects in your lap or close to you. Hand Doug one object at a time and tell him where to put it, saying, "Put the cup *on* the table," "Put the penny *in* the cup," and so on. Continue with this process, using each of the prepositions in the first goal above at least once. (The string can be used for *around* the cup, *around* the ball, etc.) When all of the objects have been used, ask Doug where each item is, one at a time. After he gives the answer, repeat it. *Example:*

You: Where is the cup?

Doug: On the table.

You: Good. The cup is on the table.

EXPRESSIVE LANGUAGE

Objective 1: To improve oral reflexes (developmental age is 6–12 months).

Materials: None

Procedure: Lip reflex. Tap gently around the angle formed at the corner of the mouth. You might use a Q-tip or the eraser end of a pencil. The response should be involuntary movements of the lips—lip closure and pouting.

Sucking reflex. Gently push and pull on a nipple or finger placed in the mouth (you might try a lollipop). The response should be alternating protruding and retracting movements of the tongue, often with elevation of the tip.

Tongue movement. Check for protruding of the tongue in response to licking (peanut butter or ice cream cone). Response desired is reaching with tip of tongue and side-to-side tongue movement.

Objective 2: To familiarize Tom with specific speech sounds ("b," "m," "k") and to encourage him to make them (developmental age is 6–18 months).

Materials: Pictures of animals or small toy animals, preferably a dog, a cow, and a duck

Procedure: Sit close enough so that you can easily reach Tom; it might be best to sit on the floor for this activity. Sing "Old Mac-

Donald," using the animals mentioned above. As you sing the name of an animal, hold it directly in front of Tom and point to it. While you're making the sound that the dog makes ("with a bow-wow here"), take your finger and flip the edge of Tom's lips, encouraging him to make the "b" sound. When you're making the sound that the cow makes ("moo-moo"), take your thumb and forefinger and press Tom's lips together. When you're making the duck sound ("quack-quack") press lightly against the top of Tom's throat. Press upward and backward while making the "k" sound.

Objective 3: To express a preference by pointing (developmental age is 1–2 years).
Materials: Raisins, bubbles, toy car, ball
Procedure: When it is time for a reward, place two of the favorite objects on the table out of his reach. Make the gesture (hands out, palms up) and ask, "What do you want?" As Jack reaches to grab one of them, quickly guide his hand to move it into a point gesture—give him the object. Once he learns this point gesture during this activity, begin to generalize it by urging him to point to things he wants at other times of the day.

Note: If Jack takes your hand to move it to what he wants (the refrigerator, for example), this is the time to help him point instead.

Objective 4: To express a need using one word (developmental age is 1½–2½ years).
Materials: Tricycle, ball, slide
Procedure: With each activity described use a very few verbs that will describe what Jerry wants to do next.

    Tricycle—push, pull
    Ball—throw, kick, bounce
    Slide—go up, go down

For example, stand Jerry at bottom of steps of slide, hold him there, and say, "What do you want to do? Go up." When he repeats "up," let him climb the steps. When he is at the top, hold him there and say, "What do you want to do? Go down." When Jerry says "down," let him slide down.

Note: It is important that you limit your language to the one-word answers suggested here. It is important for Jerry that you give him as many cues and promptings as necessary until he can use these words spontaneously. Don't be afraid to give him the answer as often as you feel necessary.

Objective 5: To increase use of object labels (developmental age is 2-3 years).

Materials: An animal puzzle (one that is good is Simple Animal Wooden Playboat made by Simplex Toys)

Procedure: Take out about three animals (cow, horse, sheep). Have John give you one of the animals on command. Ask him what it is. After he identifies it, ask him what sound it makes. If necessary, give him the sound. *Example:*

You: Give me the horse. (John gives it to you.)
You: What's this?
John: Horse.
You: What does the horse say?
John: Neigh.
If John can't answer, give him the answer:
You: What does the horse say? Neigh.
John: Neigh.

When he has done this, give him the puzzle and have him put the three pieces back at your command.

You: Put the horse in. (John puts it in.)

Objective 6: To increase word use and word understanding (developmental age is 2½-3½ years).

Materials: Pictures of objects and the objects, which should meet these requirements: 1) things Jerry uses or needs to use, 2) things he plays with, 3) things he can have frequent experience with, 4) things you can generalize to everyday use (e.g., comb, brush, toothbrush, pieces of clothing, articles of furniture, toys, eating tools, washing things)

Procedure: Lay the articles out on the floor of the room. Hold the pictures and sit with Jerry. Hold up a picture and ask Jerry: "What's this?" "What do you do with it?" "Show me." (Have Jerry pantomime the function.) Have Jerry go get the corresponding object and give it to you. Repeat the three questions and have him answer.

Spend a few minutes with each object doing things like:

a.   Soap—smell it
b.   Towel—dry different body parts
c.   Eating tools—"Give me a bite" or go get something and let Jerry eat with the tool
d.   Truck—roll it back and forth
e.   Ball—throw, roll, bounce, kick it, and have Jerry do this on command

Note: Give Jerry all the cues necessary. The purpose is to stay within the language and concepts he has, organizing them and using them in meaningful situations with real objects.

Objective 7: To pantomime actions (developmental age is 3–4 years).

Materials: Table, play stove, pans, play-do, spoons, bowl, apron, broom, and dust pan

Procedure: Have Mary sit across the table from you. Explain that you are going to make some cookies to bake. Explain that first she needs to put on her apron so we can stir the cookies. First, you imitate for her—put on the apron, get the spoon and bowl, and stir the cookies. Then say, "Okay, now you put on the apron and stir the cookies." You then say, "I'm going to pretend I have an apron and a bowl and spoon." Then you pantomime while Mary does it. Then say, "Okay, now I'm going to take the apron and the bowl and spoon and you pretend you have them." Then verbalize the actions encouraging Mary to pantomime. (It might be necessary for you to imitate with her and then for her to do it alone, but only if she is hesitant still at this point.) Go through the procedure of you imitating with objects, Mary acting with objects while you pretend, Mary pretending (or, if necessary, you pretending again as imitation for her to encourage her to pantomime alone). Do the following sequence after stirring:

1. Roll the play-do and pat into cookie sheets, put them in pan, then in the stove.
2. Wipe up the table and wash the bowl and spoon.
3. Sweep the floor.
4. Take cookies out of oven and off pan.
5. Eat cookies, then wash pan.

Objective 8: To increase spontaneous conversation and Peter's ability to relate experiences (developmental age is 3½–4½ years).

Materials: Pictures of family activities, scenes, events—pictures you can use for a simple story; objects like a ball, a shirt, an apple, a cotton ball, a glass

Procedure: Show Peter a picture or object and tell him about it. *Example:*

A ball—"Peter, this is a red ball. It is soft. It bounces. You can play catch with it. You can throw it and kick it."

Picture of the boys—"Peter, these are your brothers. There's John. He's 9. There's Billy. He's 2. There's Jay. He's 6. There's Eddie. He's 7."

Picture of a man tripping over a turtle—"Peter, this is Mr. Mooney. He was walking on [your street]. He was looking at the sky. Suddenly he tripped over a turtle. The turtle bit his toe because Mr. Mooney hurt him."

Next help Peter tell you what you said. Don't be concerned about the order. Your information should help him organize what he sees. If he bogs down, help him by giving him the things he hasn't said. Use only one or two objects and pictures for a while until Peter can say quite a bit back to you about them. When you think he's ready, withdraw your part and ask him to tell you about the object or picture. Let him add or create if he wants.

Note: The "story" pictures should be done only after Peter has begun to relate information about object or family or similar real pictures. Help Peter relate a real experience using the language structure he has learned in telling story sequences.

Objective 9: To increase dramatic gestures (developmental age is 4–5 years).

Materials: Objects (coffee pot, razor, magazine); pictures (faces with expressions like crying, laughing, scowling)

Procedure: Put three objects on the table. Go to the rug (stage) and act out using one of these objects. Ask Bruce, "What am I pretending to use?" Help him by using the real object, putting it back, and repeating the pantomime. Give Bruce a turn.

Do the same with the pictures. Put them on the table and name them (sad, happy, angry). Go to the stage and pretend one of these feelings. Ask Bruce to guess, "How do I feel?" Give Bruce a turn.

SELF-HELP

Objective 1: To grasp a utensil (developmental age is 6–18 months).
Materials: Plastic or wooden spoon
Procedure: Put the spoon into Mary's hand (overhand grasp). Help her grasp it and move it down into a bowl of sugar. Praise her, then repeat this many times.

To teach her to grasp and scoop, you will need to hold your hand over hers at first so she feels the motion of scooping. Scoop sugar up and onto a dish.

To teach her to scoop up to her own mouth, you will once again need to guide her hand at first. Use her favorite, chocolate pudding, for this step. Gradually give less and less help. Withdraw your hand to her wrist, then just give a light touch, and finally you may only need to help her get started.

Objective 2: To pull off socks (developmental age is 1–2 years).
Materials: Mary's sock, a man's sock, a jar or bottle
Procedure: Pull a man's sock down over the top of a bottle or jar in which you have poured her favorite drink. Take her hand and help her grasp the end of the sock and pull it off. Then give her a drink. Repeat this many times, giving her hand only as much help as she needs. You are working for her to grasp and pull by herself.

Now do the same thing using her foot. (You still use a man's sock, one that will come off easily.) You need to be sure that Mary is balanced well, perhaps sitting on a sofa, so that she can reach her foot without losing her balance. When she can do this without help, you can use her own sock.

Put her own sock on just a little way, so she can get it off with one pull. You can then gradually put it farther and farther on her foot. It is important to be sure that she can succeed without too much struggle so she won't give up.

Objective 3: To button and zip (developmental age is 2–3 years).
Materials: Dressy Bessy doll
Procedure: Sit at the table with Dressy Bessy doll in front of you and Ginny. Have Ginny touch face parts on Bessy and you. *Example:*
You (pointing to yourself): "Touch Mommy's nose."
Ginny does it (guide her hand or use a gesture to your nose if necessary).
You (pointing to doll): "Touch Bessy's nose."
Ginny does it.
Do this for hair, eyes, ears, mouth.
Have Ginny unzip, then zip, Bessy. Guide her by pointing or taking her hand as you tell her "Unzip" or "Zip." When Ginny can zip and unzip, move to buttons. Have her unbutton first. Don't try buttoning until she can unbutton. When doing unbuttoning, push the button half way through and then get Ginny to complete unbuttoning. Give her the command "Push button." Then work up to letting her unbutton completely. Break down buttoning the same way. Give her the command "Pull button."

Objective 4: To put on shirt (developmental age is 2½–3½ years).
Materials: Shirt
Procedure: Place Jim's shirt in front of him. Say, "Give shirt," holding out your hand and pointing to shirt. Have Jim hand you the shirt. Put it on, saying "On" and getting him to move his arms as much as possible. Pull shirt halfway over his head, take his hands, and pull it down, saying "Down." Take the shirt off, saying "Off," but leave it half off to let Jim finish taking it off himself, if possible.

Do this as many times as you can tolerate it. Try to increase the amount of movement Jim makes in getting the shirt on and off, steadily decreasing your help.

Objective 5: To complete toileting when alone in bathroom: pull off clothes, raise lid, flush, dress again (developmental age is 3–4 years).

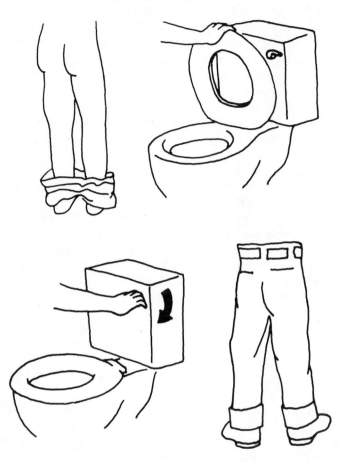

Figure 30.   Pictures to help Jim remember the toileting sequence: pants down, lift lid, flush, pants up.

Materials: Four pictures: pants down, lift lid, flush, pants on (see Figure 30)

Procedure: Jim can do each of these actions without help, but he forgets and gets sidetracked. Let's give him a visual reminder that will help organize him when you are not in the room.

Tape the four pictures in sequence on the wall behind the toilet. Teach Jim what each means by telling him, having him repeat (read) them, and pointing to each in turn as he performs the actions. Stand in doorway watching Jim, reminding him to look at the pictures, and praise him as he remembers each step.

Stand out of sight, but remind him to look at the pictures and do each one. If he forgets a step, you will notice it when you go in to check after he is through. Show him which one he forgot. When he completes this task without forgetting all four steps several days in a row, you can take down the pictures.

Objective 6: To answer phone (developmental age is 5–6 years).
Materials: Toy telephone, or best would be a set of toy phones that actually connect one room with another (available for approximately $10 from phone company)
Procedure: Practice the routine with Ethan, sitting with him at the table. You may need to write out the social greeting (since he reads and then can both read and hear the usual conversation simultaneously). Then pretend a phone call, coaching him on what to do. Next try the same thing from a different room. Once he gets used to this, let him answer the phone as often as possible. You might even ask his grandmother to call in the afternoon to give him practice with the "real thing."

SOCIAL SKILLS

Objective 1: Increase interaction (developmental age is 6–18 months).
Materials: String toys; thin, short rope; truck
Procedure: *Note:* While we regard Jimmy's strong interests in rocking and string play as nonconstructive, we can work with them rather than try to disregard them entirely.

String toys: Help Jimmy manipulate a pull-string doll, pull-string talking toy or music box, or attach a string to a sound or movement toy that you can help Jimmy pull along on the floor.

Tug-of-war: Use a short, thin rope with a loop handle tied at each end to play with in a game of pull and release.

Pat-a-cake: Play this game in a loosely structured way in the context of a rocking motion (on your lap, with hands held across from each other on the floor, seated in front of Jimmy on his rocking horse). The objective is some social response from Jimmy, such as a gestural movement to indicate that he wants to continue rocking, holding your hands as you clap. Keep his legs unfolded since this seems to distinguish rocking alone from rocking together. Exaggerate your facial expressions, sing a song, insert pauses in the rocking, and have a good time with this.

Objective 2: To increase eye contact (developmental age is 1–2 years).
Materials: Large shirt or towel
Procedure: Peek-a-boo game. Sit facing Susan, knees touching. Put shirt over her head. Say "Peek-a-boo. Where's Susan?" and slowly pull down shirt. When you see her eyes, tickle her. Repeat several times until she anticipates the tickle. Help her learn to pull down the shirt. Always wait until you see her eyes before tickling. Put shirt over your head, help her pull it off you; again tickle when she looks at you.

Objective 3: To increase affectionate contact, hugging (developmental age is 1½–2½ years).
Materials: Food rewards
Procedures: Stand Billy a short distance from you, facing you. Hold out your arms and say, "Come." When Billy comes to you, reward him with a hug and kiss and/or a piece of candy, or whatever you use as a reward. Put him back again and repeat this a number of times.

Note: Sit close enough at first so you can physically control him. When he comes every time, move back a little and do it again. Whenever Billy ignores you or seems to want to wander off, get his attention back by turning his head or raising your voice.

Objective 4: To enjoy taking turns (developmental age is 2–3 years).
Materials: Several blocks for stacking
Procedure: Pick one block from the box and place it on the table. Show Henry you want him to do the same, putting his block *on* yours. Now take *your* turn and build a tower. Continue with these turns. Make noises and gestures of excitement as the tower gets ready to fall. Encourage Henry to "look" when it is your turn. Give him physical tickles or hugs when it falls so that the game becomes exciting for him.

Objective 5: To increase awareness of others; to enjoy reversing roles (developmental age is 2½–3½ years).
Materials: Food reward, whistle
Procedure: The "I say" game is a gross motor imitation task like the game Simon Says. Sit in a chair giving verbal and physical cues to direction, e.g., "I say clap hands, I say arms up, I say jump." When Larry is leader, 1) help him give verbal directions and/or gestures, or 2) try imitating whatever movement he makes if he is calm enough to remain in the vicinity of the chair or leader's space.

"Which hand?": Hide a piece of candy or favorite object in one hand and hold out both hands fisted, saying "Find it." (The object in this game is not for Larry to track and find the object but, more important, for him to hide for you.) Reverse roles and help Larry hide object.

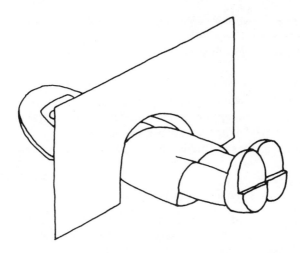

Figure 31.   Doll placed halfway through screen.

Hunt the whistle: Hide an object in the room. Have Larry look for the whistle. Help him hunt. As he gets near the object hidden, say "Oh, yes, yes, it's near here." When he finds it, let him blow it. Once he begins to understand the game, give him a turn to hide the whistle. You look. Ask him, "Is it near here?" and teach him to answer yes or no without actually telling you where it is.

Objective 6: To understand another's point of view (developmental age is 3-4 years).
Materials: Screen with hole: doll, truck, stuffed animals
Procedure: Name parts of objects (head, feet, front, back, etc.). Place object halfway through screen (see Figure 31). Ask John, "What do you see?" Then, "What do I see?" Help him at first by letting him come around and look at the object from your side of the screen.

Objective 7: To predict what someone else needs (developmental age is 4-5 years).
Materials: Watch, kleenex, comb, apple, sweater
Procedure: Place objects on the table. Make a statement with panto-mime ("I'm cold," "I'm hungry," "My hair's messy," "What time is it?") Look at Danny, saying, "What do I need?" When he points (or says) the object, reply "Good, that's what *I* need. Help me!" Let him give you the object. Pretend to use it, saying "Thank you." Now let Danny have a turn.

Objective 8: To work independently, calling for help when appropriate (developmental age is 4½–5½ years).

Materials: Puzzles or simple coloring or tracing worksheets that Jim can do

Procedure: Put the material in front of Jim. Tell him to do it. Move away, keeping watch. Let him do it himself. Remind him only as necessary. Don't hurry him. If he stops or seems frustrated, tell him to say "Help me." When he repeats this, come and help. When he is finished, have him say "All finished" and then return to him and reward him.

Note: You should start with very short tasks (1 minute) and gradually increase the length of the task.

Objective 9: To understand rules of a game, to inhibit impulses not to follow rules; to notice if others are following the rules (developmental age is 5–6 years).

Materials: Higgledy-Piggledy Game (or any other board game you have)

Procedure: Tim knows about taking turns but he relies on you to remind him. He needs to take more responsibility if he is going to play with the other children in school.

Write down the rules and have him repeat them. Play the game with him, but, instead of speaking the rules to remind him, just point to the list of rules and have him say them, e.g., "Take *one* turn." Now begin to make some mistakes yourself. If he doesn't notice, ask him "Was it my turn?" Teach him to say "Stop" when you make a mistake and tell you the rule. Sometimes delay taking your turn to see if he will take two in a row. If he does, then remind him of the rules. Say "Stop" and then ask him "What did you forget?" Make him do the thinking.

Appendix A.
Behavioral Norms
of Development

The following list of behaviors observable in most children at different ages or levels of development is grouped by function area (for a discussion of the nine function areas see especially Chapter 12). Many of the behaviors involve other areas than the one in which they are listed. For example, the 2-year-old's ability to initiate drawing a line also requires the ability to hold a crayon. Although we list line drawing under "imitation," it also involves fine motor and eye-hand integration skills.

None of the behaviors in this list occurs at a specific time period or sequence for all children. Human development is not that precise. It depends on the opportunities for expressing behavior, previous learning and experience, variations in biology, and a host of complex factors. Not the least of these are the manner and conditions under which the child's behavior is elicited. For example, a 6- to 12-month-old infant may orient to the sound of a whistle, but this response will vary according to how loudly the whistle is blown, how close it is to his ear, background noise, and what else the infant is doing. For these reasons, the age norms for these behaviors are given as age ranges approximated from tests of development, listed at the end of this appendix. Even standardized test norms are only approximations of behavior outside the test situation, however.

In spite of these variations there are regularities of developmental rates and sequences. These occur at relatively more precise periods during infancy than they will in the older child. Therefore the age ranges are expressed in 6-month intervals during the first year, and in a yearly range subsequently.

In spite of all qualifications about the precision of the scales, our parents and teachers have found them extremely helpful both for understanding and for defining appropriate teaching goals for their children.

Skills are so frequently uneven and unusual in their development that the special assessment procedures described in Chapter 2 become a necessity. The following scales are a valuable supplement to that assessment. They are helpful for the parent-teacher in three respects. First, they permit a reading on the developmental level of behavior, not directly measured by the formal testing. Accordingly they are helpful in forming appropriate expectations. Second, when emerging skills have been identified for a child, the scales can be used to find skills at the same developmental level, which may be incorporated into the teaching objectives. Third, the scales can be used as a reminder of prerequisite skills to be evaluated or trained before a particular teaching program can be used effectively.

IMITATION

Developmental Age Range	Skill/Behavior
5–12 months	*Verbal Imitation* Imitates cough, click (nonspeech) sounds Imitates speech sounds, babble Imitates new words *Motor Imitation* Imitates taking cube from a cup Imitates banging objects
1–2 years	*Verbal Imitation* Imitates two of four words Imitates crying Imitates laughing *Motor Imitation* Imitates putting object in box Imitates simple actions Imitates folding paper Imitates drawing single lines
2–3 years	*Verbal Imitation* Imitates naming objects and body parts Imitates simple sentence Imitates sequence of two or three digits or words *Motor Imitation* Imitates simple rhythmic movement Imitates use of rhythmic instrument Imitates drawing several connecting lines Imitates other's play (parallel play)
3–4 years	*Verbal Imitation* Imitates series of digits (three to four)

Imitates six-word sentence
Motor Imitation
Imitates wriggling thumb with fist
   closed
Imitates building bridge using blocks
Imitates making shapes with clay

4+years   *Verbal Imitation*
Imitates complex sentence using con-
   tractions:
"I don't know why he's crying."

PERCEPTION

Developmental Age Range	Skill/Behavior
0–6 months	Looks at movement of hands Reaches for object close by Turns head to sound of bell close by Turns to sound of human voice
6–12 months	Watches movement of bubbles Discriminates strangers Shows awareness of wet diaper Listens to music and voice intonation Orients to sound of whistle and clapper Orients to own name
1–2 years	Sees hole in pegboard Tracks movement of ball Sees object across room Discriminates shapes: circle, square, triangle Responds to hand gestures Discriminates facial expressions: laughing, crying Looks at pictures in books Discriminates speech sounds Shows awareness of toilet needs Discriminates tastes: edibles from inedibles
2–3 years	Discriminates nongeometrical forms in puzzles Discriminates designs: cross Looks at TV and films
3–4 years	Discriminates colors Discriminates rhythms Discriminates complex geometric forms
4–5 years	Discriminates rhyming words

GROSS MOTOR

Developmental Age Range	Skill/Behavior
3–6 months	Rolls over Sits up Stands, supported
6–12 months	Walks with help Crawls rapidly Walks alone
1–2 years	Throws ball Kneels, stoops to pick up object on floor Walks sideways and backward Stands on one foot briefly Carries object short distance Gets down from chair, walks down steps supported Walks up steps without help Jumps in place Can pedal tricycle
2–3 years	Learns to run Walks on tiptoe Balances on one foot for 5 seconds Balances when squatting Jumps down from bottom step
3–4 years	Throws ball overhead Catches bounced ball Goes down steps using alternating feet Hops on one foot Balances on one foot for 10 seconds Maintains momentum on swing, if started Skips on one foot
4–5 years	Walks on balance beam Hops five times successively Climbs up (ladders, trees) Packs mud or snowball, attempts aim of throw
5–6 years	Jumps rope Skips on alternating feet Runs on toes Uses skates Rides bicycle with training wheels Hits ball with bat or stick Dribbles large ball

FINE MOTOR

Developmental Age Range	Skill/Behavior
3-6 months	Grasps Pulls Bangs objects
6-12 months	Hand-to-hand transfer of object Pincer grasp Holds crayon
1-2 years	Releases object Scribbles Holds two objects in one hand Pushes button, turns knob Squeezes toys, toothpaste, sponges Turns pages of book Stacks two to six cube blocks Opens box, dumps contents
2-3 years	Manipulates clay or mud Manipulates egg beater Opens lids Finger paints Uses scissors Threads beads
3-4 years	Holds crayon in fingers Copies shapes with several different strokes Stacks blocks, nine cubes
4-5 years	Draws (pencil or crayon) simple pictures Screws together nuts and bolts Stacks blocks, more than nine cubes Folds paper more than once Identifies objects in bag by feel Makes animal from clay (two to three parts) Laces shoes

EYE-HAND INTEGRATION

Developmental Age Range	Skill/Behavior
3-6 months	Watches movement of own hands Reaches for and grasps objects Feeds self a cracker (hand to mouth)
6-12 months	Transfers cube from one hand to other Hits cup with spoon Puts finger in small hole Puts cubes in cup

EYE-HAND INTEGRATION—*continued*

Developmental Age Range	Skill/Behavior
1–2 years	Makes scribbling marks Holds cup, lifts and drinks Places round peg in round hole Completes form boards (circle, square, triangle) Places square peg in square hole Imitates several strokes, horizontal, vertical, circular
2–3 years	Uses dial on play telephone Paints dots, strokes, shapes on easel Cuts with scissors Copies cross Completes picture puzzle (simple interlocking)
3–4 years	Strings four beads Copies cross Traces diamond shape Catches bounced ball Completes interlocking seven-piece puzzle Colors within boundary line
4–5 years	Cuts out and pastes simple shapes Prints some letters (capitals) Draws simple house (square and diagonals) Draws man, two to three body parts Copies star (square) Adds three parts to incomplete pictures
5–6 years	Cuts out pictures with accuracy Copies diamond Prints lower case letters, and numbers Places details on pictures (house, person) Hits nail with hammer

---

COGNITIVE

Developmental Age Range	Skill/Behavior
3–12 months	Learns to control movement of hands and feet Controls objects: drops, throws, pulls Shows anger when toy is removed (remembers short time) Experiments with sounds and gestural expression

1–2 years	Learns simple cause/effect (light switch)
	Arranges objects in purposeful pattern
	Uses object (stick) as tool to reach toy
	Matches identical objects
	Recognizes own name and some belongings
	Recognizes and names mirror image
	Names one to five body parts
	Matches word to common object
2–3 years	Listens to simple stories
	Understands abstract words (big/little, wet/dry)
	Increases knowledge by asking questions (What's that?)
	Associates two objects by use (shoe/sock)
	Begins to see other person's point of view
	Answers "No" to absurdities ("Do we eat rocks?")
	Aware of amount (more/less, empty/full)
	Aware of time sequence ("It's time for...")
3–4 years	Develops language for attributes: shape, color, texture, taste
	Knows purpose of objects ("Why do we have stoves?")
	Understands comparitives (closest, biggest)
	Identifies people's sex by family role ("He's a daddy")
	Understands time using tenses past and present
	Can duplicate pegboard pattern or sequence
	Oral counts to 5, number concepts to 2
4–5 years	Knows age and address (street)
	Matches word to color attribute (four colors)
	Makes analogies (hat is to head as shoe is to foot)
	Understands absurdities in pictures
	Recalls set of three objects, states what is missing
	Categorizes people by sex (boy/girl, man/woman)
5–6 years	Knows source of 15–20 actions ("What bounces?")
	Knows parents' names and occupations

COGNITIVE—*continued*

Developmental Age Range	Skill/Behavior
	Understands rules in terms of "fair play"
	Counts orally to 20
	Adds and subtracts 3, using counters
	Can solve riddles ("What's red and good to eat?")
	Uses logical thinking ("What happens if. . .?")
	Predicts what will happen next from story or sequence
	Sight reads 10 words
	Identifies left/right on body parts

RECEPTIVE LANGUAGE

Developmental Age Range	Skill/Behavior
3–12 months	Turns to direction of voice
	Responds to name, shows recognition
	Responds to voice/gesture: "come, up, bye-bye"
	Listens to conversation, music
	Recognizes some objects: ball, kitty
	Claps hands on verbal request
	Follows simple verbal commands with gestures
1–2 years	Gives several common objects on command
	Looks at pictures named for 2 minutes
	Knows some body parts when named
	Points to familiar person, animals, toys on request
	Points to familiar pictures when named
	Carries out one-step directions
	Responds to negative information ("Don't touch")
	Associates simple words by category (food, clothing)
2–3 years	Rapid increase in receptive vocabulary
	Understands complex sentence ("When we get home, I'll. . .")
	Understands association by function, ("What do you wear?")
	Understands some common adjectives, three prepositions
	Listens to "how" and "why" explanations

Understands about 3,000 words
Performs two related successive com-
   mands
   ("First..., then...")

3–4 years
                 Understands color words ("Get the red
   ball")
Carries out three-step directions using
   prepositions
Listens to long sequential stories
Carries out two-part noun/adjective
   directions ("Give me the red block
   and the blue ball")

4–5 years
                 Locates or places items using behind,
   beside, between, next to
Selects actions when either/or is in
   command
Performs three successive commands
Understands "if" statement ("If you are
   a boy, stand up")
Understands the passive voice ("The
   dog was hit by the ball")

EXPRESSIVE LANGUAGE
Developmental Age Range   Skill/Behavior

1–6 months
                 Vocalizes vowel sounds (ah, eh, uh)
Babbles, coos, alone or when talked to
Imitates adult intonation
Combines several vowel sounds

4–12 months
                 Uses single consonants, babbles using
   several syllables
Imitates sounds or words without
   association
Jabbers with expression
Associates first word with person/thing
   (Mama, ball)
Uses greeting ("Hi," "Bye-bye")

1–2 years
                 Uses three meaningful words besides
   Mama, Dadda
Repeats single syllables
Imitates sounds of animals, cars, etc.
Vocabulary increases to 20 words
Names object when asked "What is
   this?"
States wants in one-word utterances,
   "go...more...up"
Refers to self by name

EXPRESSIVE LANGUAGE—*continued*

Developmental Age Range	Skill/Behavior
	Begins two-word phrases ("go car," "Mama come")
	Begins use of pronouns and possessives (me, mine)
2-3 years	Repeats a three- or four-syllable sentence ("See the kitten")
	Vocabulary increases to 200 words
	Can memorize a few nursery rhymes
	Adds "ing" to verbs
	Combines phrases to form short sentences
	Begins to use pronouns and possessives (her, him, hers, Daddy's)
	Forms unsolicited questions ("That a car?")
	Utters negative statements (besides "no" or "don't want")
3-4 years	Vocabulary increases to 900 words
	Asks many questions, reversing order correctly ("Is that a car?")
	Talks to self in long monologues, including make believe
	Describes recent events
	Uses six- or seven-word sentences
	Uses some irregular plurals and verbs correctly
	Controls speed and volume of voice for emphasis
4-5 years	Uses compound sentences
	Tells familiar stories without need for picture clues
	Recounts experiences in some sequential order
	Describes objects in terms of use
	Articulation no longer "babyish"
5-6 years	Asks the meaning of abstract words
	Uses future and past tenses correctly
	Describes many events of past experience
	Uses "yesterday" and "tomorrow" correctly
	Speaks fluently and correctly

SELF-HELP SKILLS

Developmental Age Range	Skill/Behavior
5–12 months	Picks up spoon Feeds self a cracker (chews) Feeds self finger foods Drinks from cup held by adult Holds arms out to assist dressing
1–2 years	Moves around house independently Sits on toilet, supervised Drinks from cup Removes garment (sock) Uses spoon independently
2–3 years	Removes coat and dress Puts on simple garments (pullover type) Pulls down pants (begins toileting) Bladder and bowel trained, daytime Puts toys away when told Washes hands with help, dries hands Unfastens large buttons and snaps Hangs up clothes on hook Avoids danger, reports injuries
3–4 years	Gets drink unaided, pours from pitcher Spreads butter, jam with knife Independent in toileting Brushes teeth, supervised Washes self (supervised), dries self (unsupervised) Undresses and dresses self, except for tying Uses school bus (gets on and off unaided) Distrustful of strangers
4–5 years	Uses spoon, fork, and knife appropriately Toileting complete (flushes and wipes) Washes, brushes teeth (unsupervised) Tries to blow/wipe nose Walks around neighborhood (no street crossings) Looks both ways before leaving sidewalk Helps with household chores (when told)
5–6 years	Complete responsibility for dressing and undressing Goes to bed unaided Runs simple errands

SELF-HELP SKILLS—*continued*

Developmental Age Range   **Skill/Behavior**

Answers telephone, gives messages
Plays simple table games
Brushes and combs hair
Crosses street safely

SOCIAL

Developmental Age Range	Skill/Behavior
2–12 months	Smiles, chuckles, socializes with anyone Expresses pleasure/displeasure to adults Socializes with primary caregiver Fear of strangers begins Demands personal attention Enjoys games (peek-a-boo, pat-a-cake)
1–2 years	Seeks help when needed Seeks to get and hold adults' attention Cooperative; waits, tries to help Begins to show pride in accomplishments Shows emotions (affection, delight, anger, jealousy) Enjoys company of peers, siblings Willfulness develops; "no" becomes chief word Plays alone if near adult
2–3 years	Initiates own play, or uses parallel play Fantasy play begins Likes to please others Imitates peers, swaps toys Plays simple group games Domestic make-believe games include peers Becomes contrary with violent emotions/temper Likes things the same each day Responds to and makes verbal greetings
3–4 years	Likes to give and take with others Likes to share belongings, can take turns Likes to make friends Entertains others with language or performs

Cooperative play skills begin
Insecurity, whining, stuttering may
  develop
Helps with adult activities in house and
  garden

4–5 years	Plays competitive games with peers
	Shows off and/or bosses and criticizes others
	May confuse fact and fantasy
	Shows concern and sympathy for others
	Respects property and privacy of others
	Performs undesirable task when asked
	Verbal rudeness or aggression may develop
5–6 years	Chooses own friends, enjoys small groups of peers
	Respects property and feelings of peers
	Conforms to adults' ideas
	Controls behavior in public places
	Has strong need for rules and fair play
	Accepts friendly teasing

Appendix B.
Resource Materials

This appendix contains three kinds of teaching resources. The first includes a list of materials we have found useful for teaching our children. They are available in the home, at school, or can be purchased reasonably in dime stores, toy stores, or general stores. Some are more readily obtainable from educational materials catalogs, a few of which are referenced later in the appendix. The second includes materials useful to the parent-teacher for either constructing teaching materials or for organizing and presenting teaching activities. The third section lists workbooks and manuals we have found to be useful sources of ideas and activities from which to develop individualized teaching programs. None of these three sections is intended to be an all-inclusive listing. However, they do include the resource materials we have used most frequently.

The items in the materials list are generally readily available and reasonably priced. They are included because most of our parents and our classroom teachers have neither the time nor the budget to invest in hard-to-find, expensive items. They can be used in a number of different activities at various developmental levels and therefore they are not quickly "outgrown" by the children. Beads, for example, can be used to teach grasping and releasing fine motor skills at an early level, for threading, sorting by color, and for training sequential arrangements at a higher level. The materials are safe and generally do not require special supervision. They are plain and do not contain irrelevant details or over-stimulating distractions. They are easy to see with simple shapes and bright colors. These materials are appealing and attractive to our children because they produce interesting movements and sounds. They are also easy for the parent-teacher to manage in structured lessons since they can be contained in boxes, cans, and trays.

Our parents and teachers find it most useful to make a number of materials, especially for use in language activities. Pictures that match concrete objects and those used to stimulate receptive and expressive language objectives help to develop the child's understanding and use of a practical vocabulary of common objects and daily events in his own life. The use and reason for making these materials have already been referred to in the text.

TEACHING MATERIALS LIST

animal, stuffed—bear, dog, rabbit, etc.
animals, plastic—small miniatures of animals the child has seen (dog, cat, cow)
balls—large 12-inch rubber; small rubber or sponge
balloons
bat—lightweight plastic
*beads—various sizes, shapes, colors
beads—large plastic "pop-it," interlocking
bean bags—4-inch squares (usually home made)
bell, small—with handle
blocks—2-inch wooden
*blocks—1-inch, multicolored
bolts and nuts—plastic multicolored
bolts and nuts—metal, large
books—with pictures of realistic and common events
bubbles—screw top jar with wand
buttons—large, various colors
cars and trucks
*chalk and chalkboard
clothespins—colored plastic or plain
clothing—belonging to child and family members
cooking utensils—cookie cutters, egg beater, baster, spoons, etc.
crayons—jumbo, eight colors
cups—plastic, china, paper; mugs, glasses
doll—large with clothes that can be removed
doll furniture—small plastic, items the child has in his home
doll tea set
*dolls—miniature representing family members
drum
food—edible treats, common foods, packages and cans of food
jack-in-the-box
jump rope
knife—dull edge, plastic
Lego blocks and Lego assembly kits
*lotto games—pictures of common objects the child knows
miniatures of common household objects (found in party favors, for example)

---

*Items with asterisks can be found in the catalogs listed on page 242.

  musical wind-up toys
*nesting cups—size-sequenced stacking toys
  paints—water color, poster paint, finger paint
  paper—newsprint, typing paper, paper bags cut up, shelf paper
  paper—colored construction paper
*parquetry games
  paste—white in jar with applicator or in squeeze bottle
*pegs and pegboards
  pipe cleaners
  pitcher—small lightweight, nonbreakable
  play-do—various colors
*puzzles—four-piece inset, of common objects
*puzzles—6- to 10-piece inset with knobs
*puzzles—4- to 15-piece interlocking
  ring-stack toys
  scissors—blunt ended
  screw top jars
*shape boxes
  silver—kitchen spoons, forks, knives
  spools of thread (used)
  swings—regular swing set, or from tires, cloth straps, etc.
  table games—played on a board requiring taking turns
  telephone—plastic toy
  Tinker Toys
  towels—all sizes for folding and sorting
  tricycle, wagons, or other rolling toys
*xylophone and other rhythm instruments

MATERIALS USEFUL TO PARENT-TEACHER
Materials for structuring the lesson:
sorting trays—plastic/cardboard from grocery store
paper bowls and plates—for sorting and matching tasks
cans with plastic lids—for shape boxes and for storage
egg cartons—for sorting activities
plastic boxes with dividers—for sorting activities
shoe boxes, plastic wash basins—for storing materials
checkers, poker chips, curtain rings—used as token rewards

Materials for making teaching games:
cardboard—for making stencils and lotto boards
contact paper, transparent—for protecting language picture cards
index cards with pictures pasted on for language tasks
rubber cement—quick drying for mounting pictures

Pictures for language materials should be realistic and without unnecessary background details. They can be found from the following sources: magazines, catalogs, old children's books, school readiness workbooks, phonics workbooks, Primer reading workbooks (used ones can be obtained from schools or from neighbors' children). Odds and ends that are useful for sorting and matching tasks and for craft projects include: scraps of material, buttons, wool, straws, popsicle sticks, colored toothpicks, curtain rings, toilet paper rolls, small boxes that open in various ways.

Catalogs:

Communication Skill Builders, Inc.
817 E. Broadway
P. O. Box 6081-E
Tuscon, Arizona   85733
(602) 882-9034

Community Playthings
Rifton, New York   12471

DLM Catalog
Developmental Learning Materials
7440 Natchez Avenue
Niles, Illinois   60648
(312) 647-7800

Educational Teaching Aids
159 West Kinzie Street
Chicago, Illinois   60610
(312) 644-9438

IDEAL School Supply Company
11000 South Laverne Avenue
Oaklawn, Illinois   60453

WORKBOOKS, MANUALS, AND REFERENCE BOOKS

Workbooks

Apple Tree: A Patterned Program of Linguistic Expansion through Reinforced Experiences and Evaluations, by Janis Caniglia, Norma Jean Cole, Wyman Howard, Emmylou Krohn, and Marcia Rice. 1972. Matched pictures and written word to develop language concepts. Available from:
    Dormac, Inc.
    P. O. Box 752
    Beaverton, Oregon   97005

The Peabody Rebus Reading Program, by Richard W. Woodcock, Ed.D., Charlotte R. Clarke, M. A., and Cornelia Oakes Davies, M.A. 1969. Uses rebus pictures to introduce reading. Available from:
    American Guidance Service, Inc.
    Publishers' Building
    Circle Pines, Minnesota   55014

Programmed Reading. A Sullivan Associates Program (3rd Ed.), by Cynthia Dee Buchanan. 1973. A beginning reading program based on phonetic analysis, using simple vocabulary and sentence structures. Available from:
    Webster Division
    McGraw-Hill Book Company
    1221 Avenue of the Americas
    New York, New York   10020

Reading, Thinking, and Reasoning Skills Program. Whispers (1974), *Raindrops* (1974), *Snowflakes* (1975), *Clouds* (1975), by Don Barnes, Arlene Burgdorf, and L. Stanley Wenck. Workbooks that use pictures to develop concepts. Available from:
  Steck-Vaughn Company
  An Intext Publisher
  Box 2028
  Austin, Texas   78767

Dubnoff School Program 1. Level 1: Sequential Perceptual-Motor Exercises, Level 2: Experiential Perceptual-Motor Exercises, by Belle Dubnoff, M.A., with Irene Chambers and Florence Schaefer. 1968. Level 1: Catalog number 21–110, Level 2: Catalog number 21–120. Workbooks that provide pre-writing exercises. Available from:
  NYT Teaching Resource Corporation
  100 Boylston Street
  Boston, Massachusetts   02116

The Development Program in Visual Perception. Revised to Include Basic Readiness Concepts. *Beginning Pictures and Patterns* (Revised Edition). *Intermediate Pictures and Patterns* (Revised Edition). By Marianne Frostig, Ph.D., David Horne, B.A., and Ann-Marie Miller, M.A. 1972. Perceptual-motor exercises. Available from:
  Follett Publishing Company
  Curriculum Materials Laboratories
  Divison of Follett Corporation
  1010 W. Washington Boulevard
  Chicago, Illinois   60607

Peabody Language Development Kits. Level #P (1968), by Lloyd M. Dunn, Ph.D., Kathryn B. Horton, M.S., and James O. Smith, Ed.D. Level #1 (1965), Level #2 (1966), by Lloyd M. Dunn, Ph.D. and James O. Smith, Ed.D. Pictures and materials for developing language skills. Available from:
  American Guidance Service, Inc.
  Publishers' Building
  Circle Pines, Minnesota   55014

Fokes Sentence Builder, by Joann Fokes. 1968. Catalog number 86–110. Kit providing materials for developing language syntax, grammatical structures. Available from:
  NYT Teaching Resource Corporation
  100 Boylston Street
  Boston, Massachusetts   02116

Emerging Language II, by John Hatten, Tracy Goman, and Carole Lent. 1976. For programming beginning language activities. Available from:
  Communication Skill Builders, Inc.
  815 E. Broadway
  P.O. Box 42050
  Tuscon, Arizona   85733

Manuals

Teaching Makes a Difference: A Guide for Developing Successful Classes for Autistic Children, by Anne Donnellan-Walsh, Lon D. Gossage,

Gary W. LaVigna, Adriana (Luce) Schuler, and Jan Traphagen. 1976. Available from:

> Santa Barbara County Autism Dissemination Project
> P.O. Box 6307
> 4400 Cathedral Oaks Road
> Santa Barbara, California   93111

Steps to Independence: A Skills Training Series for Children with Special Needs. Early Self-Help Skills, Intermediate Self-Help Skills, Advanced Self-Help Skills. By Bruce L. Baker, Alan J. Brightman, Louis J. Heifetz, and Diane M. Murphy. 1976. Techniques for training all levels of self-help skills. Available from:

> Research Press
> 2612 North Mattis Avenue
> Champaign, Illinois   61820

Parent-Infant Communication: A Program of Clinical and Home Training for Parents and Hearing Impaired Infants, by Valerie Sitnick, Nancy Rushmer, and Roberta Arpan. 1977. Looseleaf notebook providing techniques for early language development. Available from:

> Dormac, Inc.
> P.O. Box 752
> Beaverton, Oregon   97005

The Signed English Dictionary—for Preschool and Elementary Levels, edited by Harry Bornstein, Lillian B. Hamilton, Karen Luczak Saulnier, and Howard L. Roy. 1975. Hardcover book illustrating signs in alphabetical order. Available from:

> Gallaudet College Press
> 7th and Florida Avenue N.W.
> Washington, D.C.   20002

Appropriate Behavior through Communication: A New Program in Simultaneous Language for Nonverbal Children, by Margaret Creedon. 1975. Program for training simultaneous use of signed and spoken communication. Available from:

> Dysfunctioning Child Center Publication
> Chicago, Illinois

Hawaii Early Learning Profile Activity Guide. Year 1. Project Director: Setsu Furuno, Ph.D.; Physical Therapist: Katherine A. O'Reilly, M.P.H., R.P.T.; Teacher: Carol M. Hosaka, M.A.; Occupational Therapist: Takayo Inatsuka, O.T.R.; Psychologist: Toney Allman, M.A.; Speech Therapists: Barbara Zeisloft, M.A., Bernard Garon, M.A.; Public Health Nurse: Betty Nakaji, R.N.; Teacher's Assistant: Mary Alger, B.S. Resource of activities for the young handicapped. Available from:

> School of Public Health
> University of Hawaii
> 1960 East-West Road
> Honolulu, Hawaii   96822

Learning Accomplishment Profile, by Anne R. Sanford. 1973. Designed to generate individual learning objectives in six areas of development. Available from:

Kaplan School Supply Corporation
600 Jonestown Road
Winston-Salem, North Carolina   27103

See also *A Manual for the Use of the Learning Accomplishment Profile,* edited by Anne R. Sanford, with Donald Bailey, W. Craig Johnson, Judith Leonard, and Peter O'Connor. 1974. Available from:

Kaplan School Supply Corporation

Learning Activities for the Young Handicapped Child, Chapel Hill Training-Outreach Project, Anne R. Sanford, Director. Prepared by Don Bailey, Betty Boling, Susan Byrum, Dot Cansler, Patricia Fullagar, Beth Gove, Janet Grim, Toby Klein, Judith Leonard, Ann Overton, Annie Pegram, Barbara Semrau, Jo Ann Sharpe, and Mary Valand. 1976. This book is made up of a set of activities designed to facilitate learning of specific target skills. Available from:

Kaplan Press
600 Jonestown Road
Winston-Salem, North Carolina   27103

Reference Books

Toilet Training the Retarded: A Rapid Program for Day and Nighttime Independent Toileting, by Richard M. Foxx and Nathan H. Azrin. 1973. Available from:

Research Press
2612 North Mattis Avenue
Champaign, Illinois   61820

Autistic Children: A Guide for Parents and Professionals, by Lorna Wing, M.D., D.P.M. 1972. Available from:

Brunner/Mazel, Inc.
64 University Place
New York, New York   10003

and:

National Society for Autistic Children
1234 Massachusetts Avenue, N.W.
Washington, D.C.   20005

Teach Your Baby, A Complete Tested Program of Simple Daily Activities for Infants and Small Children, Designed to Develop Learning Abilities to the Fullest Potential, by Genevieve Painter, Ed.D. 1971. Available from:

Simon & Schuster
Rockefeller Center
630 Fifth Avenue
New York, New York   10020

Learning through Play, by Jean Marzollo and Janice Lloyd. 1972. Available from:

Harper & Row
10 East 53rd Street
New York, New York   10022

References

REFERENCES FOR THE DEVELOPMENT NORMS

Bayley, N. 1969. Bayley Scales of Infant Development. The Psychological Corporation, New York.

Bzoch, K. R., and League, R. 1970. Receptive-Expressive Emergent Language Scale (REEL) for the Measurement of Language Skills in Infancy. The Tree of Life Press, Gainesville, Fla.

Cattell, P. 1950. The Measurement of Intelligence of Infants and Young Children. The Psychological Corporation, New York.

Doll, E. A. 1965. Vineland Social Maturity Scale: Condensed Manual of Directions. American Guidance Service, Circle Pines, Minn.

Frankenburg, W. K., Dodds, J. B., and Fandal, A. W. 1967, 1970. Denver Developmental Screening Test. University of Colorado Medical Center, Denver.

Gesell, A. L., Halverson, H. M., Thompson, H., Ilg, F.L., Castner, B. M., Ames, L. B., and Amatruda, C. S. 1940. The First Five Years of Life: A Guide to the Study of the Preschool Child. Harper & Row Publishers, New York.

Hedrick, D. L., Prather, E. M., and Tobin, A. R. 1975. Sequenced Inventory of Communication Development. University of Washington Press, Seattle.

Hurlock, E. B. 1956. Child Development. McGraw-Hill Book Publishers, New York.

Pupil Developmental Progress Scale. Monterey County Office of Education, P.O. Box 851, Salinas, Cal.

Schopler, E., and Reichler, R. J. 1979. Individualized Assessment and Treatment for Autistic and Developmentally Disabled Children. Volume I: Psychoeducational Profile. University Park Press, Baltimore.

Slosson, R. L. 1963. Slosson Intelligence Test (SIT) for Children and Adults. Slosson Educational Publications, New York.

Stutsman, R. 1948. Guide for Administering the Merrill-Palmer Scale of Mental Tests. Harcourt, Brace & World, New York.

White, B. L. 1975. The First Three Years of Life. Prentice-Hall, Inc., Englewood Cliffs, N.J.

REFERENCES

Ayers, A. J. 1973. Sensory Integration and Learning Disorders. Western Psychological Services, Los Angeles.

Azrin, N. H., and Holz, W. C. 1966. Punishment. In W. K. Honig (Ed.), Operant Behavior. Appleton-Century-Crofts, New York.

Baroff, G. S. 1974. Mental Retardation: Nature, Cause, and Management. Hemisphere Publishing Corp., Washington, D.C.

Bornstein, H., Hamilton, L. B., Saulnier, K. L., and Roy, H. L. (Eds.). 1975. The Signed English Dictionary—For Preschool and Elementary Levels. Gallaudet College Press, Washington, D.C.

Cantwell, D., Baker, L., and Rutter, M. 1978. Family factors. In M. Rutter and E. Schopler (Eds.), Autism: A Reappraisal of Concepts and Treatment. Plenum Press, New York.

Dubnoff, B. 1968. Dubnoff School Program. Teaching Resources, Boston.

Federal Register, 1977. Vol. 42, No. 163, Tuesday, Aug. 23.

Foxx, R. M., and Azrin, N. H. 1973. The elimination of autistic self-stimulatory behavior by overcorrection. J. Appl. Behav. Anal. 6:1–14.

Frostig, M., and Horne, D. 1964. The Frostig Program for the Development of Visual Perception. Follett Publishing Co., Chicago.

Grossman, H. J. (Ed.). 1977. Manual on Terminology and Classification in Mental Retardation. American Association on Mental Deficiency, Washington, D.C.

Harris, S. L., and Ersner-Hershfield, R. 1978. Behavioral suppression of seriously disruptive behavior in psychotic and retarded patients: A review of punishment and its alternatives. Psychol. Bull. 1352–1375.

Haywood, H. C. 1979. What happened to mild and moderate mental retardation? Am. J. Ment. Def. 83:429–431.

Kanner, L. 1943. Autistic disturbances of affective contact. Nerv. Child. 2:217–250.

Laufer, M. W., and Gair, D. S. 1969. Childhood schizophrenia. In L. Bellak and L. Loeb (Eds.), The Schizophrenic Syndrome. Grune & Stratton, New York.

Lichstein, K. L., and Schreibman, L. 1976. Employing electric shock with autistic children: A review of the side effects. J. Aut. Child. Schizo. 6:163–173.

Lovaas, O. I., Koegel, R., Simmons, J. Q., and Long, J. S. 1973. Some generalizations and follow-up measures on autistic children in behavior therapy. J. Appl. Behav. Anal. 6:131–163.

Mann, L., and Goodman, L. 1976. Perceptual training: A critical retrospect. In E. Schopler and R. J. Reichler (Eds.), Psychopathology and Child Development: Research and Treatment. Plenum Press, New York.

Ornitz, E. S., and Ritvo, E. R. 1968. Perceptual inconstancy in early infantile autism. Arch. Gen. Psychiatry 18:76–98.

President's Committee on Mental Retardation. 1977. MR 76: Mental Retardation Past and Present. U.S. Government Printing Office, Washington, D.C.

Reichler, R. J., and Schopler, E. 1971. Observations on the nature of human relatedness. J. Aut. Child. Schizo. 1:283–296.

Reichler, R. J., and Schopler, E. 1976. Developmental therapy: A program model for providing individualized services in the community. In E. Schopler and R. J. Reichler (Eds.), Psychopathology and Child Development: Research and Treatment. Plenum Press, New York.

Rimland, B. 1964. Infantile Autism. Appleton-Century-Crofts, New York.

Rutter, M. 1968. Concepts of autism: A review of research. J. Child Psychol. Psychiatry 9:1-25.

Rutter, M. 1978a. Diagnosis and definition of childhood autism. J. Aut. Child. Schizo. 8:139-161.

Rutter, M. 1978b. Diagnosis and definition. In M. Rutter and E. Schopler (Eds.), Autism: A Reappraisal of Concepts and Treatment. Plenum Press, New York.

Rutter, M., and Schopler, E. (Eds.). 1978. Autism: A Reappraisal of Concepts and Treatment. Plenum Press, New York.

Schopler, E. 1965. Early infantile autism and receptor processes. Arch. Gen. Psychiatry 13:327-335.

Schopler, E. 1966. Visual versus tactual receptor preference in normal and schizophrenic children. J. Abnorm. Psychol. 71:108-114.

Schopler, E., Brehm, S. S., Kinsbourne, M., and Reichler, R. J. 1971. Effect of treatment structure on development in autistic children. Arch. Gen. Psychiatry 24: 415-421.

Schopler, E., and Loftin, J. 1969a. Thinking disorders in parents of young psychotic children. J. Abnorm. Psychol. 74:281-287.

Schopler, E., and Loftin, J. 1969b. Thought disorders in parents of psychotic children: A function of test anxiety. Arch. Gen. Psychiatry 20: 174-181.

Schopler, E., and Reichler, R. J. 1971. Parents as cotherapists in the treatment of psychotic children. J. Aut. Child. Schizo. 1:87-102.

Schopler, E., and Reichler, R. J. 1972. How well do parents understand their own psychotic child? J. Aut. Child. Schizo. 2:387-400.

Schopler, E., and Reichler, R. J. 1979. Individualized Assessment and Treatment for Autistic and Developmentally Delayed Children. Volume I, Psychoeducational Profile. University Park Press, Baltimore.

Sulzer-Azaroff, B., and Mayer, G. R. 1977. Applying Behavior Analysis Procedures with Children and Youth. Holt, Rinehart & Winston, Inc., New York.

Turnbull, A. P., Strickland, B., and Brantley, J. C. 1978. Developing and Implementing Individualized Education Programs. Charles E. Merrill Publishing Co., Columbus, Oh.

Vargas, J. S. 1977. Behavioral Psychology for Teachers. Harper & Row Publishers, New York.

Index